Praise for *Mosul Eye*

"When our city, Mosul, fell silent—when the law itself had no voice and disorder ruled Mosul—there were those who worked, quietly and faithfully, to document what was happening and to preserve the record intact, against the day when justice would return.

As members of the judiciary in Nineveh, we regard *Mosul Eye*, by Omar Mohammed, as far more than a personal account. It is an essential document—one that exposes the nature of the crimes ISIS committed, grounded in verified evidence and observable fact.

What Omar Mohammed achieved is a work of serious documentation that helped safeguard a critical part of this period's memory, and its contribution to the pursuit of justice was already apparent before liberation was complete.

We had the privilege of witnessing this work take shape, and we supported it in the belief that the judiciary's duty does not end at settling disputes—it extends to defending truth and ensuring that memory survives.

This book honors the victims of Mosul. It tells future generations that what happened here will not be forgotten, that justice does not expire, and that Mosul will always be a city of learning and law.

We offer this testimony in recognition of this remarkable effort, and in memory of those who gave their lives to restore Mosul."

—Honorable Judge Raed Al-Muslih, , president of the Nineveh Court of Appeal, Supreme Judicial Council of Iraq

* * *

"I first learned of the blog Mosul Eye during the darkest period of ISIS's reign over northern Iraq, when the world was searching for any reliable voice from inside the city. That voice—anonymous then—belonged to Omar Mohammed, a young historian who refused to let his city be destroyed in silence. In *Mosul Eye: A Clandestine Scholar's War Against Isis*, he gives us a meticulous and unflinching work of witness. May it inspire a new generation to defend the freedom and transparency he risked everything to preserve."

—Hillary Rodham Clinton

"What Omar Mohammed accomplished defies the ordinary categories of courage. Through his blog, a sentinel in the night, he transmitted to the world fragments of truth torn from the darkness and the fog of propaganda. I cannot help but think of the clandestine historians of the Warsaw Ghetto, who, at the heart of annihilation, documented daily life under the Nazi yoke. Their archives, buried in milk cans, already carried this tragic intuition: They might not survive, but their words had to. In *Mosul Eye*, Omar belongs to that rare and precious lineage of those who refuse to let the night have the last word. Perhaps this is, in the end, the most silent and most profound victory: that, in the face of the will to erase, a voice persisted. And that this voice inspires the renaissance."

—Audrey Azoulay, director-general of UNESCO

"Reading Mosul Eye was a revelation. Omar's courage exposed the horror of ISIS and the struggle for survival in a world of vicious cruelty. It was unique and powerful. This book belongs alongside those chronicling the terrors of the last century. He did it in real time and at huge personal risk. It serves as a reminder that courage can stand against evil, and must, if we are not to see such terror return. Omar is extraordinary, and his work and courage will long outlive those whose hatred enslaved Mosul."

—The Rt Hon Tom Tugendhat, MBE, VR, MP—Conservative MP for Tonbridge, former security minister, former chair of the UK Parliament's Foreign Affairs Committee, and a commissioner of the Commonwealth War Graves Commission

"There is physical courage. There is intellectual courage. And there is moral courage. All of these were in evidence in Mosul under the brutal rule of the so-called Islamic State—Da'esh in the contemptuous Arabic acronym. Omar Mohammed, the man behind Mosul Eye, the anonymised blog that recorded so much of what was happening—the daily life, the fear, the atrocities, the casual sadism of the men and women who thought God had commanded them to become blood-soaked criminals, the stubborn resistance of ordinary people—has now written his account of that period. It is an incredible story: of courage, hope, and the power of human solidarity in the midst of catastrophe. The Abrahamic religions tell us that we stand on the edge of an abyss. This book reminds us, as we need reminding constantly, not just of that truth but also that we are not God; no truly divine revelation can command savagery, and only faith in our shared humanity can ultimately save us."

—Sir John Jenkins KCMG LVO, former British Ambassador to Saudi Arabia; former director-general for the Middle East, UK Foreign Office

"*Mosul Eye* belongs among the manuscripts I carried out of the fire. What Omar Mohammed has given Mosul will outlast her captors, as our manuscripts have outlasted theirs."

—Mar Najeeb Michaeel Moussa, O.P., Chaldean Archbishop of Mosul

"This is, to paraphrase Dickens, A Tale of a City and a Man. The city? Mosul, in Northern Iraq, under the dire rule of ISIS between June 2014 and June 2017. The man? Omar Mohammed, a.k.a. Mosul Eye, a local scholar who, at tremendous risk to himself, single-handedly set up an intelligence network and diligently recorded ISIS's horrid exactions. Yet rather than let himself be instrumentalized by this or that intelligence service, Omar Mohammed made all this precious information public, for the good of all. In so doing, not only did he hasten the demise of ISIS's rule in the city, but he also gave hope to its crushed people. And when the day of reckoning finally came for ISIS, and the people of Mosul found themselves caught in the crossfire, his network further helped save scores of innocent lives. A most moving and well-written personal account by someone who has experienced the events firsthand."

—Percy Kemp

"A man of undaunted courage with the foresight to organize and prepare, and the hindsight to bring understanding amidst chaos. Omar is a treasure to Mosul, his city, and to Iraq, his country."

—U.S. Central Command

"Omar Mohammed has shown enormous personal courage in the war against ISIS. He risked his life every day to tell the terrible truth of ISIS's occupation of Mosul through Mosul Eye. Its stories were inspiring. I am honoured to have been able to work with Omar."

—Martyn Warr OBE, head of the Counter-Daesh Communications Cell in the UK's Foreign, Commonwealth, and Development Office

"In the summer of 2014, as the UN Security Council was locked in intense and complex debates over how to navigate the unprecedented crisis of ISIL's rise, one mysterious name kept surfacing: Mosul Eye. On the ground and under constant threat of death, Omar Mohammed was the lone voice providing the world with 'evidence from hell on a problem from hell.' As the only eyewitness risking his life to testify from within the heart of the caliphate, he unmasked the chilling banality of ISIL's evil. I read his reporting regularly—on more than one occasion it was the clearest report I had on the brutality of ISIL. This book is a harrowing history of those crimes and a powerful testament to the courage of a single human spirit determined to let the truth survive."

—Dr. David Scharia, UN Security Council · Counter-Terrorism Committee Executive Directorate (CTED)

"When ISIS seized Mosul in 2014, the city went dark. Independent reporting all but vanished. Then a blog appeared, written anonymously by a historian of Mosul, shining a light on what was happening within his occupied city. In Mosul Eye, Omar Mohammed delivers an extraordinary firsthand account of life under ISIS's brutal occupation—the story of a man who refused to let his city's suffering go unrecorded, chronicling ISIS's crimes in real time at enormous personal risk. It is a story of courage, humanity, and hope."

—Emma Sky OBE, director of Yale's International Leadership Center, author of *The Unraveling: High Hopes and Missed Opportunities in Iraq*

"Omar Mohammed is the bravest and most admirable man I have met—and this is a book fully worthy of him. It is at once a thriller and a meditation; a warning and a reassurance; a story that is both as dark as the darkest night and radiant with the light of hope."

—Tom Holland, historian and broadcaster; author of *Dominion: How the Christian Revolution Remade the World*

"Paeans to the Paris and Warsaw resistance to the Nazis are fundamental components of twentieth-century historical canon. Omar Mohammed's chronicle stands alongside those tales by revealing the moral defiance and extraordinary human bravery of Iraqis in the face of Islamic State's terror."

—Margaret Coker, author of *The Spymaster of Baghdad*

"Mosul—a city unlucky in so many ways—is fortunate to have a chronicler as sensitive and humane as Omar Mohammed. This book is an act of witness."

—Graeme Wood, staff writer at *The Atlantic*; author of *The Way of the Strangers: Encounters with the Islamic State*

"For years, Omar Mohammed—known as Mosul Eye—risked everything to document life under ISIS. More than a witness—a voice for the voiceless. His book is a powerful lesson in history: with a scholar's rigor and a journalist's keen eye, it immortalizes one of humanity's darkest passages. In the name of truth."

—Delphine Minoui, Le Figaro

"Mosul in the hands of ISIS was a black hole of history. For the two years of the siege, we journalists knew only its borders, defined by the Iraqi troops slowly advancing to liberate it. Inside, you could sense the fanaticism, the violence, but the city of the Islamic State was a mystery, an unknowable elsewhere. And then we discovered Mosul Eye—that anonymous figure who was writing its daily stories on social media, and about whom you asked yourself: Is he telling the truth? And then: Does he really exist? One evening, I remember reading his account of how, his eyes full of the horror he had witnessed, he would shut himself in his room and, in secret, with headphones on so as not to be heard, listen to classical music—Mussorgsky, *Pictures at an Exhibition*, one of the favorite pieces of my father, who had recently died. Music, beauty, in order to endure. And all at once that pseudonym—whose real name and face I did not know whether I would ever come to know—was not a figure in the war's chronicle, a more or less reliable source, a piece of testimony. That citizen of Mosul was one like us. Like me. His story is a source of inspiration and an extraordinary adventure."

—Riccardo Chartroux, RAI TV

"When Omar Mohammed's hometown, Mosul, was overtaken by ISIS in 2014, he began documenting everyday life under the brutal regime. What he only realized much later was that his archive chronicles not only life during war, but the destruction of an ancient cosmopolitan city made up of buildings with people containing memories. *Mosul Eye* is not the ultimate account of Mosul, because the city still rests on the banks of the Tigris River. But the book gives life to the famous saying by the Jewish sage Tarfon: 'It is not your duty to finish the work, but neither are you free to neglect it.'"

—Kathrine Tschemerinsky, culture editor, *Weekendavisen*

"Considering the risk to the author's life, it is astonishing that this book, *Mosul Eye: A Clandestine Scholar's War Against ISIS*, was ever written. Through his pseudonym Mosul Eye, Omar proved not only that resistance was possible but also that ISIS's actions were being observed and documented. His blog gave the people of Mosul something they thought they had lost—hope. It was an inspired gift. Now the world can read this remarkable story."

—James Bluemel, director of *Once Upon a Time in Iraq*

"Mosul is a layered city that has weathered trials and tribulations. This account is a personal record, one among many that exist, that can salvage a city when its very voice is being silenced."

—Sultan Sooud Al Qassemi, founder of Barjeel Art Foundation

"For too long, the best accounts on the ISIS group relied on distant analysis and captured documents. This is less than ideal; our understanding was deprived of authentic local voices. The exception to this was the mysterious Mosul Eye, now known to us as the distinguished Omar Mohammad, native of Mosul. This book fills the gap in the story of one of the most dangerous and diabolical insurgencies in history. I'm grateful for his work in telling the rest of the story."

—Dr. Craig Whiteside, coauthor of *The ISIS Reader*, US Naval War College

"It was 2014, and I followed a Twitter account that people said gave good updates on the situation in Mosul. Only then did it dawn on me that there were real people still inside Mosul who were trying to survive. When Omar was safe and went public, I knew I wanted to share his story, so I reached out and asked if he would speak to my students—a few minutes later he called. His story is a beautiful portrayal of human strength and courage, and yet so raw and full of pain. It offers a stark warning of how quickly religious radicalization breeds extremism, and the danger of ignoring messianic political messaging. It is a lesson in history not only because it tells the story of how Mosul survived in brutal detail, but also because it shows that history is never forgotten."

—Dr. Tova Norlén, the Defense Security Cooperation Agency (DSCA)

"In 2014, ISIS committed genocide against the Yezidis in Iraq. Many of the atrocities against Yezidi captives occurred in Mosul. In the aftermath of the Yezidi Genocide, we wanted to see national solidarity and support for Yezidis from other communities. One of the reliable allies we found was Omar from Mosul. He spoke at our virtual Yezidi Genocide commemoration events. Omar has never hesitated to highlight the crimes committed against Yezidis and the need for Iraqis, including the Iraqi state, to do better for our people. Many neighbors turned on Yezidis in 2014 and committed unspeakable atrocities. We need more common humanity and respect in Iraq, across religions and ethnicities. We are happy to have Omar as a friend and ally."

—Pari Ibrahim, the Free Yezidi Foundation

"Omar Mohammed's work reminds us that cultural resistance is not abstract: it is lived, breathed, and paid for at the highest personal cost. In a city where music was silenced, instruments destroyed, and artists persecuted, his determination to document and ultimately revive Mosul's musical life stands as one of the most profound acts of defiance of our time. Music is not a luxury. It is the deepest expression of what it means to be human: our identity, our dignity, our refusal to be erased. By preserving its memory through the darkest years of occupation, and nurturing its return after liberation, Omar Mohammed safeguarded not only a tradition, but the living soul of a city that refused to disappear."

—Paolo Petrocelli, founder and president, EMMA for Peace (Euro-Mediterranean Music Academy for Peace)

"The passion, courage, and empathy he showed were outstanding. During my life in the city of Mosul, in that underestimated city, it was rare for me to feel connected to someone's philosophy. The Jurassic changes the city witnessed shaped the community in many ways, creating a complex formula that made it seem impossible to plant a seed and expect it to grow. Omar, the Ghost, Mosul Eye—the dream planted tree seeds that have grown shaded, housed, and fed many. An ancient tree with deep roots seeks wisdom, and high branches seek light. Sharing many beliefs, crossing many paths with him made me realize that whatever crazy ideas could sound, Omar would push them further and make them happen. The world owes him a lot!"

—Ameen Mokdad, violinist and composer, Mosul

"I first met Omar when he was forced to flee Mosul, afraid for his life, but perhaps even more afraid for the erasure of his beloved city from public memory. This book shows us the weight and incomparable value of documenting a place, a history, and a life through destruction, displacement, and rebuilding. To cherish a city like Omar cherishes Mosul is a love we should all be so lucky to have—and we are fortunate to bear witness through his writing."

—Sarina Simon Rosenthal, Scholars at Risk – New York University

MOSUL EYE

A SCHOLAR'S CLANDESTINE WAR AGAINST ISIS

OMAR MOHAMMED

FOREWORD BY HIS HOLINESS
POPE FRANCIS

INTRODUCTION BY
GENERAL DAVID H. PETRAEUS

Skyhorse Publishing

10 9 8 7 6 5 4 3 2 1

Library of Congress Cataloging-in-Publication Data is available on file.

Cover design by Brian Peterson
Cover photo: Ahmad Al-Rubaye/Staff via Getty Images

Print ISBN: 978-1-5107-8567-0
Ebook ISBN: 978-1-5107-8568-7

Printed in the United States of America

For the river.

A city remembers. So will the world.

CONTENTS

FOREWORD

BY POPE FRANCIS

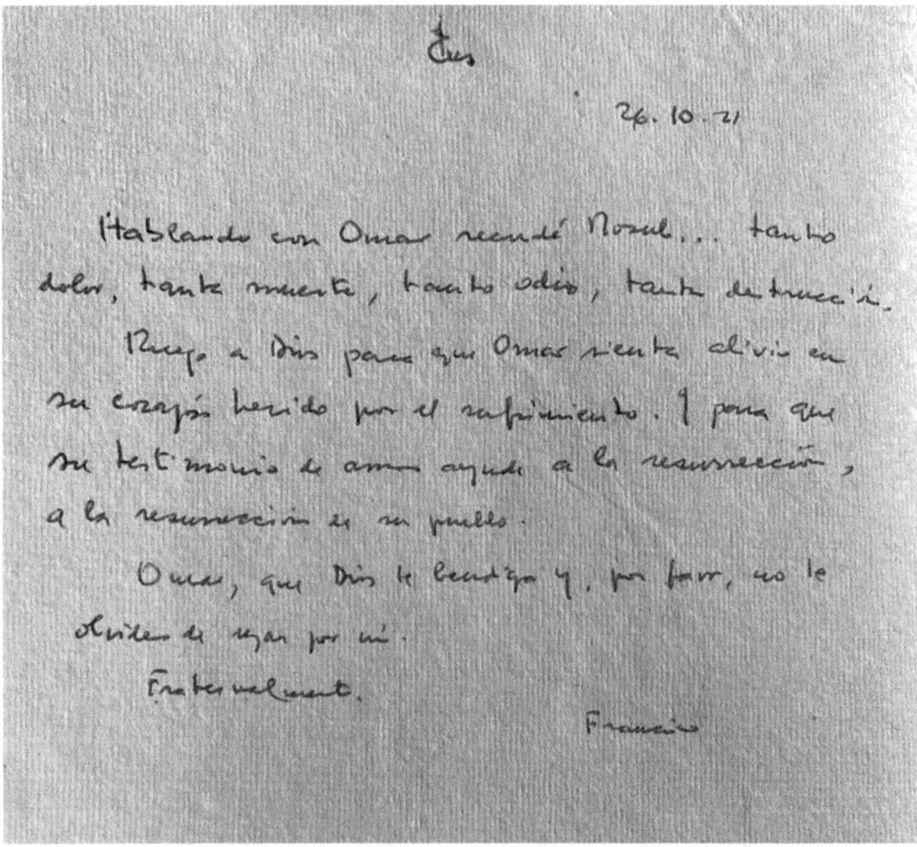

26.10.21

Hablando con Omar recordé Mosul... tanto dolor, tanta muerte, tanto odio, tanta destrucción.

Ruego a Dios para que Omar sienta alivio en su corazón herido por el sufrimiento. Y para que su testimonio de amor ayude a la resurrección, a la resurrección de su pueblo.

Omar, que Dios te bendiga y, por favor, no te olvides de rezar por mí.

Fraternalmente,

Francisco

26 Ottobre 2021
Casa Santa Marta, Rome

Hablando con Omar recuerdo Mosul . . . tanto dolor, tanto muerte, tanto odio, tanta destrucción.

Ruego a Dios para que Omar sienta alivio en su corazón herido por el sufrimiento. Y para que su testimonio de amor ayude a la resurrección, a la resurrección de su pueblo.

Omar, que Dios te bendiga y, por favor, no te olvides de orar por mí.

Fraternamente,

Franciscus

Translation

Speaking with Omar I remember Mosul . . . so much pain, so much death, so much hatred, so much destruction.

I pray to God that Omar may feel relief in his heart, wounded by suffering. And that his testimony of love may help the resurrection, the resurrection of his people.

Omar, may God bless you and, please, do not forget to pray for me.

Fraternally,

Franciscus

His Holiness Pope Francis (1936–2025)

(Written by hand for the author, Casa Santa Marta, Vatican City, October 26, 2021)

I wanted the city to have an eye that saw what was being done to it.

—Omar Mohammed

June 17, 2014

INTRODUCTION

GENERAL DAVID H. PETRAEUS, U.S. ARMY (RET.)

Ana Moslawi.

I am a Moslawi. I have said this many times over the years, and I have meant it—not as a claim of birth (I was born in Cornwall, New York), but as a declaration of attachment. In Arabic, the phrase carries more than geography. It says: "This place is part of me. And Mosul is part of me".

The months I spent there from late April of 2003 through mid-February of 2004, when I commanded the 101st Airborne Division and was responsible for Ninewa Province (of which Mosul is the capital) and the three Kurdish provinces, were among the most consequential of my life. The people I came to know—their warmth, intelligence, resilience, and civilizational depth—left a permanent mark. In truth, those of us who served in Iraq, especially those who served many years there (four years in my case) may eventually have left, but Iraq never left us. The people of Iraq—the Shaab al-Iraqi—have, ever since my final tour in the Land of the Two Rivers, remained on my mind and in my heart. And that is especially true of the Moslawis.

I first saw Mosul from the open door of a Black Hawk helicopter in late April 2003. The wheat was ripening along the Tigris—green, turning golden, against pale brown earth—and even from the air the city announced itself as extraordinary: the river bending wide through it, the density of the Old City rising from the western bank, minarets and church steeples crowded together in a way that spoke immediately of age, heritage, complexity, and consequence. I had studied Iraq—its history, its fault lines—but Mosul was not a monograph. It was alive. And it was about to become my responsibility.

We had not planned to go north. The 101st Airborne Division (Air Assault)—the famed Screaming Eagles—was to be based around Baghdad after the fight north from Kuwait that toppled the Saddam Hussein regime. We needed the vast hardstand and facilities at Baghdad International Airport for our large helicopter fleet, which needed a respite from the desert that had taken a toll on rotor and turbine blades during the fight to Baghdad from Kuwait. But on very short notice in late April, we were ordered north to Ninewa Province. The directive was clear: Get to Mosul within thirty-six hours and restore control. A small Marine unit had been unable to quell growing violence, and seventeen civilians had been killed in a demonstration the day prior.

We did not even have maps of Ninewa. Our topographic engineers printed them overnight as we prepared for one of the longest air assault operations in history. It commenced on April 22 and employed the majority of our more than 250 helicopters. Mosul, then a city of 1,700,000 people, was a shambles—ravaged as much by terrible looting as by the war. There was no electricity, no running water, no garbage removal. Shops were closed. Police had vanished. Public buildings were looted or destroyed. Parts of the city were still burning. And Ninewa contained virtually every fault line that defined Iraq—Arab and Kurd, Sunni and Shia, Christian and Yazidi, Turkmen and Shabak—along with tribal structures, intra-religious and political party rivalries, and grievances that predated modern borders.

There was no one else to do it. So we did it.

We surged forces into Mosul. Soldiers moved rapidly from our landing zones at the airport into the city as attack helicopters overwatched overhead. Our intent was to signal clearly that authority had shifted—that there was now a new governing force in Ninewa and that we had both the capacity and the will to impose order. As the commander of an occupying force under the Geneva Convention, I was, in effect, the senior executive, legislative, and judicial authority in the area. I was also the Sheikh of the strongest tribe in Ninewa Province, and we intended to use my authorities and our military capabilities.

We went to work immediately: establishing security, restoring basic services, rebuilding infrastructure, and developing a framework for governance. My intent was rapidly to establish an interim provincial government that reflected the full diversity of Ninewa—ethnic, sectarian, tribal, and political—with representation proportional to the respective elements and majority rule, while safeguarding minority rights. Within two weeks, we organized a caucus that produced a representative provisional council and governor.

We found funds to pay government workers. We reopened the Syrian border to restore the flow of goods before the salaries were resumed (to prevent the inflation that otherwise would have ensued). We brokered oil-for-electricity arrangements with Syria and Turkey. We repaired roads, took control of vast ammunition storage facilities, and occupied former Iraqi air force and other military bases. We refurbished the Olympic swimming pool. We established a soccer league with over 150 teams. We reopened the police academy. We repaired and reopened the main hospital and amusement park. We brought a derelict irrigation system (that served 280,000 acres of western Ninewa) back into operation. We even established truck stops to support the revival of commerce from Syria and Turkey, auctioned off two heavily damaged hotels and a massive stockpile of sulfur, and rebuilt the hotel and brought back translators to enable the return of international tourism at the historic Assyrian ruins at Hatra. Ultimately, we completed over five thousand reconstruction projects. And every evening, we visited local leaders in their homes—building relationships, listening, and discussing what kind of future might be possible. There was considerable optimism about the future of Iraq and Mosul without Saddam Hussein and his brutal regime.

"Money is ammunition," I told Ambassador Paul Bremer, the head of the newly established Coalition Provisional Authority, during his first visit to Mosul in late May—meaning that small, rapidly executed reconstruction projects could often consolidate security gains more effectively than additional patrols (though they also continued). That principle would later be codified in the Army and Marine Corps Counterinsurgency Field Manual drafted in 2006, but it was born in Mosul from lived experience.

One of our most consequential efforts was the rehabilitation of Mosul University. It had been heavily looted, and the terribly misguided De-Ba'athification policy was announced by Ambassador Bremer (especially as it did not include an agreed reconciliation process). It had removed the university's leadership—including every dean of the nearly twenty colleges of the university and over 120 tenured faculty members, many of whom were quite secular and Western-educated, and had joined the Ba'ath Party at the lowest levels simply to advance professionally. The result was institutional collapse.

I assigned an aviation brigade commander the mission to rebuild the university. He assembled a very capable team, and they restored infrastructure, rewired the campus, and reestablished its technical backbone. I secured from Ambassador Bremer an exception to the De-Ba'athification policy to allow a reconciliation commission (the only one in Iraq) to evaluate and reinstate faculty (as well as thousands of other bureaucrats thrown out of their jobs, whom we needed to help run a country we still did not sufficiently understand) where appropriate. Rebuilding the university mattered deeply to the new Provincial Council members and me. It was the intellectual heart of northern Iraq, and I believed then—as I do now—that a functioning university is one of the most powerful stabilizing forces in any society.

The spring and summer and much of the fall of 2003 were, in many respects, very hopeful. Americans and Moslawis worked closely together, and progress was tangible. The people of Mosul demonstrated what they had always been: resourceful, intelligent, proud, and deeply committed to their city. And they appreciated what our soldiers did; they even named a highway for the 101st Airborne Division.

But over time, near the end of our time, it began to come apart.

The disbanding of the Iraqi army—without a plan to support former soldiers—together with de-Baathification had helped fuel the insurgency. In Mosul, this had led to weeks of increasingly dangerous demonstrations. At one point, more than 10,000 former soldiers gathered around the provincial headquarters, some of them armed. The situation was dicey, and I addressed them directly, promising to press for stipends if they dispersed. I flew to Baghdad that day and argued forcefully for that policy change. It was implemented shortly after that—but only after considerable damage had been done.

As these and other decisions took hold, and as the Iraqi people's (often unrealistic) expectations went unmet, conditions began to deteriorate—particularly in the Sunni areas of Iraq, ultimately including Ninewa Province. And toward the end of our tour in early 2004, when the 101st Airborne Division, with its substantial resources and relationships, was replaced by a much smaller force, one-third our size, the gains we had achieved proved difficult to sustain. The security situation worsened. Our governor was fired shortly after I left, by authorities in Baghdad who felt he needed to be reined in (we had exercised too much initiative in the eyes of the authorities there). And, tragically, his successor was assassinated months later, in the spring of 2004. The seeds of insurgency were able to take root.

Over the following years, Iraq experienced cycles of progress, decline, and recovery, including the enormous improvements of the 2007–2008 Surge, that I was privileged to command, that were sustained over the subsequent three-and-a-half years. But after the withdrawal of the final U.S. four-star commander and the last of our combat forces in December 2011, and after disastrous subsequent Iraqi political decisions that reawakened sectarian divisions, conditions again deteriorated alarmingly. And, then, in the midst of enormous Sunni demonstrations, the Islamic State was able to reconstitute and build considerable combat power in the early years of the Syrian sectarian civil war. The result for Iraq was catastrophic.

In 2014, the Islamic State seized Ninewa Province, and Mosul became the capital of the caliphate established in northern Iraq.

When I learned of Mosul's fall, I understood the magnitude of the loss. This was not simply a military failure. It was the capture of one of the oldest continuously inhabited cities in the world by an organization intent on erasing its history, enslaving its people, and imposing an extremist ideology. The city we had worked to rebuild—its services restored, its governance reestablished, its university revived—was now under the control of extremists determined to destroy its identity.

Or so it seemed.

During the years of ISIS control, an anonymous figure began reporting from inside the city under the name Mosul Eye. The reporting was detailed, disciplined, and consistently credible. I remarked at the time that it was like having a spy on the ground. I did not say that lightly. I had spent years relying on the best intelligence capabilities in the world—first in five combat commands as a general officer, later as director of the CIA. What Mosul Eye produced matched the quality of the finest intelligence reporting—yet it came from a single individual, operating alone.

That individual was Omar Mohammed, a historian who studied at Mosul University.

He was not a trained intelligence officer. He had no formal support, no extraction plan, no institutional backing. What he possessed was a historian's discipline—the ability to verify, cross-reference, and preserve evidence with precision. Under extraordinary danger, he transformed scholarship into resistance.

He observed carefully, built networks quietly, preserved information securely, and transmitted it through channels that ultimately reached social media, coalition commanders, and the world. What he created was human intelligence in its most elemental and powerful form: one individual embedded in his own society, trusted because he was of it, effective because of his rigor, and irreplaceable because no external system could replicate what he provided.

Ultimately, he had to flee, but during the Battle of Mosul, he continued this work from exile—integrating his network with satellite imagery and ground reporting and even helping coordinate the rescue of civilians.

His brother Ahmad did not survive the conflict. And the al-Hadba' minaret—the enduring symbol of the city—was destroyed.

I returned to Iraq this past October, visiting the Kurdistan Region and Baghdad. In my conversations in the north and in the capital, I confirmed what history had shown repeatedly: Mosul endured. It was rebuilding, as it had after every attempt to break it. The Moslawis I spoke with carried scars, but also determination, intelligence, and pride. I saw that in 2003. I see it still.

This book tells the story of a man who preserved Mosul's truth when the city could not speak for itself. It is written with the precision of a historian, the awareness of someone who understood the risks, and the moral seriousness of a witness safeguarding the memory of a civilization under siege. What Omar Mohammed achieved—scholarship fused with survival and resistance—has few parallels in modern conflict.

Ana Moslawi. It is an honor to introduce this book. And it is a privilege to know the man who wrote it.

He is my hero.

—David H. Petraeus
General, U.S. Army (Retired)

EDITOR'S NOTE

Over the course of editing *Mosul Eye*, I found myself drawn into a work of unusual depth and resonance. Omar Mohammed traces not only the ordeal of a city under violent occupation, but also the difficult terrain between private conscience and public witness. The narrative moves across shifting layers of memory, history, and lived experience with a rare literary sensibility, carried by recurring images and echoes that gather force as the pages unfold. What emerges is not simply an account of events, but an immersion into a world shaped before, during, and after catastrophe.

At moments, the customary distance between reader and subject seemed to dissolve entirely. I was struck not only by the precision of the writing, but by its emotional and intellectual gravity. Twice, while editing these pages, I found myself setting the manuscript aside and walking for hours along the Hudson River, needing time to absorb where the work had taken me. Encounters with nonfiction of this caliber are exceedingly rare.

—Hector Carosso
Skyhorse Publishing

PREFACE

On June 10, 2014, the city of Mosul—Iraq's second largest, home to nearly two million people, built on and around the ruins of the Assyrian capital Nineveh—fell to the Islamic State in a single night. The Iraqi Army dissolved. Soldiers abandoned their uniforms in the streets. By morning, a city that had been continuously inhabited for seven thousand years belonged to a force that intended to abolish everything it had been.

I was inside the city when it fell. I am a historian. When ISIS took Mosul, I made a choice that would define the next three years of my life and reshape everything I understood about myself. I stayed. I documented. I refused to let the occupiers become the sole authors of what was happening to my city.

What followed—what I built, what I carried, what I lost, and what it did to me—is this book.

It is not a policy analysis, though it contains evidence that policymakers will need. It is not a military history, though it documents the largest urban battle of the twenty-first century. It is not a spy memoir, though the work it describes required deception, concealment, and the daily possibility of death.

It is the record of a historian who was compelled by the fall of his city to become something he had never intended to be. I have written it because the record demands it. Because the dead deserve to be counted by someone who knew them as people, not as categories. And because someone should say, clearly and without evasion, what it costs a human being to carry a city's truth through three years of terror and come out the other side uncertain whether the man who came out is the same man who went in.

Trust no one. Document everything.

That was the rule. This is the book.

—Omar Mohammed
Paris, 2026

AUTHOR'S NOTE

I began documenting the occupation of Mosul on the night it fell. The blog I named Mosul Eye began on June 17, 2014, seven days later. For the time I documented the occupation, I wrote under an anonymous name from inside the city. The archive has been preserved, and portions have been provided to international bodies pursuing accountability for what was done there.

Some names and identifying details have been changed to protect people still living in Iraq. These substitutions are consistent throughout. No events have been invented. Where dialogue appears, it reflects direct memory or notes made at the time.

Some of what I gathered does not appear in this book. What remains undisclosed remains so because the people it concerns are still alive.

***

For years, I carried the archive without knowing it was waiting to become a book. That changed at the Munich Security Conference in February 2025, at a gathering hosted by the BMW Foundation. There, after remarks by US Vice President JD Vance, I found myself seated next to Marco Vicenzino, a geopolitical expert and accomplished literary agent with a rare instinct for the deeper significance of a story. We began a conversation that ultimately led to this book. Marco became my agent, and a trusted friend—the person who saw this book before I did and brought it into the world.

—Omar Mohammed,
Paris, 2026

Woe to the city of blood, full of lies, full of plunder, never without victims.

Nahum 3:1 (seventh century BC)

From this place they marched to a great stronghold, deserted and lying in ruins. The name of this city was Mespila, and it was once inhabited by the Medes.

Xenophon, *Anabasis* III.4 (401 BC)

The city is a large and ancient one, fortified and imposing, and prepared against the strokes of adversity.

Ibn Jubayr, *Riḥlat Ibn Jubayr* (1184)

By ruse and treachery, the Mongols captured Mosul, massacred its inhabitants, and went on plundering and looting for nine days. They then razed the town to the ground, and the survivors fled.

Yāsīn ibn Khayr Allāh al-Khaṭīb al-'Umarī, *Munyat al-udabā' fī tārīkh al-Mūṣil al-ḥadbā'*, f. 32v

The river knew what the occupation did not: that conquerors are temporary.

Lui-même, Mosul (2014)

THE CITY THAT DISAPPEARED

There was one man who did not run. I heard him. From inside the house, beginning at three in the morning on June 6—the hour the attack on Mosul began—I could hear sustained gunfire from a single position. It did not stop when the other positions fell silent. Through the hours that followed, I heard ISIS fighters calling out to him, telling him to surrender, promising that if he gave himself up, he would live. Each time they called, he answered with gunfire. The exchange repeated itself for hours—the voices, the offer, and then the shots that refused it. Around six in the morning, the shooting from his position stopped. I do not know whether his weapon jammed or whether his ammunition was simply gone. What I heard next was a storm of gunfire directed at him—a concentrated volley from multiple weapons at once. Then silence. He was the last man to stand against ISIS in Mosul. I never learned his name.

The emergency bell at the University of Mosul rang at the wrong time—and it had never worked before, not once in all my years on that campus; when trouble came we got warning shots from security if we were lucky, and if we were not we found ourselves caught in the cross fire between soldiers and terrorists, but on June 5, 2014, the bell that had never rung actually rang—and then an ambulance was burning with a policeman's body still inside it, and then the city I had spent my life studying began to disappear. Not slowly. Not in stages that could be debated, contested, and perhaps reversed. It disappeared the way a man disappears when soldiers abandon their uniforms and walk away from their posts: all at once, and with a silence underneath the noise that was worse than the noise itself.

The beginning of Mosul's fall does not return to me as a clean sequence of facts. It comes back first as a disturbance. Heat. Dust. A bell ringing at the wrong time. A city loses confidence before it understands that it is losing itself.

Mosul sits on the Tigris River in northern Iraq, roughly halfway between Baghdad and the Turkish border. The Tigris is one of the two rivers of ancient Mesopotamia—the land between the rivers, the territory that textbooks call the Cradle of Civilization—and Mosul is built on and around the ruins of Nineveh, the Assyrian capital that fell to Babylon in 612 BC, a city whose name appears in the Hebrew Bible and whose stones are still visible from across the streets. For most of the modern era, it was Iraq's second-largest city, home to more than a million people, and it was the kind of place that carried its age consciously. The Tigris runs wide there, the color of hammered tin, and the old city rises from its western bank in a dense layering of neighborhoods that have been inhabited continuously for centuries. Moslawis—the city's people—had a word for those who did not understand this: They were people who had not yet sat long enough by the river.

My family had sat by that river for a long time. My grandfather on my father's side came from generations of wool traders who had shipped their goods south to Basra along the Tigris, with England as the ultimate destination—families whose trade news had once flown between Mosul and Basra by pigeon, long before any nation called Iraq existed.

The family home was in the city's oldest neighborhood, a few minutes' walk from the water. My grandfather on my mother's side had been an unrepentant communist under first a monarchy and then a succession of military dictators, sentenced to death four separate times for refusing to bend to prevailing political winds. Each time, a change of government spared his life, and he died in his seventies—a normal death, I would later say, after Mosul had spent years learning what abnormal deaths looked like. Between them, these two men gave me something I would not fully understand until my city was occupied: the wool trader's patience with systems, routes, and the slow accumulation of practical knowledge, and the communist's insistence that it was possible to refuse the terms imposed by powerful men, even when refusal seemed futile. I grew up in a house that loved the sound of music—a house where music was part of the air, part of how the family understood itself, long before anyone thought to forbid it.

I was born in 1986 during the Iran-Iraq War, the middle child of five brothers and five sisters. Ahmad was the eldest of the brothers—protective, quick-tempered, the one who had taught me to ride a bicycle by refusing to accept that I could not. He ran a shop where he made curtains, and he carried himself with the weight of someone who had assumed responsibility early. He did not understand my obsession with archives and old manuscripts. He did not need to. What he understood was that a younger brother required looking after, and he never stopped. Under Saddam Hussein's dictatorship we could not ask questions, but I was a child who asked them anyway. One of my teachers told me: You ask too many questions—when you become an adult, then you can ask these questions. I thought about those words for years afterward, and when the extremist groups that followed the American invasion began killing people for loving music and for asking questions, I understood that questions could kill. By 2014, I was a scholar of history at the University of Mosul, having completed my master's and begun doctoral work, spending whatever time remained in the city's archives, where I was most at home. The focus of my research was Mosul in the nineteenth century: the Ottoman period, the layered record of a city that had always been more than its rulers understood it to be. History was not, for me, a matter of detached analysis. It was the way I made sense of the place I lived and the people I lived among.

For years we had lived between checkpoints and assassinations, rumors and reprisals, bombings and denials. The American invasion of 2003, which toppled Saddam Hussein's government, had not brought order to northern Iraq; it had dissolved the existing order and left behind a violent contest for what would replace it. Through the years that followed, Mosul became a crucible for that contest. Al-Qaeda in Iraq operated there, then splintered, then reconsolidated under new names. Sunni Arab militias and Kurdish forces competed for territory. The Iraqi Army, which replaced the old security structure with men who owed their positions more to political loyalty than to military competence, struggled to hold the city. Bombings, targeted killings, and abductions became part of the texture of daily life. Families learned to read the city's moods through small signals: which streets to avoid, which hours were safer, how to move and speak and calculate without provoking the wrong attention.

When instability continues long enough, people stop living in permanent alarm. They adapt. They keep studying, shopping, planning, grading papers, speaking about salaries and rent and the approaching holy month of Ramadan. The extraordinary becomes ordinary, and when the true break finally comes it first resembles one more variation of the same disturbance. That is one reason those first days were so hard to read correctly.

The city's preparation—if you can call it that—began not on a single day but in a sequence that was difficult to read at the time. Roughly a week before the fall, on or around May 30, the Army of the Men of the Naqshbandi Order—a Sunni insurgent group led by former Ba'athist officers with roots in the Sufi Naqshbandi tradition—seized control of Mosul for more than twenty-four hours. Then the attack ended as if nothing had happened. The armed men withdrew. The city resumed its ordinary shape. I did not understand then what it meant. I learned later that seizure had been a rehearsal—a test of the city's defenses and the army's response, carried out in coordination with or in preparation for what ISIS was planning. That Mosul could be taken for a full day and returned without consequence should have told everyone what was coming. It did not.

Then, at dawn on June 5, ISIS struck Samarra,* a city south of Mosul whose most sacred site is a Shia Muslim shrine, one of the most important

* Samarra is one of the oldest continuously inhabited sites in Iraq, with traces of settlement dating to approximately 5300 BCE. In the ninth century the Abbasid caliph al-Mu'tasim made it the capital of the Islamic empire, renaming it Surra

in Iraq. The attack was quick, almost bizarre—fighting flared in the city and subsided, and in Mosul we had no idea what was really happening. It was a provocation designed to inflame sectarian tension across the country. Samarra was not Mosul. But news travels through relatives, phone calls, and the shorter circuits of rumor, and in Mosul, which was majority Sunni Muslim but had always contained Shia communities, Christians, Kurds, Turkmen, and Yazidis alongside one another, any event that stoked sectarian violence sent a specific kind of chill through the population. We had seen how that violence could reach into a city and reorganize it. By noon that day the security forces had declared a curfew.

I was at the university when the order came. The security forces issued clear instructions: Everyone must go home. We began running. It is never safe to stay on the streets when Mosul locks down, and even before I understood why this curfew felt different from the others, I could see it in the faces of the people around me. They were not moving with the annoyed haste of people managing another interruption. The sky was dusty and red.

The University of Mosul—where I had spent that afternoon before the curfew emptied it—was one of the largest universities in Iraq. Founded in 1967, it occupied a sprawling campus on the eastern bank of the Tigris, and for decades it had been the intellectual center of the city—the place where Mosul's historians, engineers, doctors, and poets were trained, where the city's future was prepared. I had defended my M.A. thesis in that same building—a study of the Egyptian historian al-Jabarti, who documented Napoleon's occupation of Cairo from inside the city.

That night the rumors arrived faster than anyone could verify them. A government employee—his name passed through the neighborhood

Man Ra'a—"He who sees it is delighted." In 847, his successor al-Mutawakkil built the Great Mosque, the spiral minaret of which remains one of the most recognizable structures in Islamic architecture. After al-Mutawakkil's assassination in 861, Baghdad reclaimed the capital and Samarra's prominence faded. Its most sacred site today is the al-Askari shrine, one of the holiest in Shia Islam; its bombing in 2006 by al-Qaeda in Iraq ignited the sectarian civil war that would reshape the country in the years before ISIS.

before his body was found—had been killed on one of the roads leading out of the city, shot at a checkpoint that had not existed that morning. Cars that had left Mosul in the first hours of the curfew had not arrived where they were going—they had driven into a space between the city and whatever was gathering outside it and had simply disappeared, neither returned nor accounted for, as though the roads themselves had swallowed them. And from Muhallabiya, a town to the west where the voices you heard in the streets had always been the voices of people who belonged there, word came that a foreign tongue had been heard—accents that were not Iraqi, not local, not from any province anyone could name. Men speaking Arabic that came from somewhere else entirely. In Muhallabiya, where foreign voices had no reason to be.

No one I knew slept that night. The curfew held the city in place while, outside the edges of what we could see or confirm, something was arranging itself in the dark.

The attack on Mosul itself began in the early hours of June 6, around three in the morning, when ISIS fighters struck the western districts of the city. On the western side, where I lived, I received it first through sound—sustained gunfire rather than scattered shots, explosions followed by intervals of silence followed by new waves, the unmistakable difference between an incident and an assault.

The heat of Mosul in June has its own cruelty. By noon, sunlight does not simply illuminate the city; it presses on it. The temperature can reach fifty degrees Celsius—a heat that enters buildings, that makes the air above the roads shimmer, that turns the normally patient rhythms of street life into something frantic. Dust enters the air, the mouth, the eyes. That day the dust and the fear seemed to assist one another. The outlines of the city itself looked unstable.

By eleven in the morning—June 6—I went outside. Near our neighborhood I passed a red car bomb that was ready to detonate. The remains of what looked like metal twisted into shapes that metal is not supposed to take, shrapnel scattered across the pavement in a radius that told you the force of what had happened before your mind could process it. An ambulance was burning. Inside it was the body of a policeman who had been trying to reach the wounded when the vehicle was hit. The fire had not finished with him. I stood and looked at it, and the smell entered me before the image did—the smell of burning rubber and burning fuel and something else underneath both of those that I did not want to identify and that my body identified anyway.

Farther down the street, a brand-new Toyota pickup sat in the middle of the road. Mounted in its bed was a heavy machine gun, dark black, with the dull sheen of something recently unwrapped. Behind it stood a man with a long beard, wearing the loose Afghan-style clothing that would soon become the uniform of the new order. He did not speak. He did not move. He stood behind the gun with his hands resting on it and watched the street with the patience of someone who already owned it.

On the side of the road, two more fighters. One was Asian—not Iraqi, not Arab, someone from a distance I could not guess—and he was eating a piece of *sammoun*, tearing the bread calmly with his fingers the way anyone in Mosul tears *sammoun* on any ordinary morning. Beside him stood a tall Black man, also armed, also silent.

The street was calm. Everything seemed calm, as if nothing had happened. Except that everything looked as though a storm had just struck and then disappeared—had torn through and taken every familiar sound with it, leaving behind only silence. Deep silence. The silence of a city holding its breath without knowing yet what it was holding its breath for.

On June 7, Nouri al-Maliki—the prime minister in Baghdad whose security forces had just dissolved—ordered air strikes on ISIS positions inside Mosul. What reached our neighborhood was not precision. It was obliteration aimed at no one in particular. Explosions struck residential streets. Houses were damaged—ours among them, the walls cracked, the windows blown inward, glass across every surface. There was no safe place. We moved from room to room as the strikes continued, trying to calculate which part of the house was farthest from the outer walls, knowing the calculation was meaningless. In the street, families who had stayed through the ground assault were now running again—not from ISIS but from their own government's aircraft. Every living thing was a target. We wanted life, and there was nowhere in the city that was offering it.

I wrote that day: We are experiencing unbearable and unimaginable things. That sentence was not dramatic. It was exact. What was unbearable was not merely the bombing but its source. The army that had abandoned us without fighting was now bombing us from a distance, and it was hitting not the men who had taken our city but the people who remained inside it.

Two days later, I learned why.

Abu Waheeb—Shakir Wahib al-Fahdawi, one of ISIS's most feared field commanders, an escaped prisoner from Tikrit who had made himself notorious for killing captives on the highways of Anbar Province—had been in Mosul before the assault began, staying secretly in the house of a Mosul tribal sheikh. The sheikh was a figure both sides knew well. For years he had served as a channel between Nineveh Operations Command, the Iraqi military authority governing the province, and various armed groups including ISIS. Both sides understood what he was. He was the man through whom messages passed when the two sides did not want to fight, when a prisoner needed releasing, when a neighborhood needed sparing, when the silent negotiations that ran beneath the public violence required a trusted intermediary. He belonged fully to neither side, which was precisely what made him useful to both.

When Maliki ordered the air strikes, it was the sheikh's channel that carried the coordinates. And it was Waheeb who supplied them—coordinates he knew to be civilian. Every target he passed through Abdulsalam was a home, a street, an ordinary piece of the city where no ISIS fighter was standing. The air strikes hit exactly where Waheeb wanted them to hit. He wanted the people of Mosul to see their own government killing them. He wanted the distance between Baghdad and Mosul to become unbridgeable—not only in military terms, but in the moral currency that matters most when a city is deciding whether to resist or submit.

The cruelest part of the calculation was that it barely needed to be made. Maliki's forces were not known for their concern with civilian casualties in Sunni cities. The coordinates could have been accurate, and the result might have been the same. What Waheeb did was ensure it, and ensure that the people of Mosul would know—or believe—that the government they were supposed to hope would save them was instead killing them from the sky.

Our house gathered us the way houses do when public language fails.

What I remember most about those hours is not one dramatic speech or one decisive domestic scene. It is the eyes.

We dragged the closet to the windows—the heavy wooden wardrobe from the bedroom, pushed across the floor and braced against the glass to absorb what the glass could not. My brothers and I did this without speaking, without anyone giving the order, because every family in Mosul knew the geometry of shelter: furniture against the windows, bodies away from the outer walls, everyone in the innermost room. My mother, my brothers, my sisters, my nieces and nephews—the children wide-eyed and quiet in the way that children become quiet when they understand, before anyone has explained it to them, that the adults are afraid. All of us in one room. I looked at their faces, and I saw a room I had been inside before.

I was four years old in 1991 when the American bombs fell on Iraq during the Gulf War, and my entire extended family had sheltered together in the house of a relative named Ibrahim—every member, every generation, crowded into one space while 116,000 air sorties struck the country in six weeks. I had returned to that room in my mind many times since. Now I was inside it again. The same geometry. The same eyes. My nieces and nephews where I had been in 1991—small bodies pressed against the people they trusted, not understanding what was happening but understanding that it was happening. One bomb and our entire history and future would disappear together.

I took out my phone and photographed the room. I am looking at that photograph now, years later, beside the memory I carry of the same moment, and they are a striking match—the faces, the positions, the light, the expression in every pair of eyes that is not panic but something harder to name: the look of people who are waiting to find out whether they will continue to exist.

The television was still on. Iraqi state television spoke in the formal register of official reassurance—a register that people who had lived through decades of Ba'athist rule had learned to translate instantly. *The situation is under control. Security forces are responding. Citizens should remain calm.* My father watched with the stillness of a man who had heard those words before and knew what lay behind them. My mother moved through what space remained, carrying tea she had made without being asked, pressing a glass into each hand—"Drink"—the way she said it when there was nothing else she could do. Her hands would not stop moving. It was not denial. It was the last structure left when the larger ones are breaking. The ordinary tending of a household against the collapse of everything outside it.

Outside, the street was silent with the quality of a place that has been evacuated rather than stilled. A street with no movement can feel more frightening than a street clogged with cars. By afternoon the silence had become heavier than the traffic it had replaced. It was not the silence of calm. It was the silence of a city that had stopped breathing.

On June 8, the governor of Mosul, Atheel al-Nujaifi—one of the most powerful political figures in the province, a Sunni Arab politician who had governed Nineveh Province, of which Mosul was the capital, for years—appeared publicly to reassure the city. The attack was limited and under control, he said. Things would return to normal. For many families those words mattered. People stayed, or returned after early flight, because a man of senior authority had assessed the situation and judged that departure was unnecessary. Later, after everything was lost, those assurances would acquire the weight that false reassurance only accumulates after the fact. At the time they worked as intended: They slowed departure, calmed some fears, and helped sustain the illusion that the state still stood between the city and disaster.

That illusion did not last.

The city was not simply overwhelmed by superior force in a straightforward battle. It was abandoned.

The Iraqi Army in Mosul had long been one of the institutions most distrusted by the city's population. Its soldiers were often poorly paid, poorly equipped, and commanded by officers whose appointments owed more to political connections in Baghdad than to military ability. Years of corruption had hollowed out its fighting capacity even as its official numbers remained large. When ISIS pressed against Mosul's defenses, what was exposed was not merely a military failure but the accumulated consequences of years in which the army had been an instrument of political patronage rather than genuine security.

Military presence disappeared from positions where it should have held. Equipment was abandoned where equipment should not have been left. The defensive line did not retreat in orderly fashion; it fragmented. On June 9, a Saudi fighter named al-Jazrawi, who had come to Iraq as part of ISIS's transnational volunteer force, drove a bomb-laden tanker truck toward the Mosul Hotel, where the Iraqi security forces had concentrated their last organized resistance. The explosion destroyed the building and ended those final lines. What followed was not a tactical withdrawal. It was dissolution: soldiers removing their uniforms, abandoning their weapons, and blending back into the civilian population or fleeing east toward Kurdish-controlled territory.

On June 12, as the Iraqi Army was dissolving across Mosul and the north, ISIS moved south toward Tikrit. At Camp Speicher—the former American air base outside the city, named after Scott Speicher, a US Navy pilot lost in the first Gulf War—approximately 1,700 young men died.

They were cadets. Air force students, most of them barely trained, many of them still in the first weeks of their service. When ISIS arrived at Tikrit, they were not inside the fortified base. They were outside it, on the roads, trying to reach safety. ISIS gathered them in groups. Some were taken to the banks of the Tigris. Some to the grounds of one of Saddam Hussein's former palaces near the river. They were told to lie face down. Then they were shot.

I heard about it in the afternoon—the day it happened. ISIS distributed the videos themselves, broadcasting them on screens across the city, announcing them on the radio. Not as atrocity but as victory. "We reached Tikrit. We took hundreds of what they called *Rafida*"—their word for Shia, meaning those who reject—"and we administered God's judgment." The videos showed the trucks. Men packed in like animals, begging, some of them saying to the camera: We didn't even train yet. We just arrived.

What I remember is not one image. It is the pistol. The man moving along the bank, methodical, shooting into the prone bodies one after another, working his way down the line with the patience of a man finishing a task that needs to be finished before something else can begin.

The number that emerged in the weeks after was 1,700. Some estimates were higher. The Iraqi government, which would eventually exhume mass graves from the Speicher site years later, confirmed the scale. The victims were predominantly Shia men from the south of the country—young men who had volunteered for military service and arrived at a base that the army had already decided to abandon. They were killed because they were there, because they were Shia, and because ISIS understood, with the clarity of an organization that had been planning this for years, that the mass killing of soldiers in the first days of the occupation would complete the message the army's dissolution had begun: The state was gone, and everything that had stood between the population and ISIS was gone with it.

The massacre at Speicher was not an improvisation. It was a statement. Made in plain sight, distributed on video, announced on radio, aimed not only at the dead but at every person watching—which in those weeks meant every person in Mosul. This is what we do. This is what we are capable of. This is what you are now living inside.

A city conquered after prolonged resistance carries one kind of historical meaning. A city left open carries another. The emotional effect on its inhabitants is different in a way that is difficult to describe. If a city falls after defense, grief may still contain a tragic dignity. If it falls through abandonment, grief is mixed with something sharper—a sense of betrayal that has no obvious object because the betrayal came from so many directions at once. By the time this became clear, choice had narrowed to its most basic human form. Stay or leave.

My family decided to leave for Erbil. We went on June 12, like many others moving east.

Erbil is the capital of Iraqi Kurdistan, the autonomous Kurdish region that occupies the northeastern part of Iraq. In 2014, it was one of the few parts of the country that had achieved something close to stability—governed by the Kurdistan Regional Government, protected by the Peshmerga, the Kurdish military forces, and separated from the worst of Iraq's sectarian violence by both geography and political arrangement. Erbil was where people went when they needed to be somewhere that was still, provisionally, safe.

By the time we left Mosul, leaving had acquired a terrible ordinary quality. Pack, calculate, move, wait, pass a checkpoint, call someone, ask someone, explain yourself, carry what you can, abandon what you cannot. Departure transforms the status of ordinary objects. Documents become precious. Cash becomes inadequate. Clothing becomes a calculation between necessity and ignorance, because no one knows whether they are leaving for days, weeks, or forever. A car becomes not transportation but triage. How many people can fit? What can be carried? What must be left behind? A family fleeing does not move in one emotional register. There is urgency, grief, irritation, small practical arguments, silence, prayer, and exhaustion, all existing together inside the same vehicle. Ahmad took charge the way he always did—counting heads, checking that the younger ones had their documents, speaking to my father in a voice that was calm on its surface and tight underneath it.

Getting into Erbil was not simple. Two friends helped. One was another researcher, from Baghdad, whose family bridged Arab and Kurdish worlds—his mother from the Talabani family, one of the most prominent Kurdish political dynasties in Iraq, his father from a prominent Baghdadi household. When I told him I needed to bring my family somewhere safe, he called someone working for the Kurdistan Regional Government, who met us behind the checkpoint and facilitated our entry. A second friend, a dentist, was also involved. Even in flight, one encounters systems rather than pure movement. Geography is never only geography.

But arrival in Erbil did not mean arrival in the full sense. I wanted to rent a house directly. We were told we needed permission from the Asayish, the Kurdish security services, whose approval was required for Mosul's displaced to establish residency in the region. Housing controls and bureaucratic obstruction intervened immediately. Refuge does not look like safety when one is forced to negotiate it through official channels while carrying panic, family responsibility, and uncertainty.

Emotionally, I could not stand the distance.

Mosul remained the center of reality. History was being made there, or unmade. The city was changing while I sat outside it. Safety separated from one's city at the moment of its transformation can begin to feel like mutilation. In Erbil I was not simply displaced. I was estranged from the site of truth, and that estrangement—from the streets where I had walked every day, from the archives where I had worked, from the people who remained and whose lives were now being reorganized by a force I could only read about from a distance—was intolerable in a way that is hard to explain to anyone who has not felt it.

I went back because I knew I would not understand Mosul from outside it.

When I returned, occupation did not announce itself through overwhelming visible force. What struck me first was not simply the presence of armed men, but the strange coexistence of armed control and apparent quiet. There were black flags—the banner of ISIS, inscribed in white with the Islamic declaration of faith—mounted on buildings and hung across intersections. There were checkpoints where fighters stopped vehicles and questioned their occupants. There were armed men at specific positions around the city. But there were also long intervals of ordinary-looking urban space: markets still open, people moving through streets, the surface of daily life not yet fully broken.

The city did not become a battlefield everywhere at once. It entered a new grammar.

By then I had already begun going out, observing, trying to register what had changed. In the early morning hours of June 10—while gunfire still sounded from the western districts—I had posted on my personal Facebook page, simply noting that I could hear the attacks. A friend messaged me within minutes, warning that I was risking everything. He was right. I did not stop taking notes, but I stopped posting under my own name. The observation continued; the exposure did not. That shift—from public voice to hidden recorder—was the first step toward what came next, though I did not yet understand where it would lead.

By June 13 and 14, one thing had become clear: These men entered Mosul not only as a military force. They came with media units, printed posters, a city constitution already drafted, pre-prepared administrative language, a structure that suggested duration rather than improvisation. An invading force that expected to leave does not print constitutions. A force that expects to govern does.

A battle can be witnessed as a civilian. An occupation must be studied as a system.

On June 17, this change in me became explicit.

I went out that morning to buy meat from a butcher I trusted—a man with a farm outside the city whose animals were properly fed, not like the other butchers. I took a minibus toward the old city, the route I had taken many times before. I noted where the old line of control ended. The last presence of the Peshmerga—the Kurdish military forces who had shared security responsibilities in parts of the city for years—was still at the familiar shared checkpoint at Gogjali, a crossing point on the city's northeastern edge that had for years marked the line between Iraqi government territory and the Kurdish region. A minute and a half farther by car, the control of the armed men began. A city can change hands within less than two minutes of driving.

From that checkpoint north toward the city's bus station, the stretch felt safe and stable—which was itself part of the lesson. Those outside Mosul who were reading reports of the fall often imagined spectacular terror operating at every corner simultaneously. Reality was more complicated.

Some areas felt eerily ordinary. People were going about their business, trying to discover who the armed men were, how long they intended to stay, what rules would now govern their lives.

No one knew. But the armed men themselves were not everywhere. They held specific positions, approximately twenty city blocks apart in some places, forty to seventy blocks apart in others. I made that calculation myself, walking. I counted the intervals. I noted which intersections they controlled and which they had left unguarded. I was no longer only experiencing the occupation. I was measuring it.

At ten-thirty that same morning, the grave of Ibn al-Athir was completely removed.

I never reached the butcher. Where the green pillars and the green dome had stood—the site I passed so many times that it became part of the city's unconscious furniture, the way a familiar building becomes invisible through repetition until the day it is gone—there was nothing. Ibn al-Athir was born in 1160 in Jazīrat Ibn 'Umar, a town on the upper Tigris, and came to Mosul as a young man, spending his life writing history at a time when the city was one of the most powerful in the Islamic world. His chronicle, known as *The Complete History*, remained a primary source for historians eight centuries later. His grave was not simply a religious site. It was a landmark of historical continuity, a physical connection to the city's intellectual inheritance. And it was gone.

The destruction was ISIS's first major act against Mosul's historical fabric. The group considered the veneration of graves to be polytheism, but the act carried something else inside it. A new order that destroys the graves of its predecessors is not merely enforcing theology. It is asserting the sole right to define what the city is, what it was, and what will be remembered about it.

I stood in front of the empty space and remembered the American soldiers removing Saddam Hussein's statues after the 2003 invasion. That had meant nothing to me—the statues of a dictator I did not love, pulled down by foreigners whose purposes I did not understand. This was different. This was the removal of a historian from his own city. And it worked inside me in a way I could not have predicted: All the historical narratives I had been studying—the Abbasids who also massacred the people of Mosul when they arrived, the Mongols who destroyed and sometimes rebuilt—began pressing against the present. ISIS was not here for political reasons alone. They brought their own narrative of the city, and they intended to replace the existing one.

I did not buy the meat. I went home. My sisters and brothers, my nieces and nephews, were in the living room watching television. I sat among them and looked at the screen without seeing anything. Later in the evening Adam and Samuel came—my two closest friends—and we sat in the garden. We talked about what was going to happen. We had experienced terrorism before. We knew what it meant to be ruled by it. But what we could not yet identify was what made these men different from the groups we had already survived. The tomb of Ibn al-Athir gave us the answer. Since they started destroying the historical sites, it meant these people were very dangerous in a way the others had not been. The Mongols, when they took Iraq in the thirteenth century, eventually renovated some of the tombs they found. These men were not renovating. They were erasing.

Deep inside myself, in the garden that night, I was going through a conflict I could not fully share with anyone present. What does it mean to know history? Is it merely to read it? Or does knowledge carry a responsibility—to preserve what is being destroyed, to record what is being falsified, to refuse the erasure? The removal of Ibn al-Athir's grave was not the removal of a statue. It was the removal of the value of the city itself. They were not bringing weapons alone. They were bringing their own version of what Mosul was.

By the afternoon of June 17, I created an anonymous blog on WordPress and wrote the words that mark the real beginning of this book. I chose the name Mosul Eye because I wanted the city to have an eye that saw what was being done to it—an eye that could not be closed by the men who were trying to replace its memory with their own. My hand was steady as I typed. The rest of me was not. What I witnessed that day was difficult to express. There were many fabrications and false stories being spread by the media, contradicted by reality on the ground. My work as a historian required an unbiased approach. I would keep my personal opinion to myself. I would communicate only the facts I saw. That was not an aesthetic preference. It was a discipline for survival and truth at once.

The next morning, June 18, I woke to another lesson in why method mattered. Around 3:10 a.m., there had been an air strike. From inside the city, I first believed the strike had hit al-Kindi Hospital, one of the city's main medical facilities. Later, I double-checked and established that it in fact targeted a building next to Project 1101 in the al-Kask neighborhood. Hearing an explosion from inside Mosul gives you only its intensity, not its location. Sound initiates inquiry; it cannot complete it.

I went through the city again that morning, and the city taught me what an occupation looks like when it is still arranging itself. The armed men were sparse—ISIS did not need to saturate every block with fighters. It was building a system, and the system was already visible in its early architecture. At al-Mufti mosque, a prominent congregational mosque in the western part of the city, two new institutions had opened: a Bureau of Grievances that received citizens' complaints, and a Council of Repentance where former soldiers and police could come forward, declare their past service, swear an oath, and receive a stamped document guaranteeing their safety. The lines at the Council were not short. Men came in afraid and came out relieved, holding papers they believed were amnesty. I watched from a distance and understood something most of them did not: The documents required names, addresses, ranks, units. The system that presented itself as forgiveness was also a registration system. What it would do with that registration, I could not yet prove. But I recorded what I saw.

One armed man told me something that complicated the image of a monolithic conquering force: They had not themselves released the City Constitution—the Wathiqat al-Madina, the document outlining the rules governing life under ISIS authority—and its stricter provisions represented thinking that he, at least, did not share. Competing registers of authority already existed within the new order.

The majority of those visible in the streets were young men from Mosul who had had nothing to do with weapons before the crisis. Foreign fighters existed—men from Arab countries, from Central Asia, from Europe—but they were rarer on Mosul's streets than many outside observers imagined. The occupation was not purely local, nor purely foreign. It was already a layered reality.

By June 28, fighters at checkpoints were carrying laptops, checking identification cards against what appeared to be preloaded civil and military records.

The checkpoint was also an archive. That single detail reorganized everything I had assumed about how the regime was learning the city. It meant they came prepared not only with weapons and constitutions but with data—names, service records, the bureaucratic residue of the state they had displaced. The checkpoint was not merely a point of knowledge. It was a point of control—which is to say, the two were the same thing.

One armed man gave me a version of events that stayed with me. Their entrance into Mosul, he said, had been planned as a revenge mission. They prepared explosives to secure their withdrawal and expected to remain for two days at most. The collapse of the Iraqi Army had not been expected. But the road opened in front of them, so they did not stop. He called it a liberation like the liberation of Mecca—invoking the Prophet Muhammad's conquest of that city, framing what had happened as the fulfillment of religious destiny. Even allowing for boasting, one thing in that statement was historically true: The scale and speed of the collapse surprised even some of those who benefited from it.

By June 20, the city's paradox had sharpened. In one sense, Mosul looked calmer. In another, it was becoming more deeply occupied. I was in the house of a Shia neighbor—a member of the Muslim community that ISIS considered its primary enemy—who had returned to his home in one of the most exposed areas of the city. His presence seemed a sign of something. I called a Christian friend to ask whether the jizya—the historical tax on non-Muslims that ISIS had claimed the right to revive—had yet been imposed on Mosul's Christians. My friend said no. The jizya had not yet come. I checked the churches I could reach and found them still standing.

These confirmations mattered in a specific way: It would have been easy, under the pressure of an occupied city, to collapse later persecution backward into these first days. Sequence is not a formality in this kind of history. What happened when determines the meaning of what happened. The full apparatus of Christian expulsion had not yet unfolded on June 20. The churches, at that point, still stood.

That same day the statue of Abu Tammam was destroyed. Abu Tammam was a ninth-century Arab poet, born near the city of Homs in what is now Syria but closely associated with Mosul, where he spent significant time and whose intellectual culture shaped his work. His statue had stood in the city as part of Mosul's public commemoration of its own cultural history. ISIS destroyed it—along with every other statue in the city—on the grounds that the representation of human figures constituted a form of idolatry. The destruction of statues was not only an act of religious enforcement. It was the systematic removal of the city's self-representation, the erasure of the figures Mosul had chosen to honor in its public spaces.

On the night of June 21, I drove through Mosul again and the paradox was almost unbearable. In the Woods—a large forested public park on the eastern bank of the Tigris, one of the places where Mosul's families always gathered on summer evenings, where children played and older people sat and where the city always expressed its ordinary social life—families filled the footpaths as if nothing had happened. Children, adults, ordinary evening movement. ISIS fighters were among them in their new cars. The roads were trafficked. The city was safe and quiet in the immediate sensory sense.

Abu Tammam's statue had disappeared. The former Counter-Terrorism Center became the main ISIS headquarters. A few of the Arab fighters I had seen in the early days—Tunisians and Algerians who came to Mosul from abroad—were guarding its gates. One of them was white-haired, in his sixties, carrying a pistol at his waist. Near the University of Mosul, on a public television set mounted in the street, an ISIS video played continuously, showing killings and kidnappings carried out on the Mosul-Baghdad road. Heavy equipment was entering the university grounds and no one knew for what purpose.

Oppression can disguise itself as relief if it first removes a prior irritant. In Mosul, the years of Iraqi Army checkpoints had not merely been inconvenient; they were a source of daily humiliation. Soldiers at checkpoints extorted money, harassed young men, and made movement through the city feel like a series of small degradations. The new order, in its first days, removed those checkpoints—or replaced them with its own, which carried a different and as yet unfamiliar kind of dread.

By the end of June 21, I wrote in my notes that this week was the most anxious and fearful week for civilians since the fall. People began doubting their earlier assessments of the armed men, especially after the destruction of statues and graves. It was the sixteenth day of the occupation and ISIS had still not clearly explained who they were, the nature of their governance, or their plans for the city. Everything remained officially unknown, even as its outlines were becoming clear. Ramadan was approaching—the month during which Muslims fast from dawn to sunset, a period of heightened religious observance that in ordinary years organized the rhythms of daily life in a predominantly Muslim city—and with it came fears that made ISIS's ideology tangible in the most practical terms. Food shortages, electricity blackouts, the possibility that generator fuel would run out by the end of the month, chaotic markets, and sharply increasing prices. Occupation was entering kitchens and fuel tanks, salaries and mealtimes, the question of whether a family could eat properly during a holy month.

That same evening, an ISIS fighter drove through a neighborhood with a loudspeaker mounted to his vehicle, announcing that every household was required to send a volunteer to join ISIS forces. The phrasing was precise: Join, defend, live in dignity and honor—or face death. Compulsory volunteering transformed the texture of the occupation because it pushed the city from passive submission toward forced participation. The Legitimate Court—ISIS's judicial body—became more active, with citizens going to its branches to resolve disputes, register property claims, or seek redress under the new legal order. Officials' houses were taken over. Young men, some not older than fifteen, appeared in a new wave of recruitment. Tribal leaders invited ISIS fighters to celebratory meals, publicly signaling their alignment. What had entered as a military conquest was becoming, day by visible day, a recruitment machine, a judicial theater, and a social sorting system.

On June 23, I wrote words that remain among the most painful I have ever written: For history's sake, the army was not the only runaway. Mosul had been abandoned by its best people, those who used to cry for justice, and Erbil became their haven. Everyone abandoned us. We were alone fighting an uncivil attack that swept Mosul and threatened our civil identity. The civil system was near breakdown.

What I feared was not simply death or occupation in the narrow military sense. I feared civil collapse—the destruction of the conditions under which Mosul could still think of itself as a city belonging to history rather than to sect, revenge, and barbarism. The city I knew was not only a political entity. It was a social fabric. Christians and Muslims had been neighbors for generations. Sunni and Shia families had intermarried, done business together, shared streets and schools. Turkmen and Arab and Kurdish communities coexisted within the same neighborhoods, sometimes in tension, but coexisted. What ISIS was doing was not only military conquest. It was the systematic dismantling of the arrangements that made that coexistence possible, however imperfectly.

At the same time, I continued checking rumors, because falsehood was becoming another front in the battle. Rumors circulated that the Mufti of Mosul—the senior Islamic religious authority in the city—was killed by ISIS. I contacted a member of his family and confirmed that he had in fact left Iraq several days before the crisis and was in Qatar. False atrocity stories, false reassurances, false claims of protection, false reports of siege, false moral panics—Mosul was drowning in all of them, and the drowning served ISIS as much as any of its other tactics. When the population cannot distinguish truth from fabrication, when fear attaches to rumors that have no basis alongside fears that are entirely justified, the result is a kind of paralysis that benefits whoever holds the guns.

To document the city truthfully meant resisting both the lies of ISIS and the sensational fantasies of those outside it.

On June 24, at 7:09 in the evening, I witnessed an air strike. An unmanned aircraft—almost certainly American—hit the former intelligence center with two missiles. ISIS fighters on the ground fired at the aircraft without success. It kept flying for a while and then disappeared, heading back over the west side of the city. Such moments carried a dual meaning. They reminded civilians that Mosul was not invisible to the outside world. They also intensified a growing fear: Air strikes killed indiscriminately, or could be made to. ISIS was already learning to manipulate the visual landscape—placing its flags on buildings that did not house its fighters, making civilian spaces and military positions difficult to distinguish from above.

That same night, the demolition of al-Fatih al-Mosuli began. The shrine, known locally as al-Sheikh Fathi, was pulled down with cranes working in darkness. Al-Fatih was a Sufi mystic who lived during the reign of the Abbasid caliph Haroun al-Rashid in the eighth century. Sufism—the mystical tradition within Islam, emphasizing spiritual experience and devotion to saints—was precisely what ISIS, with its rigid scriptural literalism, regarded as idolatry. The shrine had been a place of Sufi pilgrimage for more than seven centuries. Writing that history into my notes that night was not ornament. If a shrine is destroyed and only its destruction is recorded, something of what was destroyed is lost again. To preserve what had been there—who it was, why it mattered, what tradition it sustained—was part of the same work as recording its destruction.

The destruction of the shrines was not random vandalism. The same logic that erased the grave of Ibn al-Athir was erasing shrines across the city. ISIS was reorganizing Mosul's relationship to its own past, removing the physical markers through which the city remembered itself. The opening move had been the grave of a medieval historian. What followed was a systematic campaign against the accumulated human time that made Mosul a particular place rather than an interchangeable territory.

To write these days honestly, I have to resist two temptations. The first is retrospective simplification—the desire to make everything seem clear from the beginning. It was not clear. Mosul in June 2014 was full of contradiction. Some people were terrified. Some were relieved—for the first time in years, they told themselves, there were no government checkpoints where soldiers demanded money. Some were seduced by the appearance of order in a city that had known so little of it. Some were confused. Some were opportunistic. Some hoped that tribal forces or former Ba'athists—members of Saddam Hussein's party who had survived within the new order—would check ISIS's power before it fully consolidated. Some believed the new rulers would leave. Some thought they represented Sunni Arab political revenge against a Baghdad government that had excluded and humiliated them for years. The city did not move as one moral body.

The second temptation is to describe the beginning of documentation as though it arrived in a single heroic moment. It did not. It accumulated.

I began by hand. Then on a laptop. I noted what I had seen, what I had heard, what I had verified, and what remained uncertain. I recorded timing, location, mood, institutions, rumors, corrections, administrative signs, and the shifting geography of control. I wrote because I understood that sequence itself was under threat. If ISIS was imposing its own language, legality, and history on Mosul—if it was producing its own account of what the city was and what was happening to it—then one answer was to preserve the actual order of events against falsification. What happened before and what happened after. What was still standing on June 20 and what was gone by June 25. Who had said what, and whether what they said matched what they did. These were not archival technicalities. They were the load-bearing elements of truth.

The notebook was not simply a container for facts. It was a defense against erasure.

Long before the outside world knew the name Mosul Eye, the method was already there in those first weeks: Observe carefully, move ordinarily, verify before repeating, separate what is seen from what is inferred, correct mistakes publicly when evidence requires it, and write everything down before fear, propaganda, and exhaustion rearrange memory into something easier but less true.

If I had to identify the exact point at which witness stopped being passive for me, it would not be the university bell alone, or the first night of gunfire, or the family's flight to Erbil. Those were stages in the city's collapse. The deeper transformation occurred when I returned, crossed into the newly controlled city, measured the distance from Gogjali to the first armed checkpoint, stood before the emptied site where Ibn al-Athir's grave had been, corrected the location of the air strike, traced the early workings of the new institutions at al-Mufti mosque, verified the burning of the church in al-Wahda, watched office furniture move into former state buildings, and understood that Mosul was being rewritten faster than most people outside it could imagine.

I stayed. Not because I was not afraid—I was afraid every day for eighteen months, afraid in the specific and draining way of someone who lives with the permanent knowledge of what happens if they are found, a knowledge that becomes the background radiation of every waking moment without ever becoming ordinary. I stayed because I understood what cities need when they are taken: They need someone who will remember them accurately. Not heroically. Accurately. Someone who will write down the name of the man executed in the public square and the name of the square and the stated charge and the date and the number of people compelled to watch. Someone who will record the price of bread and the closing of the schools and the burning of the library and the empty Christian quarter and the executions after prayers.

Someone who will not let the conquerors write the only history.

Mosul was fatherless. Someone had to stay.

Ibn al-Athir had written from inside a city shaped by invasions, dynasties, warfare, and the ambitions of men who believed force could outlast memory. He had died centuries before I was born. In June 2014, his grave was erased from the city he had spent his life trying to preserve. I opened a notebook and continued his work.

I did not know then what that choice would demand of me. I did not know how long I would have to continue, how elaborate concealment would become, or how many layers of fear would settle over daily life. I did not know the names that would later dominate Mosul, the systems that would harden out of those first checkpoints and councils, the punishments that would make private thought dangerous, or the number of dead who would disappear into rumor and category unless someone insisted on fact.

I only knew that Mosul was occupied, that memory was already under attack, that reality itself was being falsified in real time, and that if someone inside the city did not start recording carefully, the occupiers would inherit not only the streets but the narrative.

Mosul had not disappeared into nothing.

It had disappeared into another order.

And where the green dome had stood, there was now only flattened earth and the faint smell of pulverized stone—the city's first wound made visible, the first absence I would spend years refusing to let stand as final.

THE CITY UNDER RUSE

My mother and I went out together in those late June days, and what I noticed first was that it was easier.

That is the hardest thing to explain to anyone who was not there, and the most important, because without it the rest of what happened during those weeks makes no sense.

Mosul was in its third week under ISIS. The organization had not yet shown most of its face. What it had shown was enough to make the city quiet: The black flags inscribed in white with the Islamic declaration of faith hung over intersections and public buildings; armed checkpoints had appeared at major roads; banks were closed; university professors and municipal employees had begun receiving notices that their conditions of employment had changed. The systematic violence was still largely out of sight. What was visible was a city in suspension—not yet fully rearranged, not yet certain what it had become—still attempting the ordinary routines of daily life while awaiting the next revelation of what the occupation actually meant.

What the city had ceased to feel, immediately, was the checkpoint of the Iraqi Army. For years those checkpoints had organized movement through Mosul in a way that is difficult to convey to anyone who has not experienced a city administered as a security object. Soldiers stopped vehicles, demanded identification papers, and in many cases extracted informal payments from drivers who needed to move without extended delay. Young men had it worst. They had learned to carry small money separately, to calculate routes, to wear expressions calibrated to avoid the particular attention of soldiers who might decide to make an afternoon of them. Those men were gone. The army had dissolved in the night, shedding uniforms in side streets, flowing north and east toward the Kurdish-controlled territory that began at Mosul's edge. Their checkpoints stood empty.

My mother and I walked out on one of those late June mornings and I watched her face. She was not happy. She was relieved. Those are not the same emotional state, and the difference between them is one of the most politically significant things I observed in those first weeks—because relief can be manufactured cheaply by anyone willing to remove a lesser irritant, and ISIS understood this with the precision of an organization that had studied the city's grievances before it entered the city.

At least the roads are open now. I heard it everywhere—from people who opposed ISIS and from people who had not yet formed a view, from those who understood exactly what had entered the city and from those still trying to decide. The sentence was spoken in the same breath as fear, by people who would not repeat it six months later, when it would have acquired a bitter inflection. But in late June—in the specific exhaustion of a city that had spent years inside a security theater that protected no one and profited some at everyone else's expense—it did real political work for the new rulers without any effort on their part. Relief does not wait for political clarity. It moves faster than thought, in the places where years of accumulated daily friction have settled.

The ruse was not a lie about who ISIS was. Everyone in Mosul knew, in broad outline, who ISIS was. The ruse was something more precise: the use of exhaustion as a political resource.

That interval was all it needed.

The Wathiqat al-Madina—the City Constitution—was issued on the eleventh of June.

One day after the black flag went up at the highest point of the city. Not after weeks of deliberation. Not after the new rulers had surveyed what they had captured and drafted a governance framework suited to what they found. The day after. The document laid out the administrative, legal, and moral order of a city they had decided to remake before they entered it. It had been written somewhere else, carried into Mosul, and issued on schedule. A conquering force that expects its occupation to be temporary does not draft constitutions before the battle ends.

Evidence of preparation was everywhere, once I began reading the city the way I had spent my working life reading archives—not for the dramatic event but for the administrative pattern behind it. Printed signs appeared on buildings within days of the fall designating offices that had been planned for specific locations before anyone occupied them. Vehicles moved furniture into former government buildings within the first week, which meant the furniture had been staged for transport before the army fled. ISIS media units arrived with the fighters, not after them; the filming of the conquest was not reactive documentation but prepared production. Printed flyers were distributed in mosques containing Qur'anic citations alongside administrative announcements—documents that require graphic design, printing facilities, and a distribution network that no military force assembles in two days.

In Mosul's mosques, a second administrative layer began taking shape almost immediately. In Arabic-speaking Muslim societies, the mosque has never been exclusively a house of worship. It has historically served as courthouse, school, and civic center as well, and ISIS drew on this tradition deliberately in establishing its first administrative offices. At al-Mufti mosque—a prominent congregational mosque on the western bank of the Tigris, near the city's older commercial districts—ISIS established two new institutions.

The first was the Diwan al-Mazalim: the Bureau of Grievances. A diwan, in classical Arabic administrative usage, is an office of state, a formal body with designated jurisdiction. The Bureau of Grievances received citizens' complaints, adjudicated disputes between residents, and presented itself explicitly as a remedy for the corruption and arbitrariness that had characterized the old state. I went to observe it on one of those early July mornings, walking past as though my route merely brought me near the building. Inside, through the open door, men sat in rows on plastic chairs. Some held folded papers—deeds, contracts, receipts from disputes that predated the fall. They had come to seek justice from the new authority because the old authority had offered them none. A man I recognized from a neighboring street was describing a property dispute with a former police officer who had extorted him for years. The ISIS official behind the desk was writing everything down. Citizens came in significant numbers. Many of them had real grievances against the government that ISIS had overthrown—against the extortion at checkpoints, against police who had taken money, against local officials who had collected payments and delivered nothing. ISIS had prepared for this. The Bureau of Grievances was not a humanitarian institution. It was an intake mechanism that converted the old state's victims into the new state's registered subjects.

The second was the al-Tawba Council: the Council of Repentance. Former soldiers and police—men who had served the Iraqi government that ISIS had just displaced—were invited to come forward and declare themselves. They could surrender their weapons, or pay a penalty if they no longer possessed weapons to hand over. They could swear a formal oath and receive in return a stamped document: Their past service would not be held against them. Their blood, in ISIS's own phrasing, would be safe.

Many came. The lines were not short. I watched from a distance during those first weeks and understood what I was actually looking at. The stamped documents required names. Addresses. Ranks. Units. Every man who stood in that line and declared himself was handing ISIS the same information the old state had held in its security files: the identity, location, and military history of every person who might pose a future threat to the new order. The system that presented itself as forgiveness was simultaneously a census of the city's former security sector. What looked like clemency was also a database of potential targets. The foundation of future arrests was being laid inside the architecture of mercy.

What I had observed at the city's checkpoints by late June confirmed this reading: fighters carrying laptops, checking each identity card against preloaded civil and military records. The database had not been assembled after the fall. It had been brought in.

The question of who exactly had entered Mosul mattered because the simplest answers were also the most wrong, and the wrong answers served ISIS's interests by making it appear more foreign, more externally imposed, and therefore more temporary than it was.

The dominant assumption among observers outside the city—and among many Moslawis who had not thought carefully about what they were watching—was that ISIS had arrived from Syria as a transnational force imposed from outside. The reality was more disturbing. Mosul had been living alongside the infrastructure of its own occupation for years. By 2012, the militia movements that had been fighting the American military before the 2011 withdrawal had reorganized, reconsolidated, and begun moving their fighters back into position. Many of those fighters had, in the intervening years, done something that required a second look to understand: They had joined the Iraqi police. Not because they had abandoned their ideologies but because the police offered cover, salary, and proximity to the city's security infrastructure. The commander of Mosul's police station before the fall had been a man who had led an al-Qaeda cell in a village near the town of Shirqat, south of Mosul. He brought sixty of his men with him when he joined the force. The arrangement was documented. The government in Baghdad was aware of it. It had been permitted.

The jihadist infrastructure had not been waiting outside Mosul to invade it. It had been inside the city, in uniform, cycling between criminal records and official positions, for years. When the fall came, these men did not need to travel. They were already there.

This did not mean the city had collaborated in its own occupation in any simple sense. It meant something harder to hold in the mind: Mosul had been governed, in the years before 2014, by a security system that had been hollowed out from the inside so gradually, and so thoroughly, that when the moment came the hollow was exactly the shape of a collapse.

The question that observers outside Iraq have asked most often—and asked with a judgment that was itself a form of ignorance—is why Mosul did not resist. Two million people, and no uprising. The question assumes that resistance is the natural response of an occupied population and that its absence must be explained by some deficiency of character or some hidden sympathy with the occupier. Both assumptions are wrong.

Armed resistance requires institutional structure: a military that has not fled, a police force that has not dissolved, a tribal system that has not been co-opted, a political leadership that has not vanished overnight. By June 11, every one of those structures was gone. The army had abandoned its posts, its weapons, its uniforms. The police had evaporated. The tribal leaders who might have organized a coordinated response had spent years navigating between the Iraqi government and the armed groups that preceded ISIS—years of calculated ambiguity that left them compromised by both sides and trusted by neither. The political class that governed Nineveh Province had fled to Erbil and Baghdad, issuing statements from hotel rooms while the population they had failed to protect remained inside the city they had failed to defend.

And then the government began bombing its own city from the air. A population trapped between an occupying force on the ground and its own military striking from above does not have the luxury of organized resistance. Individual acts of defiance occurred—and I documented them, one by one, throughout the occupation. A man shot a fighter in Bab al-Toub. Another used a niqab as disguise to assassinate a commander. These were acts of extraordinary courage. They were not a resistance movement, because a resistance movement requires what Mosul no longer had: coordination, communication, leadership, supply, and a population that is not simultaneously being targeted by both sides.

The absence of armed uprising was not consent. It was the arithmetic of a city from which every structure capable of organizing collective action had been removed—by design, by corruption, by years of institutional decay—before the first black flag was raised.

Other men joined after the fall for reasons that had nothing to do with prior organizational membership. ISIS opened volunteering centers across the city and advertised with the precision of an organization that had studied which pressures it was addressing. Monthly salaries were promised. Improved living conditions. And—named explicitly, offered as a structured benefit to unmarried young men—arranged marriages. In a city where male identity had been eroded by years of unemployment and the feeling of being excluded from any future the Iraqi state was theoretically building, that combination was not accidental. The salary addressed the economic pressure. The marriage addressed the social one. Together they constituted a proposition that was less theological than it appeared: ISIS would make you a man who could provide, and who belonged. Some who came were committed believers. Some needed the money and told themselves the conviction would develop later. Some had been known for criminal behavior before the fall and appeared now in new authority because power had moved to a new address, and they had walked to find it.

One afternoon in the Al-Dawasa neighborhood—the area along the old city's western edge, beside the Tigris—I was sitting with a friend at a café when four ISIS fighters entered. I could tell from their accents they were from the villages outside Mosul, not from the city itself. They took the seats beside us and spoke at the volume of men who have decided they are no longer subject to ordinary social pressure. They were discussing the newly announced prohibition on smoking and shisha—the water pipe that had been one of the fixtures of café life in the city for generations. One turned to the other with what appeared to be genuine concern and asked how he was going to manage. He smoked four packs of cigarettes a day.

His friend laughed without embarrassment: I am not included in this decision.

They were enforcing a prohibition that did not apply to themselves, and they said so aloud without dropping their voices. This was not carelessness. It was the public performance of a differential standing that ISIS was extending across every dimension of city life: The rules existed for Mosul's inhabitants. Those who had come to govern occupied a separate category. I recorded this exchange and sat with it for several days before publishing. One event, observed directly. But it contained, in compressed form, the logic of everything else I was watching.

Around that time I also spoke with a group of women who had been active in Mosul's civil society before the fall—educators, organizers, women who had spent years working toward a city with functioning institutions and public life. One told me she felt injustice and indifference; ISIS did not differ from the government, as both treated people without humanity, both served the weapon rather than the human being. We wished for the human to govern us, not the weapon. Another said she was afraid of what would happen if the situation continued. She did not want to become, she used the exact word, a gift to one of ISIS's criminals. A third said she had not left her house since the first days. She felt like a prisoner. She wished someone would tell her how to stop worrying.

I wrote down what each of them said and did not immediately publish it. They had not offered their words for circulation, and in a city where words could be retrieved and used against the person who had spoken them, honoring that boundary was not a formality. It was a form of protection, one of the first disciplines the occupation had imposed on documentation.

On July 4, approximately one hour before the Friday sermon at al-Nuri mosque, mobile phone service across Mosul was cut.

It returned two hours after the event ended.

Al-Nuri mosque stands in the old city on the western bank of the Tigris, and to understand what happened there that afternoon, the building beside it matters as much as the mosque itself. The Hadbaa—the name means Humpbacked, for the pronounced lean that has characterized it for centuries—is a minaret completed in 1172 during the period when the Zengid rulers governed northern Iraq and made Mosul one of the most powerful cities in the Islamic world. For more than 850 years, it had been the most recognizable mark in the city's skyline, an architectural fixture so identified with Mosul that the city itself had an old nickname, al-Hadba', the Humpbacked. The mosque beside it had served as the central congregational mosque of the western bank for generations. To appear at al-Nuri was not to appear at an ordinary building. It was to appear at the symbolic center of Mosul's religious life.

Abu Bakr al-Baghdadi understood this precisely.

He came in a black robe and climbed to the pulpit. Around him stood the fighters of al-Sadeeq Battalion—that designation, written in white Arabic script on the right shoulder of each man's uniform—armed, arranged, the visual frame of a claim that had been prepared far longer than the conquest that preceded it. He declared himself caliph.

The caliphate is the office of supreme leadership of the Muslim community—combining religious and political authority in the person of a single ruler regarded as the successor to the Prophet Muhammad. The institution had existed in various forms from the seventh century through the early twentieth, when the Ottoman Empire, which had held the title, collapsed after World War One and the caliphate was formally abolished in 1924. For ninety years, no one had held the position. When Baghdadi stood in al-Nuri mosque and declared himself Caliph Ibrahim, he was not merely claiming authority over a territory. He was claiming the leadership of all the world's Muslims and situating the violence of ISIS's military campaign inside a religious framework of cosmic significance: not a local insurgency but the fulfillment of a divine obligation.

He said that all those who had previously declined to announce the caliphate were sinners. He said he promised not luxury but jihad. He called on Muslims everywhere to offer their bay'a—the oath of personal allegiance that, in classical Islamic legal tradition, a Muslim owes to a legitimate caliph. Following the prayer, a group of fighters moved forward inside the mosque and performed the oath in public.

The phone blackout tells you almost everything about how this event was understood by those who staged it. What happened at al-Nuri on July 4 was not released into Mosul's ordinary communication. Civilians could not document it on their own terms during the hour it took place, nor could they share commentary through the informal circuits of rumor that survive even under occupation. The filming was ISIS's. The distribution would happen on ISIS's schedule. The one-hour window of disconnection before the sermon was the equivalent of controlling the room before the performance begins. ISIS could shut down an entire city's telecommunications at will, and it had done so for a speech. That fact alone was a demonstration of total infrastructure control more frightening than the sermon's content.

For the vast uncertain middle of the city—not the committed, not the resistant, but the majority of people who had not yet decided what this occupation was or whether it would last—the sermon at al-Nuri closed something that had been held open since the fall. The question of duration had been, for many, a survival strategy: Keep the future unresolved, keep all possibilities technically present, and the paralysis of the present becomes manageable. A man standing in the city's most important mosque, surrounded by armed men in uniform performing a religious oath, calling himself the leader of all Muslims, was not conducting an occupation that was expected to end. He was instituting a civilization. Some in the city heard this and felt the ground solidify under ISIS's authority—not because they agreed with what was being built, but because certainty, even alien certainty, has its own gravity when it fills the vacuum left by the collapse of everything familiar.

That evening, I sat in the living room with my mother and my brother Ahmad and said nothing about what the sermon meant. Ahmad, who was older than me, had his own interpretation of what was unfolding around us, and I could see him turning it over in the silence the way people do when language has not yet caught up with what they have understood. My mother poured tea. The television was showing whatever ISIS's media channel had decided the city should watch. What I was thinking—what I would write later that night in my room with the door closed—was not something I could share with either of them. The gap between what I knew and what I could say in my own house was already becoming its own form of weight.

The day after the sermon, on July 5, ISIS began excavating the shrine of Prophet Younis.

The caliphate that Baghdadi declared was not merely Sunni in character. It was built on a theological foundation that divided the world into categories of the faithful and the condemned. To understand what would follow—in Tel Afar, in the Christian quarters, in every community that fell outside the regime's definition of acceptable belief—requires understanding a division within Islam that is central to everything ISIS was doing. Islam's two major branches, Sunni and Shia, trace their origins to a dispute over succession following the Prophet Muhammad's death in the seventh century. For most of the fourteen centuries since, Muslims of both traditions have lived as neighbors without systematic violence. But the jihadist theology from which ISIS emerged regards Shia Muslims not merely as a rival branch but as apostates—people who have abandoned the true faith and whose blood is therefore religiously permissible to shed. ISIS called Shia Muslims *Rafida*, a derogatory term meaning those who reject the first three caliphs. In ISIS's framework, killing them was not violence against fellow believers. It was the purification of the faith.

The caliphate had its theology. What followed was the application.

Rumors reached me about Tel Afar.

Tel Afar is a town roughly seventy kilometers west of Mosul, predominantly Turkmen in population—the Turkmen being a community descended from Turkish settlers who arrived in the region over many centuries and who form a significant minority across northern Iraq. A large portion of Tel Afar's Turkmen community is Shia Muslim. In the framework, Baghdadi had just proclaimed from the pulpit of al-Nuri that they were not a civilian population. They were a theological target.

The same categorical violence reached the Shabak—an ethno-religious community, many of them Shia, whose villages lay on the Nineveh Plain east of Mosul. Their shrines were destroyed. Their villages were emptied. They joined the Turkmen, the Christians, and the Yazidis in the registry of communities that ISIS defined not as populations to be governed but as populations to be erased.

The reports arriving in Mosul about what had happened there were specific in the way that atrocity accounts from occupied places always are: They carry the structural shape of truth inside a distortion of scale or sequence that makes them dangerous to repeat before checking. I called a Sunni source in the town. I was careful not to display sympathy during the conversation. When a listener is visibly sympathetic, a speaker often edits toward what the listener can bear. I did not want the edited version. I needed to hear what the source considered ordinary.

He did not hesitate. After ISIS took the town, he said, he and others had entered streets where the Shia community had lived—streets that had been closed to them before. He described what they found: burned bodies in the open, beheaded bodies, blood at the thresholds of houses, women lying in front of their doors. When the smell from the dead became unmanageable, he said, ISIS dug pits and buried tens of bodies in them. He used the word *Rafida*. He used the word Magi—an additional slur comparing Shia Muslims to followers of Zoroastrianism, the ancient Persian religion, implying that they are not truly Muslim at all. His voice did not change when he described the bodies.

He had not been a witness to atrocity. He had been a participant in something he considered a justified act of God.

I published his account two days later, after the broad outline had reached me through a second route.

On August 3, 2014, ISIS moved against the Yazidis of Sinjar.

I had written about it before it happened. On August 3, the day itself, I recorded in my notes: news from inside Sinjar that the Peshmerga had withdrawn in the morning, that ISIS had entered very quietly, that their entrance means a massacre will happen soon to the Yazidi residents. I wrote: ISIS treats Yazidis by the principle of death or Islam, without a third option. There are news which says ISIS had spread flyers saying that residents don't have any choice except slaughter.

I wrote this before the massacre happened. This is what the logic of the occupation produced. Everyone in Iraq understood what ISIS would do with the Yazidis, because the suffering of the Yazidis had been the same for centuries, not from ISIS, but from everyone. Al-Qaeda had committed massacres against Yazidis in earlier years that had emptied them entirely from Mosul. These men were continuing something that had never properly been interrupted.

The Yazidis are among the oldest communities in the region, an ancient ethno-religious minority whose faith draws from Zoroastrian, Christian, and Islamic traditions, and who ISIS had declared devil-worshippers, polytheists whose existence could not be tolerated within the caliphate. They had lived in the Sinjar region for centuries. When the Peshmerga—the Kurdish military forces who had been their nominal protectors—withdrew without warning, the Yazidis had nowhere to go and no one coming.

What happened in August 2014 in Sinjar was genocide. The United Nations determined this. The Iraqi parliament determined this. Courts across Europe have since adjudicated it as such. The men were separated and shot. Thousands of women and girls were taken into slavery—distributed among ISIS fighters as a theological entitlement, bought and sold at markets, passed between men whose theological framework had calculated that these women were not fully human and therefore not entitled to ordinary protections. Children were taken for indoctrination and military training. Thousands of people fled to the top of Sinjar Mountain, where they were trapped without food or water for days until American air strikes opened a corridor.

The number of dead has never been fully established. Estimates begin at five thousand. The number enslaved was at least five thousand more. Mass graves continue to be found.

I heard about it from inside Mosul on the day it began—through the same circuits of rumor and informal network that carried everything else. I confirmed what I could confirm. I wrote what I could verify. And I experienced something I had not fully experienced in the two months since the fall: a shame that was different from grief. Not only was this happening, but it was happening here, in my region, in the territory that had fallen partly because of the city I lived in, carried out by men who had taken my city as their capital and my streets as their home.

I have Yazidi friends. I have never found the words for what to say to them about what happened in their name, on their land, in the weeks after Mosul fell. I do not have them now. What I have is the record. The dates. The numbers. The testimony of Dr. Hafiz about the girls brought to the hospitals. The names of the mass graves as they were identified, years later, by the people who survived to go back and look.

The world did not prevent the genocide at Sinjar. It was happening while the world was still deciding how to respond to Mosul. I was inside Mosul, writing it down, knowing that writing it down was not the same as stopping it, and continuing anyway because stopping was not the option available to me.

The delay was not timid. Mosul was filled with rumors faster than any individual could process them. Fear generates stories at a rate that outpaces events, and in a city where the population cannot freely investigate—where asking too many pointed questions marks you as someone who asks questions—information traveled through the shortest available circuits, accumulating distortion with each transfer. If I repeated everything I heard, I would become another node in the regime's own circuit of confusion. Uncertainty serves whoever holds the weapons.

The discipline I had been developing since June had, by those weeks, hardened into a private set of rules I applied to every piece of information before using it. Did I see this directly? Who told me, and how would they know? Can I obtain a second confirmation via a route that does not intersect the first? Is this something ISIS announced officially, or something being inferred from fear? If two sources confirm the same event but disagree on a specific detail, what does the disagreement reveal about each source's position? These were not academic questions in any sense. In a city where credibility was the only medium through which truth could travel, a false report would do permanent damage to the record being built. In a city where the route of information could be traced backward, a true report published carelessly could reveal as much about how it had been obtained as about the fact itself.

The route always mattered as much as the destination.

If one wanted to see, in its most concentrated form, how ISIS intended to govern—the full apparatus at once, administrative and theological and coercive, each layer reinforcing the others—the correct place to look was at what was being done to Mosul's Christian community. But the event can only be understood correctly if you begin where it actually begins, which is not in July.

Christianity reached Mesopotamia in the first centuries of the common era, carried along the same river routes and trade roads that had connected the Mediterranean with the East long before the faith existed. By the time Christian communities took permanent root in this region, Mosul was already ancient: built on and around the ruins of Nineveh, the Assyrian capital whose destruction in 612 BC is recorded in the Hebrew scriptures and whose stones were still visible from the city's western bank. The Christian community that ISIS catalogued as an administrative category on June 11, 2014, had been living continuously in this city for more than 1,700 years. It had survived the Mongol invasions of the thirteenth century, the Ottoman centuries of ambiguous tolerance, the violent oscillations of post-Ottoman Arab nationalism, and the sustained chaos that followed the American invasion of 2003. Ancient presence of that duration produces a confidence that usually operates below the level of conscious thought—a background assumption, never examined, that what has always been here will continue to be here. ISIS had decided to administer that assumption out of existence.

The surveys began on June 11, the same day the Wathiqat al-Madina was issued. Men moved through Christian neighborhoods with official-looking purpose, documenting properties: homes, shops, businesses, buildings, and their ownership. The information was entered into records. Most people at the time did not register what they were watching. Administrative activity looks like administrative activity until the purpose behind it becomes apparent.

On June 30, ISIS moved into the Orthodox Archbishopric—the headquarters of one of Mosul's main Christian denominations, located in the al-Shurta neighborhood—and raised their flags over it despite the presence of its Archbishop and several families inside. That same day, ISIS issued an order excluding all Christians from the payroll lists that were about to distribute salaries to public employees. In a city where the government payroll had been one of the main economic arteries, removal from it was not merely financial. It was a signal that the community's civic existence had been formally revoked.

By July 17, stickers appeared on Christian homes and properties throughout the city: the letter N, for Nasrani—the Arabic term for Christian—a marking drawn from ISIS's own administrative alphabet. Separately, properties belonging to Shia families and to those on ISIS's wanted lists received different markings: Islamic State Property. ISIS announced through intermediaries that all markings were statistical, for counting purposes only. Simultaneously, ISIS informed the tenants of Christian and Shia properties to redirect their rent payments to ISIS, as the new owner. The statistical markings were also title transfers. Both statements were simultaneously, contradictorily true, and the contradiction was the point.

On the eighteenth of July, the Friday sermon at mosques across the city formally announced the imposition of jizya on Mosul's Christians.

The jizya was a tax historically levied on non-Muslim communities living under Islamic governance—a practice codified in classical Islamic jurisprudence during the first centuries of the faith and applied, in various forms, across the medieval Muslim world. Under the traditional arrangement called *dhimma*, non-Muslims who accepted subordinate legal status and paid the tax were regarded as protected subjects of the Islamic state: permitted to practice their religion, exempted from military service, but excluded from certain civic functions and required to observe specific social restrictions. The institution had fallen largely out of use centuries ago. ISIS claimed the religious standing to revive it, and framed its revival as mercy: Christians would be recognized, subordinated, and protected, rather than simply expelled or killed. Three options were formally named—conversion to Islam, payment of jizya, or death. The sermon presented jizya as the most generous.

ISIS had already tested this model. Six months before the fall of Mosul, in January 2014, the organization had imposed the same framework on the Christians of Raqqa, its Syrian capital. The Christian leaders there had signed the *dhimma* covenant. They accepted subordinate status, agreed to pay jizya, and received in exchange the formal protections of Islamic law as ISIS defined it. Their names were kept anonymous—ISIS agreed to conceal the identities of the signatories—but the document itself was published and circulated as evidence of Islamic governance in action. The Raqqa *dhimma* was the first functioning covenant between the caliphate and a non-Muslim community. It was proof of concept: proof that ISIS could govern as historical caliphates had governed, that the institution Baghdadi had declared from al-Nuri was not a militia with a flag but a legal order capable of administering the classical relationship between the Islamic state and the People of the Book.

When ISIS came to Mosul's Christians with the same offer, the expectation was the same result.

I recorded this at 8:34 in the evening.

At 11:05 that same night I received word that two Christians had been killed in Mosul, in front of their families. Their money had been taken.

What followed requires understanding a sequence that was not public at the time but that I was able to document. On June 16—a month before the jizya sermon—a meeting had taken place between Christian leaders and ISIS representatives, including tribal leaders delegated by the organization. The purpose was direct: ISIS wanted the Christians of Mosul to accept the *dhimma*, as the Christians of Raqqa had done. They wanted a signed covenant. They wanted the relationship between the caliphate and Mosul's oldest religious minority to be formalized under classical Islamic law—a recognition that would carry legal, theological, and political weight far beyond the question of a tax. The Christian leaders were offered terms. They were told that accepting the *dhimma* would guarantee their physical safety, the protection of their churches, and their right to remain in the city where their communities had lived for seventeen centuries. They were given time to consult their leadership and respond.

The response was due on July 17. The Christian leadership rejected the offer. They refused to sign.

That same evening—the evening of the jizya sermon, which now became the public announcement of a process that had already been decided behind closed doors—a document was distributed across the city. The wali, ISIS's appointed governor of Mosul—a man who had himself served three years in Badoosh prison, the old Iraqi state penitentiary west of the city that ISIS had converted to its own purposes, and who was known for severe extremism even within ISIS's own ranks—issued the evacuation order. It was called the 'Ahd al-Jalaa, the Deportation Order. All Christians must leave Mosul. Without property. Without belongings. Without even a watch. A fourth option had been added to the original three—what ISIS called the gift of the Caliph: permission to leave alive, carrying nothing. The deadline was noon on Saturday, the nineteenth of July. Those who remained after that hour would be killed.

ISIS wanted the refusal hidden. If the Christians were deported, ISIS preferred to say that they had disobeyed the law of the *dhimma*—that the community had been offered the protection of the caliphate and had chosen, through its own stubbornness, to forfeit it. The narrative ISIS needed was not expulsion but disobedience: not that the caliphate had driven its Christians out, but that the Christians had refused the caliphate's mercy. That framing required that the refusal itself remain invisible.

The sequence—surveys on June 11, property database completed by early July, jizya formally announced on July 18, expulsion ordered that same night for July 19—had been structured so that the entire administrative machinery was in place before the legal theater began. The offer of jizya was not a genuine choice. It was the final scene in a process whose outcome had been determined five weeks earlier, when the first survey teams walked through Christian streets with clipboards.

I heard from a Christian friend in the days after he crossed out of the city. He spoke with the flattened affect of a man for whom feeling has not yet found its form. They had stripped everything at the checkpoints, he said: mobile phones, money, the clothes from his children's bodies. ISIS told the Christians they were not permitted to travel in cars. They walked out of the city they had lived in for seventeen centuries, on foot, with nothing.

In the days that followed, families from displaced communities in other parts of Iraq—from Diyala and Salah al-Din, areas where ISIS had also driven people from their homes—began moving into Christian houses in

Mosul. I watched this happen in Al-Dawasa. Men whose accents identified them as from outside the city walked through doorways that had belonged to families who had opened those doors for generations.

What I understood then, and what I believe history must record, is that the offer of jizya operated on two levels that must not be confused. On the material level—property, revenue, territorial control—ISIS won regardless of what the Christian community decided. If the community fled, the administrative apparatus that had been running since the surveys began on June 11 absorbed the abandoned properties through Bayt al-Mal and the Real Estate Diwan. The filing systems had been built for precisely this outcome. On that level, the theater of legal process arrived after the machinery was already running. The theater gave the machinery its justification after the fact.

But on the level that mattered most to ISIS—the level on which the entire caliphate project depended—the Christian refusal was a defeat.

The *dhimma* was not primarily about revenue. It was not about the jizya as a tax. It was about legitimacy. A caliphate, in classical Islamic political theology, is not merely a territory held by force. It is a legal and spiritual order—one that governs Muslims and non-Muslims alike under a recognized framework of Islamic law. The *dhimma* is the institution through which that governance extends to the People of the Book. Without a functioning *dhimma*—without a Christian or Jewish community that has voluntarily accepted subordinate status and received the caliphate's formal protection—the caliphate lacks one of the classical proofs of its own legitimacy. It is an army with a sermon, not a state with a covenant. ISIS understood this. It is the reason the organization tried so hard in Raqqa and tried again in Mosul. It is the reason the Raqqa *dhimma* was published. And it is the reason ISIS wanted the Mosul refusal hidden.

The Christians of Raqqa had signed, and in signing they had granted the caliphate its first functioning covenant with a non-Muslim community—its first evidence, in the language of Islamic governance, that it was what it claimed to be. Mosul was supposed to follow. Mosul was the prize. The city of Nineveh, the seat of Assyrian civilization, the place where

Christians had lived since the first centuries of the faith—a *dhimma* signed in Mosul would have carried a weight that Raqqa's could not. It would have meant that the caliphate governed the oldest Christian community in Mesopotamia under the same terms the Abbasids and the Umayyads had used. It would have been continuity—not merely with the early Islamic state, but with the deep history of the land itself.

The Christian leadership refused. And in refusing, they denied ISIS the one thing its property machinery could not manufacture: the voluntary recognition of a subject community. The Christians lost everything. Their homes, their churches, their savings, the weight of seventeen centuries of continuous presence in the city. They walked out of Mosul on foot, stripped at the checkpoints, carrying nothing. But by refusing to sign, they struck at the caliphate's claim to legitimacy in a way that no military force had yet managed from inside. They did not defeat ISIS on the battlefield. They defeated it on the ground where ISIS had chosen to fight—the ground of Islamic governance, of historical continuity, of the right to rule. The deportation was ISIS's punishment. But the refusal was Mosul's verdict.

What the Christians saved, at the cost of everything they owned and everything they had built, was the city's identity as something ISIS could not claim to govern. Mosul remained, in the historical record, a city whose oldest community chose exile over submission. That choice cannot be taken back. It cannot be revised by force or erased by occupation. The Christians of Mosul, by refusing the *dhimma*, saved not only their own dignity but the city itself from the one fate worse than destruction—the fate of having consented to the caliphate's terms. Mosul was destroyed. But it was never legitimized. And that difference—between a city that was occupied and a city that was claimed—is the difference the Christian refusal made permanent.

On July 21, ISIS carried out mass arrests of militia faction leaders who had refused to pledge allegiance to the caliphate. Separately, on the same day, men who had objected to the Christian expulsion were arrested. Some were being held for ransom. Even internal opposition to ISIS's methods was being processed through ISIS's own administrative system.

On July 22, I confirmed what I heard the previous day. Dr. Mahmoud al-Assli had been killed.

He was a professor of law at Mosul University, a man who had spent his professional life in the exacting work of legal scholarship—teaching, writing, and thinking carefully about what law is for and what it means when the gap between legal principle and political reality becomes absolute. He was known in the faculty for a particular quality of stubbornness: the insistence that legal reasoning must be applied precisely because circumstances make it inconvenient to do so, not in spite of that inconvenience. He objected, directly and in person, to ISIS members, to the looting and burning of Christian homes. His cousin had been killed a few days before him for the same reason. He understood what the objection might cost. He made it anyway.

I wrote his name. His position. The date. The cause. In a city where ISIS was producing its own official account of every death—where each killing could be reclassified as the punishment of someone who had violated divine law, where every expulsion could be narrated as the lawful administration of the caliphate's governance—the specific name of a law professor killed for defending his neighbors' property had to exist in the record as a fact rather than a category. Not as symbol. Not as representative of a type. As the person he was, anchored to the day he died.

The compression of daily life moved through July by stages, and the staging mattered as much as the content, because incremental change is harder to resist than sudden transformation. Each new condition had to be absorbed before the next one arrived.

On July 17, the Legitimate Court—ISIS's judicial body, which had begun holding sessions in several locations around the city—administered its first formal flogging in Mosul. Two men had been arrested in al-Ghaba, the large, forested park along the eastern bank of the Tigris where Mosul's families had always gathered on summer evenings. The men were arrested for a verbal dispute that had become physical. The Legitimate Court sentenced them to fifty lashes each and three days in prison. The sentence was publicly announced. The punishment was administered. A judicial apparatus that had been operating in ISIS's Syrian territories for months was now functioning in Mosul with the procedural regularity of an established court. This was not ad hoc violence. Administered violence implies a state.

That same day, twenty-one men were imprisoned for eating publicly during Ramadan—the month during which Muslims fast from dawn to sunset, one of the five pillars of the faith, and in a majority-Muslim city like Mosul a period that had always organized the rhythms of daily life in visible ways. ISIS sent fighters on regular patrols to enforce the fast. In Al-Sirchikhana, men were arrested for wearing shorts.

On July 19, women's clothing shops received written instructions. Any garments that did not conform to ISIS's specifications—clothing that exposed the arms, fit the body's contours, or displayed color in ways ISIS deemed immodest—must be removed from sale within five days, returned to suppliers or surrendered for confiscation. Sewing factories were ordered to report to the *hisba*, ISIS's moral enforcement police, to receive the new material and construction standards.

On July 24, the niqab was formally imposed on all women in the city. The niqab is the full-face veil—a covering that conceals the face entirely, leaving only the eyes visible or in some interpretations covering those as well. ISIS's version came with specific material requirements, approved construction specifications, and mandatory compliance. Failure to comply would be met with arrest.

On July 24, ISIS destroyed the shrine of Prophet Younis.

Younis is Jonah—the figure known from the Hebrew scriptures and the Qur'an alike, the prophet who fled his divine commission and was swallowed by a great fish, held for three days in its belly, and released to carry God's message forward. His story appears in roughly the same form in the Jewish, Christian, and Islamic traditions, and his tomb in Mosul had been a site of pilgrimage for believers from all three faiths for more than a thousand years. The shrine stood on a hill on the eastern bank of the Tigris, rebuilt and re-venerated across many generations. It also stood on something older: Beneath it lay the ruins of the palace of Sennacherib, the Assyrian king who ruled Nineveh in the seventh century BC. ISIS had begun excavating the site on July 5, the day after Baghdadi's sermon at al-Nuri. Archaeologists who were watching from whatever distance they could manage already feared what lay beneath, and what would be done to it.

On July 24, ISIS also seized the Monuments Museum—the institution that housed Mosul's collection of antiquities spanning thousands of years of the region's history.

On July 25, the shrine of Prophet Sheet was demolished.

Sheet is Seth in the Hebrew tradition—the third son of Adam and Eve, a figure whose tomb in Mosul had drawn pilgrims for centuries. When ISIS's demolition team arrived at the mosque surrounding the shrine, the residents of the neighboring streets gathered in front of it. They did not have weapons. They had only their collective presence, and the hope that the physical presence of people might constitute an argument. After a period of negotiation, ISIS agreed: The site would be closed rather than destroyed.

Two hours later, cranes arrived and took the mosque to its foundations, leaving only the minaret and the front wall.

The negotiation had been a staging interval, not a concession.

That same Friday's sermon—which much of the city had expected would provide public theological justification for the Christian expulsion the previous week—instead broadcast a document authored by Turki al-Bana'ali, a Bahraini scholar who served as one of ISIS's principal ideological authorities. The document argued that Abu Bakr al-Baghdadi was descended directly from the household of the Prophet Muhammad—not from the Abbasid dynasty that had ruled the Islamic world from Baghdad for five centuries, but from Ali ibn Abi Talib, the Prophet's cousin and son-in-law, and Fatima al-Zahraa, the Prophet's daughter. Every dynasty that had claimed Islamic authority throughout history had eventually needed to establish its genealogical connection to the Prophet. The caliphate was manufacturing its credentials. The document existed on paper. The shrine of Prophet Sheet existed in rubble.

By July 24, section fourteen of the Wathiqat al-Madina, the city constitution issued on June 11, had been fully executed. Two sections remained. Those final sections, ISIS announced, contained the complete implementation of Islamic law and the formal declaration of the caliphate's completion as a state. The document carried into Mosul on June 11 was nearly fully operational. Forty-three days from the flag going up to the constitution nearly done. The schedule had been kept.

The more clearly I could read this system, the less visible that reading could be.

Observation under occupation is not the same as observation in ordinary circumstances. Ordinary curiosity has an acceptable face. The curiosity I needed was another matter. It required the appearance of ordinariness while practicing something entirely different underneath, and the gap between the two had to be maintained at every moment, because the city itself was learning to read such gaps in other people. ISIS informers and frightened neighbors and exhausted civilians were all developing the skill of interpreting small signals. I could not afford to emit the wrong ones.

I went to markets. I visited relatives. I moved through the streets in the patterns of a man going about his ordinary business. I lingered, but not too long in any single place. I asked questions but with the inflection of idle conversation rather than directed inquiry. I listened without displaying the appetite for information that I actually felt. Some of this was physical—where I stood, how long I remained, which routes allowed observation without making me observable. Some of it was a management of expression: the discipline of receiving disturbing information without the expression that disturbing information normally produces.

The opposite pressure was equally real. If I waited indefinitely before publishing, memory blurred, sequence broke, and ISIS's own public communications—its court announcements, its Friday sermons, its administrative proclamations, its claims that what was happening in Mosul was law rather than coercion—began to inherit the narrative by default. Against that apparatus, a single hidden recorder who delayed without end would eventually be documenting the past rather than countering its falsification in real time.

The balance between those two dangers was not a formula. It was a judgment remade each time I sat down to write, usually alone, always with consequences I could not calculate in advance.

He was from the neighborhood.

Two doors down from one of my closest friends. After 2009, I had seen him nearly every day. He had been a taxi driver before the fall. In 2008, he was arrested by a Shia militia and spent nine months in their custody. He was married, had a daughter. After June 10, he became an official member of ISIS. His brother joined. His cousin—I would learn this gradually over those months—was among the most dangerous men ISIS had in the city.

We still sat together sometimes in the evenings, the four of us: Adam, Samuel, he, and I. In the neighborhood, without prior arrangement, the way old acquaintance insists on continuing even when everything surrounding it has become unrecognizable.

He told me about five hundred women.

He told me this, I understood as he spoke, because of the arguments we had been having for months before the fall—in which I had been critical of Islamist ideology and he had not. He was not confiding. He was not seeking approval or testing my reaction. He was making a point—demonstrating the shape of something he had concluded I consistently failed to understand. He said ISIS had kept the women before the killing. He had spoken to one of them himself. He asked her why she would do what she did. She answered: Whether you kill me or not, I will continue. He told me he had not believed her.

Then: Now we cleaned the city from these germs.

I did not accept the number. Five hundred I filed as something requiring verification—a figure from a single source with evident investment in the scale of his own account, needing a second route before I could treat it as established. That was the first discipline, and by that July it was automatic.

But the number was not what moved through me.

In Arabic, certain uses of the act of cleaning—in specific registers, spoken with specific inflections, invoking what he was invoking—carry inside them a claim to a kind of authority that has no ordinary human equivalent. You are not removing dirt in the way a person removes dirt. You are exercising the ultimate power: the power that belongs, in classical Islamic understanding, to God alone—the power to determine what is permitted to exist and what must be removed from existence. To say we cleaned, in this register, is to speak from a position outside ordinary human standing. It is to claim that you are not acting as yourself, subject to human limitation and human judgment, but as an instrument of divine determination. He was not speaking as the man from the neighborhood—the former taxi driver who had spent nine months in prison and wanted to get married. He was speaking from a position the ideology had made available to him: not Abraham, as his friends had always known him, but something that differentiated itself from ordinary human capacity. The ideology had not only changed what he believed. It had changed the position from which he understood himself to be acting.

What I could not file was the calm. The complete absence of any need for my reaction—for my approval or my horror or even my attention. He was not confessing and not performing. He was correcting a factual error he thought I had been making. His voice had the evenness of a man explaining something to a person who has not yet understood it.

I kept my expression level. I asked a question or two that implied curiosity rather than the thing moving through me. I had learned enough by then to know that what flowed through him—what he had access to, what his pride would eventually say without intending to, what his need to be understood as significant would disclose over time—was worth more than the immediate relief of ending the conversation. Every interaction under occupation had to be weighed against what it might yield. This was one of the things the occupation had made me.

He was the first human opening I found into the system from the inside. Not the public surface of ISIS—the constitutional documents, the court sentences, the Friday sermons, the administrative requirements for women's clothing—but the private language of the men living within it: the way they described to themselves what they were doing, and from what position they understood themselves to be acting, and what they said when they believed they were among those who understood.

I sat in the neighborhood in the late July evening, the occupation settling into everything around me, and I listened. The river was somewhere behind the houses. The air was beginning, slightly, to cool. Adam and Samuel had gone home. Abraham stayed. He was off duty, trying to inhabit the portion of his life that had preceded ISIS: the part that still contained late conversation and familiar company and the particular quality of the air in late July when the day's heat has finally begun to release. He did not come in uniform on those occasions.

I did not know then what that opening would cost to maintain, or what it would eventually demand of me.

THE CITY AS MAP

The cigarette ban had been in force since late July, about six weeks after ISIS seized Mosul, and by August the city had developed its own way of living with it. The ban itself was simple enough: Smoking in public was forbidden, shops caught selling cigarettes would be raided, offenders taken to the *hisba*—the morality police ISIS had established to enforce its interpretation of Islamic law on the streets. What emerged in response was something more complicated.

You did not ask for cigarettes directly. You went to the right shop—and which shops were right was itself a kind of social knowledge that circulated through neighborhood networks by word and gesture. You said you had chest tightness, needed to sit down for a moment. The shopkeeper, if he was still willing to run the risk, would tell you to wait, then disappear to wherever he kept his stock—always somewhere other than his own premises, because *hisba* officers could arrive within minutes of a telephone call from anyone on the street. One man told me his visit was recognized by a watcher on a bicycle circling the block. The *hisba* car arrived in under a minute. The shopkeeper had already moved his cigarettes. They found nothing. When the officers left, the man returned, paid, and walked home with one pack. One pack only—the shopkeeper told him he had to keep some for others who needed them.

This was the texture of the city by August. The ban was not fully working, but its partial enforcement was precisely the point. ISIS did not need to eliminate every cigarette in Mosul. It needed people to experience their desire as furtive, illegal, dependent on the cooperation of strangers who could at any moment become informants. The pleasure of an ordinary thing was converted into a transaction of risk.

That is how the tightening worked—not through one catastrophic transformation but through sequential small ones, each arriving before the last had been fully processed. The amnesty papers that seemed like safety in the first weeks—the stamped documents from the Repentance Council that I had already recognized as a registration system—began producing their real purpose. The arrests of those same registered men had started. A road that was made easier to pass made another space newly forbidden. A sermon was standardized before a punishment went public. The logic was always the same: Offer something that looks like stability, then use that stability as the foundation for the next constraint. By the time most people understood the shape of what they were inside, they were already inside it.

The city moved differently by late summer. Pauses in conversation grew longer. Men who once lingered at shop thresholds in the early evening did not linger now, or stood differently, with a different quality of attention. Women moved through the streets in the new coverings—the black that ISIS required, the niqab that concealed the face, the gloves that concealed the hands—and the streets themselves looked different because the women in them had been made to disappear behind fabric. You could walk through a market and see a hundred women and recognize none of them. The faces that had given the street its human character were removed from view, and what replaced them was a uniformity that was not modesty but erasure. Children still played in the side streets, but the games had changed: Boys imitated the fighters, carrying sticks as rifles, staging mock checkpoints. They learned the new logic faster than anyone. The call to prayer had always been part of the rhythm of daily life in Mosul, a predominantly Muslim city where the call rang from dozens of minarets five times a day. Now it carried an edge of coercion it had not carried before, because attendance at the mosque was not a choice but a requirement, and the *hisba* circulated during prayer times to note who was absent. The beard that every man was required to grow changed the way faces looked in the street—the familiar rendered slightly foreign, the individual face disappearing inside a mandated uniformity. The trousers shortened above the ankle in the style ISIS prescribed changed the way men walked or the way they felt about walking. Every morning the body performed obedience before the mind had decided anything. You dressed according to the regime's specifications, you grew the hair the regime required, and by the time you stepped into the street you were already wearing submission on your body. I wore it too. I wore the beard and the shortened trousers the way a historian wears a cover: to get close enough to the thing being studied without being seen to study it. But the cover was also the thing. There was no neutral body in that city.

Fadi, a shopkeeper I knew from the Dawasa market—a covered bazaar in the commercial center of the city—told me that he had begun to pray faster. He used to go to the mosque because he wanted to. Now he went because he had to, and while he prayed, he thought about his shop. He was afraid someone would come in and steal while he was forced to be somewhere else.

What Fadi understood was what many people in Mosul came to understand without being able to say it cleanly: ISIS had gotten inside the ordinary forms of life. The mosque was no longer only the mosque. The Friday sermon—in Islamic practice, the weekly congregational prayer on Friday, when an imam addresses the community on religious and civic matters—was no longer only a sermon. Preachers across the city were receiving identical written instructions each week specifying what to emphasize: the obligation to support the Islamic State, how even the Ramadan fast should be framed in its terms. You could go to any of the thirty or forty mosques in Mosul on a Friday and hear the same vocabulary, the same themes, the same sequence of arguments. It was made into a broadcast system. To listen to a sermon was to hear not a local act of religious guidance but a directive the regime had decided the city needed to receive that week.

The city was being formatted. That is the word I kept returning to. A damaged but recognizable city waiting for political resolution—that was not what this was. The regime was not occupying the existing city. It was replacing it, piece by piece, with a different version of itself. The acoustic landscape of the markets changed. The background noise of a Mosul market had always included radio from the stalls, popular music between the voices of vendors, the ordinary city sound of people in commerce. That sound was gone. What replaced it was not silence but a different kind of noise—the call to prayer amplified through new speakers, the sound of vehicles that did not belong to merchants, the absence of the music that had been as much a part of the market's identity as the goods it sold. On the shelves, certain categories of things disappeared: music, certain electronics, books that predated the approved curriculum, anything that carried an image of a human face. The shape of what was missing was itself information.

On September 19 and 20—four months into the occupation—crowds filled the markets in a rush that looked almost like ordinary life. They moved through Sarjkhana, a covered market that had served the old city's lanes for generations; through the open stalls of Bab al-Saray and Bab al-Toub; along the Corniche, the promenade following the western bank of the Tigris; and around al-Meydan, the main public square. Merchants said entire shipments had cleared in hours. One trader told me he distributed six truckloads of goods and was asked within days for more.

I went out in those markets too. In the same street where women stacked cloth and men carried cooking oil, I watched an ISIS fighter who appeared to be Uzbek or Azerbaijani walk with his wife and two small children—even the daughter, very young, wore a niqab. He carried a medical prescription and was heading to a clinic. I recorded it that night in a field note, in the plain register I used for such things. Family life, conquest, medicine, commerce: one frame. Mosul had not frozen under occupation. It continued, and the continuation was part of how the regime had deepened its hold.

In the first weeks after the fall, I could still learn an enormous amount by walking. The spacing between checkpoints. Which government offices had changed their functions. The visible city was generous with information in those early weeks.

By August, it stopped being transparent. The surface was still full of signs—the black flags at major intersections, the checkpoints where fighters stopped vehicles and pedestrians, the *hisba* officers on motorbikes who circled through markets and side streets—but the surface was now only the visible portion of a much larger machine. What the machine was actually doing had moved somewhere else. The database I saw building at the checkpoints since June—each identity card checked against preloaded records—was now operating across the city. But the machine's deeper workings were invisible from the street.

I learned this on September 5, when ISIS killed three young men from the Intesar district in eastern Mosul, charging them with apostasy—the renunciation of Islam, which ISIS treated as a capital offense. The men were not the ones in question. ISIS later sent notes to their families acknowledging the error, calling the dead men martyrs. The notes were not apologies. They were administrative notifications: The system had processed the wrong names, and the system was recording that fact. What they revealed was a regime that had gathered categories and was acting on them, imperfectly but relentlessly—one in which being entered into the wrong column of a list was enough to get you killed, and being removed from that column after death was considered a resolution.

After September 5, I understood that the public executions I witnessed were not the event itself. They were the final step in an earlier process that had already happened somewhere I could not see. The cameramen were in position before the killing because the killing had been scheduled. The crowd was directed to a specific space—Bab al-Toub, an open square in central Mosul that had become the primary site for public punishment, or the stretch of pavement outside the old national insurance building—because the staging had been planned. The violence was the visible end of an administrative sequence: categorization, registration, judgment, sentence, display. And display was the word. At Bab al-Toub square I witnessed an execution I cannot put aside—not the killing itself but what preceded it. They brought a man out in the orange uniform ISIS used for its prisoners, the costume borrowed from the photographs of Guantánamo Bay and repurposed as a stage prop. Three cameramen stood around him. While the man waited for the moment that would end his life, the cameramen talked to each other about angles. No, not from there—try the other side. One of them moved. Another adjusted his position. They discussed the shot the way a film crew discusses a shot, while a human being stood between them waiting to die. The condemned man was not the subject of the scene. He was the prop inside it. The cameramen were producing content. When they were satisfied with the framing, the execution proceeded. By October, I had entered more than a hundred such events into the file. I knew their names. I knew their charges. Someone had to remember.

The eye alone could no longer master what the city had become. I needed people. And I needed methods that went beyond observation.

A document can expose you. A hard drive can. A badly kept note. But a person can expose you in ways objects cannot—through misreading, through careless speech, through the panic of someone who believed they were protecting you and discovered they had exposed you instead. That changed the questions I had to ask. Not only: did this happen, where, when, who saw it. Now also: Why is this person telling me this? What do they think this conversation is? If I publish what they have given me, can the chain be traced from the published fact back to their door?

This was not paranoia. A city governed by a violent intelligence regime is a city in which the route of truth matters as much as truth itself. An entirely accurate fact, published too directly, can kill the person it came from.

Since June, I had been moving through the city in various characters. Often just a man with no obvious destination, wandering streets full of other men wandering without obvious destination, because in an occupied city, moving is neutral. Stopping, or having a visible purpose, is not. Some days I decided not to go out at all—not because of a specific threat but because I had been seen too often in the same streets in the same week. I did not want my face to be familiar. A man who appears regularly in the same places acquires a legibility that a man who appears irregularly does not. The discipline of absence was as important as the discipline of presence.

But some of the characters had more structure.

At the bakery near Forest Street—a tree-lined promenade that ran beside the Tigris in eastern Mosul—I had claimed to work. I did not bake. The owner was a man I paid for the arrangement—not a friend, not a relative, a man I had known before the fall who was willing to accept the risk for money. The bakery was a small space, low-ceilinged, with a clay oven set into the wall and flour dust on every surface that light could reach. People entered, waited, spoke to each other and to whoever stood behind the counter while the bread was prepared. The conversations were not directed at me. They were the ordinary speech of a neighborhood conducting its morning business—complaints about prices, questions about which streets were passable, the particular silence that fell over the room whenever a man in ISIS dress walked past the open doorway. What I heard was not intelligence in the formal sense. It was the sound of a city thinking aloud in the one register it still trusted: the brief, careful, elliptical speech of people buying bread from a man they recognized.

One morning a woman came in and asked, in the way you ask about weather, whether the road to the hospital was open. Her son had been taken the night before. She did not say taken by whom. She did not need to. The question about the road was the question she could ask. The question about her son was the question she could not. I answered her about the road. She stood at the counter for a moment after I spoke, not moving, not asking anything else. Her hands were folded in front of her, very still. The silence between us held everything she was unable to say. Then she adjusted her niqab, thanked me, and left without buying bread. I recorded the arrest in my notes that evening—not her name, not her son's name, but the neighborhood, the date, the fact that a man had been taken and that his mother had to disguise her inquiry as a question about traffic.

The bread came out in the early heat. The smell of it—the yeast, the char from the oven's lip, the particular warmth of flour and water transformed—filled the small space and drifted into the street. People entered that smell and relaxed inside it, because bread is older than any regime and the body responds to it before the mind can intervene. That is what intelligence looked like at the bakery: not a secret passed in a whisper, but the shape of what people could not say pressing against the shape of what they did say. The smell of bread was the last neutral thing in the city.

At al-Jumhuriya Hospital, I had a friend who was a doctor. We had known each other before the fall, and one afternoon—joking around, the way friends joke when the alternative is to think clearly about the situation they are in—I convinced him to lend me his white coat. I put it on and walked through the wards. The coat changed the way people looked at me. Patients spoke as though I were a physician. Nurses shared numbers they would not have shared with a man in street clothes—how many ISIS casualties had been received that week, from which direction, with what injuries. The wards held intelligence that the streets did not: The doctors and nurses who processed the wounded were among the only people in the city who saw the organization's losses rather than its displays of strength. On the day I wore the coat, the hospital received seventeen bodies of slain ISIS members from the fighting fronts in western Nineveh. The coat told the staff I was one of them. What they told me gave me the most accurate counts of ISIS casualties available to anyone outside the regime's own records. I did not use the coat every day. It was an advantage I took when the moment permitted—because sometimes your appearance gives you access to things you cannot reach in your ordinary life.

At other times, I drove a taxi through the city's eastern districts—the cover of a driver whose passengers talked to each other as though the man behind the wheel were furniture. People in the back of a taxi discuss things they would not discuss in a market or a café, because the transaction is brief and the driver is anonymous and the movement of the car creates a temporary space that feels, incorrectly, private. I listened. I said nothing. I drove the route and heard what the route contained.

There was also a method that required no costume at all. It is not easy to talk to ISIS fighters. There is only one way, and that is through religion. I had read Islamic history, studied it, taught it. When I used that knowledge—when I spoke to fighters in the mosques using the language of theology, citing sources they recognized, engaging them in the register they trusted—I was not disguised as a clergyman. I was using my own scholarly training as a key. They did not suspect a man who could discuss the hadith—the recorded sayings and actions of the Prophet Muhammad, a primary source of Islamic jurisprudence—with fluency and precision, because such a man belonged, in their understanding, to their world. I would go with this face—Omar the religious man—and in the mosques I would speak to them. Not always to extract sensitive information. Sometimes to understand how they thought, what ISIS looked like from the inside of its own belief, what its fighters said to each other when they believed they were among the faithful. The knowledge of Islam that I spent years acquiring as a historian became, under occupation, an operational tool.

Other mornings I moved differently. A rumor would reach me—through a neighbor, through a conversation at the market, through the informal circuits that moved faster than any official communication—and I would go to check it. Most often the rumors concerned air strikes. A report would circulate that a building in a certain neighborhood had been hit overnight—but which building, and what had it been used for, and who was inside? The difference between an air strike on an ISIS command post and an air strike on a family house was the difference between a military operation and a war crime, and in a city where both were happening, the distinction could not be left to rumor. I would walk to the site the next morning, on the opposite side of the street, at a pace that did not distinguish me from any other man going somewhere he had a reason to go. I noted the damage—its shape, its radius, what it suggested about the size of the ordnance. I noted who was clearing the rubble: ISIS fighters or civilians, which told you who had owned the building. I circled the block once and returned by a different route. What I saw was not proof. It was corroboration—one more data point that, placed alongside a second report from a different route, would either confirm the rumor or reveal it as the kind of fear-generated fiction that multiplied daily. This was the method: hear a claim, walk to the place, observe what the place shows, check it against a second source that does not know about the first. Most of what I recorded in those months passed through this process before it reached the page.

I also learned to photograph without appearing to photograph. The *hisba* posters that appeared on walls—rules about dress, about prayer, about the penalties for violation—were documents that belonged in the record. A man standing in front of a wall with a phone pointed at it was a man whose intentions were legible to anyone watching. I learned to hold my phone at waist height, to frame without looking, to keep walking while the shutter operated. The images were imperfect. Some were blurred, some badly angled. But they existed, and in a city where the regime's own documents were designed to be read and obeyed and not preserved as evidence, their existence was the point. I had seen a man arrested in al-Meydan market earlier that summer for holding his phone in a way that looked like he was photographing ISIS members. They accused him of spying. The lesson was not lost on me.

What made all of this possible was that ISIS in Mosul was not composed entirely of strangers from elsewhere. A significant part of its membership was local men from Mosul, or from the surrounding towns and villages of Nineveh Province. Their relatives still lived in familiar houses. Their brothers still had shops on familiar streets. The occupation didn't erase the social world of the city; it rearranged who held power within it. And social texture, even when deformed, can be read. I had known this city all my life. I knew its neighborhoods, its old families, its informal hierarchies. I knew which streets led where and who was likely to be found on them. That knowledge was now something else: a working map of how the new order had embedded itself inside the existing one.

Access came through ordinary relation. A walk with my brother to our uncle's workshop where he repaired vehicles—a route I had taken many times before the fall—was also a reading of the neighborhood: which buildings had changed their function since June, which doorways were now guarded by men who had not been there three months earlier, what the pattern of vehicles at certain addresses suggested about what was being organized inside them. The ordinary visit and the intelligence work occupied the same afternoon, the same street, the same pair of eyes.

This demanded reading people in two registers at once: who they had been before June 10, and who the occupation had made them. A man I had known as entirely unremarkable might now have a position of real value to me. A man I had once considered worth listening to might now be too frightened to speak at all. Access and reliability were different things. A person could be close to information and still narrate it badly—out of pride, out of fear, out of the desire to appear more important than they were. A disciplined man discloses little. A vain one discloses function, hierarchy, resentment, and atmosphere, often without understanding what he is giving away.

There was always a threshold at which the usefulness of a contact and the danger of the same contact began to converge. That continuity was a door I could use. It was also a door through which I could be found.

By the end of September, I had developed a headache that arrived each evening and did not leave until morning.

The financial architecture of the occupation was becoming visible at the same scale. Around September 17, ISIS moved through the markets and collected what it called zakat from every merchant and businessman in the city. Zakat is one of the five pillars of Islam, the religious obligation to give a portion of one's wealth in charity. ISIS reframed it as mandatory taxation, set the amount at two million Iraqi dinars per person—roughly $1,600 at the exchange rate then prevailing—and collected it as a single round across the entire commercial sector. A source with access to the organization's Zakat Department confirmed that from that one collection, ISIS gathered approximately five million dollars from the city's merchants alone. In a city where the average monthly income had collapsed since June, where unemployment had driven families to sell possessions for food, five million dollars extracted in a single pass was not taxation. It was systematic seizure dressed in religious obligation.

I watched the collectors move through Bab al-Saray on the morning of the collection. They carried lists. They moved from stall to stall the way a landlord's agent moves through a building collecting rent—not with the urgency of men taking what does not belong to them but with the administrative patience of men who believe they are exercising a right. One merchant I knew—a man who sold electronics near the entrance to the covered market—counted out the bills with the deliberate slowness of a man who wants the act of compliance to be seen as something other than surrender. The collector waited without impatience. He had been doing this all morning. He would do it all afternoon. The merchant placed the money on the counter between them rather than handing it directly—a gesture so small that only someone watching for it would have noticed, but I noticed, because small gestures were all that remained of refusal. The collector picked up the money, wrote a figure in a ledger, stamped a receipt, and moved to the next stall. Two million dinars. The merchant looked at the receipt the way a man looks at a fine he has paid for a crime he did not commit. Then he folded it and put it in his pocket, because the receipt was also protection—proof that he had already paid, in case a second collector came. What had been a criminal protection racket in the years before the fall—violent organizations demanding payment from merchants under threat—was now legalized by theology, and the legalization came with receipts.

I want to say something about what the merchant's gesture represented, because I watched versions of it across the city for months, and because the world outside Mosul never understood the position these people were in.

The population of an occupied city does not divide into resisters and collaborators. That is the binary of people who have never lived under total control. The reality is a spectrum so compressed that the distance between cooperation and refusal can be measured in the angle at which a man places money on a counter. A father who sent his son to the rewritten school was not endorsing ISIS's curriculum. He was calculating that a distorted education was less damaging than no education at all, and that a boy seen on the streets during school hours would attract the attention of the *hisba*. A shopkeeper who paid the zakat was not funding the caliphate by conviction. He was buying another day of operation with the only currency the regime accepted. A woman who wore the niqab was not submitting to the ideology. She was navigating a city in which her uncovered face was a punishable offense and her covered face was survival.

These were not moral failures. They were the daily calculations of prisoners performing the routines their captors required in order to remain alive. Every person in Mosul who was not a member of ISIS and did not flee was making these calculations every day—at the checkpoint, at the market, at the mosque, in their own homes. The occupation did not offer a third option between compliance and death. It offered compliance, and it punished everything else.

On June 18—eight days after the fall, while the city was still absorbing the shock of the collapse—ISIS called the faculty of Mosul University to a meeting.

Eight days. The army fled on June 10. The black flags went up. The Repentance Council opened its doors. And already the regime was reorganizing the university. That speed told me something about what this occupation was. It was not improvising. It had a plan for every institution, and the plan for the university was ready before the university had even closed for the summer.

The meeting was held inside the College of Arts, in the conference room—the building where I had studied, where I had defended my thesis, where I had taught for six months before the fall. The room was one I knew. The chairs were the same chairs. The man sitting at the front was not.

His name was Dhu'l-Qarnayn. He was a German Egyptian—not Iraqi, not from Mosul, not from any city whose university he was now appointed to lead. ISIS made him the president of the University of Mosul. The university that had trained Mosul's historians and doctors and engineers for fifty years was now being given to a man who had come from abroad, carried no connection to the institution or the city, and owed his authority entirely to the regime that placed him there.

He explained what the university would become. All classes would be restructured to conform to the strictest interpretation of the Quran and the Sunna—the recorded practices and teachings of the Prophet Muhammad. Subjects that contradicted Islamic law as ISIS defined it would be removed.

The goal, he said, was to produce a generation of strong Muslim fighters, not the kind of graduates the old system had produced.

Strong Muslim fighters. Not scholars, not professionals, not citizens. Fighters. The university that had trained generations of Mosul's intellectuals and civil servants was being told, in the room where I had studied history, that its purpose was now to produce soldiers for a caliphate.

Then one of my former colleagues spoke. A professor I had known for years—a man who had built his academic reputation teaching about freedom, liberty, and secularism. He raised his hand and addressed Dhul-Qarnain with a suggestion: The new university should offer more Asian languages, he said, because the caliphate had many non-Arab Muslims from those regions. He framed the suggestion as practical, helpful, forward-looking. He was volunteering his expertise to the regime that had just abolished his discipline. I sat and watched a man I had once respected offer his services to the system that was dismantling everything he had claimed to believe. I recorded what he said. I did not record what I felt.

Many people I knew joined ISIS in those months. Many. But one stays with me.

He had been my student—a young man whose exam I graded in the history of the Middle East just months before the fall. He was smart. I still have his exam paper. I do not know what happened to him, what pressure or conviction or despair led him from my classroom to their ranks. He was killed after a few months of joining. I learned this the way I learned most things in the city—through the short circuits of neighborhood knowledge, a sentence spoken in passing, a name that stopped being mentioned. His exam paper is still in my files. He had written about the siege of Mosul by Timur in 1393—the last time the city had been taken by force before ISIS arrived six hundred years later. It belongs to the university that no longer exists, graded by a teacher whose position was abolished, written by a student who was consumed by the system that abolished it.

October brought the implementation.

Announced on the twenty-first: The colleges of law, political science, fine arts, and archaeology were closed. The departments of philosophy and tourism were dissolved. From the remaining curriculum were removed democracy, human rights, cultural education, the study of drama and the novel. Exam questions must no longer reference patriotism, ethnicity, geographic divisions that contradicted sharia, or what the decree called "forged historical incidents"—meaning most of what I had spent years studying and teaching. Every textbook was to replace the words "The Republic of Iraq" with "The Islamic State." Every administrative heading that once read Ministry of Higher Education would now read Chamber of Education.

What followed was worse than the decree. ISIS forced all teachers and university staff into the central library building of Mosul University—the same library where I had spent years among the archives, where the city's intellectual inheritance was stored on shelves that now served as the backdrop for its own erasure. The faculty sat there from eight in the morning to eight at night, for months, rewriting the school textbooks. Twelve hours a day, the scholars of Mosul's university dismantled the education they had spent their careers building and replaced it with what the regime required. Some resisted quietly, writing slowly, producing as little as possible. Some cooperated. Some did both on different days, because in an occupied city the line between resistance and compliance runs through the same person at different hours.

And among those leading the rewriting—I learned this later, through the circuits of information that moved through the university's surviving networks—was the woman who had sat on my thesis panel and accused me of defending secularism. The same woman. The accusation that had nearly ended my academic career was now the qualification for redesigning the university. She had not changed her convictions between the day she challenged my thesis and the day she began writing for ISIS. The convictions simply found a regime that shared them. What ISIS brought to the university was not entirely foreign to the university. It was something that had been present inside the institution, waiting for the conditions that would allow it to become policy.

I stood in the hallway of the College of Arts after the October decree was posted—the same hallway where I had walked to my thesis defense, where I walked to my first day of teaching, where the light through the high windows falls in the particular way it falls in buildings designed for thinking. The decree was mounted on a wall beside a noticeboard that still held announcements from the previous academic year—examination schedules, office hours, a faded poster for a student conference on archaeological methodology. No one had bothered to remove the old notices. They hung beside the decree like the artifacts of an extinct civilization displayed next to the weapons that had destroyed it.

But then something happened that, in all those months of documenting the occupation's advance, gave me one of the few moments of genuine hope.

The parents of Mosul refused to send their children to the new schools.

It was not organized resistance. No one announced it. No committee met. The parents simply did not send them. The schools opened under the new curriculum, and the classrooms were empty. ISIS threatened the teachers. They forced the school principals to report under threat of punishment. Two teachers were killed. But the parents did not break. The children stayed home.

I called it, in my notes, the soft resistance. It was one of the most important things I witnessed inside the city, because it proved that the occupation's power, for all its administrative sophistication and its willingness to kill, had a limit. The limit was the door of a family's house, and the decision made inside it. The regime that had rewritten the curriculum, forced the faculty into months of labor, abolished entire disciplines, and appointed a German Egyptian to lead the university—that regime could not make the families of Mosul deliver their children to it.

This was one of the moments I came closest to something that resembled happiness inside the occupation. I had been close to giving up. Nothing was changing. No one was rising against ISIS. The tightening seemed absolute. Then the families of Mosul did something ISIS could not force or undo, and they did it without weapons, without organization, without a single public statement. They simply kept their doors closed.

The archive was not a repository. It was a living problem.

Earlier it had been a record kept against erasure—a way of preserving what was happening against the possibility that no external account would survive. By October, it had become something heavier: a collection of linked exposures, each piece of documented truth connected to the person through whom it had arrived, and that connection itself a danger.

The practical infrastructure of the work was fragile and had to be rebuilt constantly. I had internet access through a friend who ran a small internet café—not an ISIS operative, a man I had known before the fall, someone I paid considerably more than the standard rate for an arrangement that required his personal risk. The café was a small room with six or seven screens, the kind of place that had existed on Mosul's commercial streets for years, where students came to check email and men came to read news and the electricity was more reliable than at home. ISIS required that anyone using public internet provide their name, address, and passwords. My friend had filled out a fake application on my behalf—a fabricated name, a fabricated address, the minimum information needed to create an account that would not lead back to me. I used the café in the late afternoon, when it was busiest, when one more man at a screen was one more man at a screen. I kept the sessions short. I composed what I needed to publish before I arrived, typed it quickly, posted it, and left. Even so, his connection was sometimes cut without warning, sometimes for hours, sometimes for days.

For mobile communication, there was another method. You drove slowly through certain areas of the city where a signal from outside ISIS-controlled territory could sometimes be caught—the organization had disrupted most civilian telecommunications, cutting off the city's normal connections with the outside world. You composed the message in advance, drove slowly, sent it while moving. You did not stop. ISIS noticed the pattern and arrested people for it. Three men were executed. After that, the method was used differently: women in the car, because ISIS officers were less likely to stop a vehicle carrying women. For a while. Then they noticed that pattern too.

The hard drive that held it all was organized the way a historian organizes a research archive—by date, by category, by source. Each entry carried the date, the location, the nature of the event, the source through which it had arrived, and a reliability assessment. Accompanying each entry was a separate file with the day's fuller observations—the things that did not fit into a single data point but that mattered to the texture of what was happening. The spreadsheet grew by several entries each day. It was the most dangerous object in the house.

Files had to be separated by exposure risk, not only by subject. Some truths stayed off the public page because the chain that led from the published fact back to its origin was too short—because only one or two people could have known what I was about to publish, and those people were still alive inside the city. Notes required abbreviations. Devices required clearing. The simplest danger was not technical sophistication on ISIS's part. It was a house search. A curious officer pulling open a laptop. A neighbor saying something he should not have said.

But the technical sophistication was also real, and it was greater than I understood at the time. ISIS's newspaper—which I obtained and read only after the liberation—contained detailed counterintelligence articles explaining how cell tower triangulation worked, how connecting to the internet from Mosul through WhatsApp or Telegram could expose a user's identity and location, how encrypted applications could be compromised through a phone's IMEI number. One article used Mosul as its example: If you connect from Mosul through any communication application and contact anyone whose communications are monitored—such as families of foreign fighters or anyone with a jihadist record—the information is enough for the intelligence services to begin building a profile of you and everyone around you.

They had dismantled the commercial cellular networks in the city as a deliberate counterintelligence measure, precisely because they understood the surveillance architecture those networks enabled. They deployed their own communications and monitored the population's digital traces with a sophistication drawn from manuals they then published openly in their weekly newspaper. They wrote about coalition drones flying at nine thousand meters—too high to hear or see—and about fake cell towers mounted on military vehicles that could intercept every phone in range.

Every precaution I had developed through instinct and necessity—rotating internet cafés, limiting sessions to fifteen minutes, separating devices, clearing browser histories—matched almost exactly the vulnerabilities ISIS was warning its own members to exploit in others. I was operating against an enemy that had written the manual on detecting people who did what I did. The distance between my life and my death was the width of a single procedural error, and the enemy had published the list of errors it was looking for.

Historians imagine archives as stable repositories, shelved and organized, waiting for the future to come and find them. My archive moved with me. It changed shape in response to what had happened each day. Some days it shrank: things deleted, things not written down, things kept only as memory because memory left no trace a search could find. Other days it expanded: a new fact confirmed, a date fixed, a name recorded against the day when names could be published safely. It was not a record of events. It was a record of what could be safely kept, which is a different thing entirely.

To stay alive carefully enough to keep the record alive: By October these had become the same obligation. I had not planned to think this way. The work required it of me and I followed. Some nights I lay awake and could not remember whether I had eaten that day. The headache became a companion. I noticed it the way you notice a sound that has been in the room so long it becomes part of the room. My mother brought tea each evening and I drank it in the same chair, in the same room, at the same hour. The ritual of the tea—the heat of the glass, the sugar stirred three times, the particular way she set it down without asking whether I wanted it—was one of the few things that had not changed since June. I held on to it without knowing that I was holding on.

Then, on the night of October 24–25, the Al-Kindi military facility on the northeastern edge of the city was hit by air strikes from the American-led coalition that had been conducting operations against ISIS positions in Iraq since September. Al-Kindi was a large complex that ISIS was using as a command center, disguised to look insignificant from the air. ISIS had taken measures to deceive the monitoring planes into believing the facility had no importance. Those measures had failed. The air strikes destroyed the facility completely. At least eight senior ISIS leaders were killed. The hospitals received at least a 145 casualties, some bodies not intact. The strikes were precise enough—no civilian casualties were reported—that the organization understood someone had provided accurate targeting information from inside.

Within days, fighters who had been moving openly through the city for months began covering their faces again, reverting to the concealment they had used before the fall. Men who had given their names to neighbors, who had been recognized at checkpoints, who had allowed themselves to be known, now wanted to be unknown again. ISIS began investigating its own ranks, focusing particularly on non-Iraqi members who had come from Syria, Europe, and elsewhere to join the organization. Local ISIS members—men from Mosul who joined after the fall—shaved their beards and returned to their previous jobs, trying to disappear back into the civilian population they had recently risen above.

The Al-Kindi strike changed the atmosphere of what followed. I could see it the next morning in the streets: The checkpoints were manned differently, the fighters standing farther back from the road, their faces newly covered. Vehicles that had been parked openly outside headquarters were moved inside compounds or dispersed among residential buildings. The confidence that had characterized the occupation since June—the open convoys, the unhurried patrols, the men who walked through the markets as though the city had always belonged to them—was gone. The city that had been learning to accommodate a visible, confident occupier was now learning to accommodate a frightened, suspicious one.

A frightened, suspicious occupier is more dangerous than a confident one: It strikes more widely and verifies less carefully.

Every method I had developed since June—the disguises, the sources, the separated files, the careful management of what could be said and what had to be held back—brought me to a place I could not have described to anyone, even if there had been someone I trusted enough to describe it to. I was inside the system now, reading it from close enough to understand its daily workings, and the system was reading me back through every checkpoint and every pair of eyes I passed on the street. The city of lists was being documented by a man who kept his own lists, in hidden files that moved through the house at night. The gap between those two operations—the regime's intelligence and mine—was the space in which the entire work existed. It was not a wide space. And after Al-Kindi, it had begun to narrow in ways I could feel but not yet fully measure.

THE CALIPHATE AS OFFICE

What does a terrorist look like when he is no longer planting a bomb but governing a city?

Not when he is killing—the world has seen that, filmed it, broadcast it, consumed it. But when he is processing a tax receipt. When he is filing the paperwork that authorized an execution he will attend after lunch. When he is sitting behind a desk with a laptop, a ledger, a list of names, a stamped document, a budget spreadsheet with twelve monthly tabs and a line item for diesel fuel beside a line item for forced marriages. When he has an office with regular hours—eight in the morning until two in the afternoon—and eats at a restaurant on the street where the bookshops used to be and walks home past the square where a man was flogged that morning and stops at the bakery to buy bread for his children.

What does terror look like when it has a health department, an agriculture department, a tribal affairs office, a police force that produces monthly statistical reports categorizing thefts and homosexuality in the same flowchart—and when it wants you to see all of it?

I know what it looks like. I lived inside it for eighteen months. I walked through its offices. I handed my identity card to its functionaries. I paid its taxes, obeyed its dress codes, attended its mandatory sermons, and moved through its checkpoints while carrying, hidden on my person or in my room, the evidence of every crime I watched it commit. Every department I describe in this chapter was a department that could detect me. Every mechanism was a mechanism I had to navigate. Every office was an office whose jurisdiction included the crime of documenting the regime that had created it.

The question that should have been asked more often—by analysts, by governments, by anyone trying to understand what happened to Mosul—was not what ISIS built. It was how ISIS built it so fast. A city of nearly two million people had a functioning parallel state within weeks of the fall. Media, police, courts, taxation, property registration, morality enforcement—all operational before most of the world absorbed the news that Mosul had been taken at all. The speed astonished even those of us living inside it.

The answer, which I came to understand only gradually, was that ISIS did not build a state from nothing. It took over what was already there. It changed the signs. It changed the stamps on the paperwork. It brought in its own managers. The government buildings were the same buildings. The filing systems were the same filing systems. The civil servants, in many offices, were the same civil servants—now working under new authority, the property deed that had once been their employment contract now serving as the threat that kept them at their desks. ISIS did not need to invent a bureaucracy. It needed to parasitize one. The existing infrastructure of the Iraqi state—its offices, its records, its personnel, its institutional knowledge—was absorbed into the caliphate the way an organism absorbs a host. The host's structures remained. The host's purposes changed.

And there was a deeper logic beneath the speed. ISIS had been functionally governing parts of Nineveh for years before the fall—collecting taxes through extortion, enforcing codes of conduct, mediating tribal disputes, and eliminating anyone whose influence competed with theirs. The formal seizure of the city in June 2014 was not the beginning of ISIS governance. It was the moment when the covert system became overt, when the functions that had been performed in shadow were given offices, stamps, and the vocabulary of a state.

Years later, after the liberation, I obtained the compiled issues of *Al-Naba*—the weekly newspaper ISIS had published throughout the occupation and beyond. In its pages, they described the fall of Mosul not as a miraculous event but as the final stage of a planned campaign. They wrote that just over three hundred fighters had defeated tens of thousands of Iraqi soldiers, and they attributed this not to divine intervention alone but to what they called strategic security work—a decade of covert operations conducted by dozens of cells inside Mosul and its outskirts. They described a sustained war of attrition: targeted assassinations of officers and policemen, car bombs at checkpoints, silenced-pistol killings on residential streets, suicide attacks against military installations. Every bomb that detonated, every bullet from a silenced weapon, every suicide attacker—they counted all of it as investment toward the day the city would fall.

They were describing, in their own triumphant language, exactly what I had been documenting for years—what my archives contained as individual incidents recorded in notebooks and hard drives. What I had tracked as daily violence, they now presented as a coherent strategy. The world saw a sudden collapse. ISIS saw a harvest. They had created the conditions of dysfunction in the existing government and then presented themselves as the cure for the dysfunction they had engineered.

I learned this system the way a prisoner learns the architecture of his prison—by walking its corridors, by counting its doors, by noting which ones opened at which hours and which ones never opened at all. I learned it at checkpoints where I handed my identity card to a boy who held a weapon in one hand and operated a laptop with the other. I learned it in markets where the tax collector arrived on schedule and left with a receipt. I learned it in mosques where the Friday sermon had been scripted by a department whose offices I could locate on a map. I learned it because learning it was the condition of surviving it, and surviving it was the condition of documenting it, and documenting it was the only thing I had decided I would not stop doing.

The sentencing tariff was not a secret document. It was not an internal memo circulated among judges. It was a professionally designed flyer—al-Hudud al-Shar'iyya, "The Sharia Punishments"—produced by ISIS's media office with the caliphate's library stamp, bearing Quranic citations and hadith references for each category of offense, and distributed to the population through mosques, through media points, through the same channels that distributed administrative announcements and recruitment propaganda. Someone with graphic design training had laid out the categories: Adultery. Slander. Theft. Drinking Alcohol. Sodomy. Highway Robbery. Each category explained the offense, cited the scriptural authority, specified the punishment. The tariff was public because the punishments were public. The dual visibility of the system was, in this document, literally a piece of paper you could hold in your hand.

For selling cigarettes: 150,000 dinars per carton, escalating above one hundred cartons to one million per carton plus confiscation of the total purchase price. For adultery, unmarried: twenty-five million dinars plus one hundred lashes. Married: fifty million plus 150. For smoking: 250,000 dinars. For theft: return of stolen goods plus ten million dinars plus fifty lashes. For failure to close a shop during prayer: five million plus twenty-five lashes. For sodomy: fifty million plus one hundred lashes, for both parties.

Each punishment combined a financial extraction with a physical punishment. The fine and the lash were part of the same sentence, administered by the same system, recorded on the same form. The money went to Bayt al-Mal, the treasury. The lash marks went home with the man. Both were visible—the treasury's ledger and the man's back.

Each prisoner required two guarantors—known residents who would vouch for the prisoner's conduct after release. The guarantor's property deed was held as collateral. The prisoner was forbidden from leaving Mosul. To be released from the system, you had to bind two other people to it. The property deed in the court's filing cabinet ensured that the binding was not metaphorical.

In the *hisba* headquarters in the Nabi Zarzis neighborhood, the detention rooms were full. Three hundred people had been arrested for smoking and for failing to attend communal prayer. The sounds carried through the walls—old men and teenagers, the rhythm of the whip, the shouting that follows each stroke. A source described the scene: a line of men waiting to enter a room from which other men emerged with the marks of the lash on their backs, their offense written on a form they carried with them as they walked home. The form was their receipt. The man walking home with the form in his hand and the lash marks on his back was himself the system's message to everyone who saw him: The state punishes, and the state keeps records, and both are written on this body.

The governor of Mosul issued a written amendment to the method of execution for homosexuality—changing it from throwing the accused off a building to burial alive. The amendment was distributed through the judicial apparatus and implemented immediately. A bureaucratic memo changed the method of killing. The memo was filed. The burial was public.

In Bab al-Toub, a man found with twenty-five bottles of alcohol was tied to a post in the center of the square. ISIS instructed the bystanders to abuse him physically. The punishment lasted three hours—conducted in the commercial heart of the city, with the population itself recruited as the instrument of enforcement. In the same square, on other days, the court's sentences were read aloud, cameras filming the executions that would be broadcast through the media points at the mosques. The square was both a courtroom and a theater. Two brothers were forced to kill one another. The survivor was tied to his brother's body for hours, smeared with his brother's blood, displayed in the street. The punishment was the display. The display was the punishment.

The cigarette economy revealed the system's deepest logic. The official responsible for confiscation in the Bab Sinjar area had collected 250 million Iraqi dinars in two days. He told his colleagues he deserved a medal. Eight hundred million dinars were confiscated from cigarette dealers in a single sweep. And the sources confirmed what the population suspected: ISIS itself was allowing cigarettes to enter the city. The prohibition was the business model. The supply and the punishment were the same revenue stream. The man flogged for smoking walked home past the route through which the cigarettes had entered under ISIS's own facilitation.

The financial apparatus I mapped across months of daily reports was the skeleton of everything else.

From the largest merchants—more than seven thousand at an average assessment of five thousand dollars each—ISIS collected approximately thirty-five million dollars. From a second tier of more than 5,800 smaller traders—approximately eleven point six million. From the wealthiest businessmen, assessed individually at more than $200,000 each—thirty-four million. From salaried employees—$470,000. These were initial one-time collections. The monthly extraction continued on top of them—10 percent of every merchant's profits, 3 percent of government salary transfers from Baghdad, and the household tax assessed on every house in the city by the number of its stories, visible from the street.

The money-transfer offices were the regime's window into every financial relationship. At the end of each week, every *hawala* operator submitted copies of identity documents for every sender and receiver to Bayt al-Mal. The transfer slip was a surveillance document.

Even leaving the city required a financial deposit: a guarantor, a property deed or car title, two thousand dollars. If you did not return within ten days, the property was confiscated and the deposit forfeited. More than 350 people left in secret in a single week, paying smugglers one million dinars each.

By late 2015, the *hisba* had been placed on self-funding—its staff salaries paid from the fines it collected. The instrument of moral enforcement and the instrument of revenue collection were the same man with the same receipt book.

Confiscated properties were managed through three offices: Bayt al-Mal absorbed financial assets; Diwan al-Aqarat processed real estate; Diwan al-Ghana'im—the Office of Spoils—handled movable property. Saint Ephrem Church, one of the ancient churches of Mosul, had been converted into a market where confiscated goods were sold at reduced prices. Citizens purchased the property of their former neighbors in a church whose cross had been smashed, at prices posted on a board, with receipts issued by an office that stamped each transfer. The cross was broken. The receipt was printed. The transaction was public.

After the liberation, Iraqi judicial investigators recovered and analyzed ISIS's own internal archives from the ruins of its administrative offices across Nineveh. What they found confirmed what I had documented from the street but added a dimension I had been able to infer only partially: the full organizational depth.

Every *wilaya*—every province under ISIS control—contained the same sixteen administrative centers, replicated without exception. The recovered documents listed them: Security. Education. Media. Real Estate. Services. Health. Police. Da'wah and Mosques. Courts. Agriculture. Tribal Relations. Hisba. Ifta. Zakat. Bayt al-Mal. Communications. Sixteen centers. Each center reported upward through its corresponding diwan to the Delegated Committee. Each received its funding from Bayt al-Mal. Each operated under the same directives, the same forms, the same procedural chain.

The documents were classified by a system of colored stamps. Red stamps—the highest level: the Delegated Committee, the diwans, the military divisions. Blue stamps—operational: administrative offices, brigades, battalions. A red stamp meant the document had been approved at the governing level. A blue stamp meant it was implementation. Every document I had seen at checkpoints, at the court, at Bayt al-Mal, carried one of these stamps. The data on those documents was encrypted using TrueCrypt—commercial encryption software repurposed for the administration of a state that wanted its internal records hidden from enemies while its public acts were displayed to the population it governed. The public punishment visible to all. The administrative record encrypted and hidden. Both produced by the same system.

The Diwan al-Jund—the Military Bureau—administered the caliphate's armed forces across all eastern provinces from its headquarters inside Nineveh. The bureau was modeled explicitly on the original diwan established by the Caliph Umar ibn al-Khattab—ISIS cited the seventh-century precedent in its founding documents. The first war minister was Abu Omar al-Shishani. After his death in an air strike at al-Shirqat, he was replaced by Iyad Abdulrahman Talib Rashid al-Ubaidi. Under the war minister, ten military divisions operated simultaneously, each named after an event or figure from Islamic history—battles for the older units (Nahawand, Ain Jalut al-Sawari, Qadisiyya, Yamana, Yarmouk) and ISIS commanders for the newer ones (Furqan, Bilawi, Abu Mu'taz al-Qurashi). Each division contained its own administration, intelligence, sharia committee, medical unit, supply chain, artillery, rockets, mortars, air defense, snipers battalion, inghimasi battalion, surveillance committee, military engineering, and booby-trapping unit. The organizational chart is not my reconstruction. It is ISIS's own document, recovered from the caliphate's own archives. The precision is itself evidence: This was a military bureaucracy that documented its own structure with the same rigor it used to document its punishments and its taxes.

That precision did not come from theology. It came from the men who built the system. The senior military and intelligence planners inside ISIS were, in significant numbers, former officers of Saddam Hussein's army and Mukhabarat—men who had been expelled from the state by the de-Baathification order of 2003, radicalized in American detention facilities like Camp Bucca, and reconstituted inside the insurgency that became ISIS. They brought with them the organizational methods of the old Iraqi state: the filing protocols, the hierarchical command structures, the intelligence compartmentalization, the instinct to document everything and classify it by color-coded access. The caliphate's language was seventh-century Islamic governance. Its architecture was twentieth-century Iraqi military bureaucracy. The diwan that ISIS named after the Caliph Umar was designed by men who had served under Saddam Hussein and learned their administrative craft in institutions the Americans had dismantled. What the world saw as the terrifying competence of a new kind of terrorist organization was, in substantial part, the competence of an old state reassembled under a new flag.

Among those sixteen centers were three that revealed the full scope of the caliphate's ambition more clearly than the courts or the checkpoints: Health, Agriculture, and Tribal Relations. Courts and security are what any armed group establishes. A health department, an agriculture department, a tribal affairs office—those are what a state establishes.

The Health Department operated inside the hospital complex at Ibn Sina—a vast compound of multiple buildings that always looked to me, whenever I walked through it, like an intelligence installation. ISIS was always present inside the complex. Prefabricated offices—metal containers of the kind you see on construction sites—had been placed outside the hospital buildings, inside the grounds. The hospital had its own architecture—the wards, the operating rooms, the morgue—and beside it, ISIS had added its own administrative layer in those containers, the way a parasite attaches its organs to a host without replacing them. Doctors were told to continue working. Those who refused were threatened with the confiscation of their homes—the same mechanism that kept shopkeepers paying taxes and teachers writing curricula. The coercion was administrative, not theatrical. No public flogging was required. The property deed in the Real Estate Department's filing cabinet was sufficient.

But the health system served the caliphate before it served the population. A shipment of medicines arrived from Turkey—surgical drugs, anesthetics, antibiotics. An ISIS doctor issued an order: The surgical drugs were reserved for fighters. Civilians could receive them only in cases of "maximum emergency," a phrase whose definition was left to the ISIS official rather than to the treating physician. Medical equipment was simultaneously being transported out of Mosul to Syria—machines, instruments, supplies stripped from the hospitals and shipped to the caliphate's other territories. The Health Department was a logistics operation that distributed medical resources according to the caliphate's priorities. The Uzbek fighter I had seen in al-Meydan with his prescription and his veiled daughter was moving through this system—the prescription issued by a military medical office, filled at a pharmacy under *hisba* jurisdiction, in a clinic staffed by a doctor who worked under threat of losing his home. The rifle, the prescription, and the property deed were all connected. Three offices governing a single transaction.

The Agriculture Department governed the vast plains surrounding Mosul—one of Iraq's most productive agricultural regions. The same 10-percent levy applied to urban merchants was applied to farmers. A farmer's wheat harvest was assessed the same way a shopkeeper's inventory was assessed: by a functionary with a ledger, applying a published rate, issuing a receipt.

The Tribal Relations office managed the allegiance of tribal leaders, mediated disputes between clans, facilitated the public pledges of loyalty—the *bay'a*—that sheikhs were expected to offer at ceremonies ISIS filmed and broadcast. A sheikh who pledged allegiance publicly became an instrument of the administration. His clan's young men were recruited through his authority. His cooperation was documented, filed, and used as leverage. The pledge was visible. The file was hidden. The office and the whip. The tribal leaders were what the system valued most—not as individuals but as nodes of influence, men whose authority over their communities could be co-opted and turned into the caliphate's local infrastructure. Win the sheikh and you win his village. Lose him and you have to garrison it.

Courts, finance, security, media—those are the departments that appear in every analysis of ISIS. But it is Health, Agriculture, and Tribal Relations that prove what the caliphate actually was. A group that builds courts is enforcing its will. A group that builds a health department, an agriculture department, and a tribal affairs office is governing a society—managing the body, the food supply, and the social fabric. The courts could be dismissed as theater. The Health Department could not. The agriculture levy could not. The tribal affairs office could not. Those three departments are the proof that ISIS in Mosul was not an insurgency that performed governance. It was a government that performed insurgency.

But even that formulation understates what the system actually was. The longer I lived inside it, the more I understood that every department, every office, every function of the caliphate served not one purpose but two. The Health Department did not merely ration medicine. It rationed medicine in a way that demonstrated the caliphate's authority over life and death. The Agriculture Department did not merely tax wheat. It taxed wheat while framing the levy as zakat—a religious obligation—thereby converting economic extraction into ideological submission. The courts did not merely punish. They punished publicly, with Quranic citation, with cameras, transforming each sentence into a broadcast that told the population: This is not arbitrary violence. This is the law of God, administered by the state of God, and you are living inside it.

Every department had two roles. The first was to enforce the caliphate's policies—whether those policies concerned real estate, agriculture, law enforcement, or education. The second was to ensure that in performing those functions, the department reinforced the caliphate's ideology. The administration was a propaganda machine. The governance was the propaganda. The tax receipt and the Friday sermon were not separate instruments. They were the same instrument, applied through different offices, producing the same effect: the saturation of every corner of daily life with the caliphate's claim to total authority. A propaganda state—not in the sense that the state produced propaganda, but in the sense that the state was propaganda, that its administrative existence was itself the message it most wanted the population to receive.

The security apparatus was smaller than anyone outside the city imagined, but its organizational depth was that of a professional military. I estimated between 900 and 1,200 fighters inside Mosul at any given time. No more than thirty to forty per neighborhood. Fourteen checkpoints on the east bank, three fighters at each. Four *hisba* patrol vehicles. Fifty military police. The numbers were small. The visibility was not. The checkpoints were on main roads. The cameras mounted on electricity poles along Kirkuk Road were installed in plain sight. The surveillance was itself a message.

Each significant facility had a security chief—an *amni*—with exactly eight subordinates. Communications used coded language: "Printer" meant the printing press location; "dictionary" meant the forest area; "tea" meant the pedal area. Certain special units were prohibited from any visible marker of ISIS membership—no face coverings, no beards, no devices. They looked like ordinary civilians. They were the one part of the system designed to be invisible, because their task was to find the people who were trying to be invisible too. People like me.

The most devastating element was the children. A source inside the organization confirmed: "The information flows to us without our asking. People cooperate with us extensively. And children are the most frequent visitors to the *hisba* offices to report cases of violations."

Twenty-five thousand dinars. The price of a child's report on a neighbor.

On March 11, ISIS arrested at least two hundred people from three districts for using mobile phones. The coverage point—a patch of signal on a street corner—had become a surveillance target. The arrests were visible. The minibuses were visible.

The media apparatus extended this visibility: two radio stations—al-Bayan at 92.5 FM in six languages, al-Zahoor at 95.3 FM. When air strikes struck the transmitter, ISIS rebuilt it immediately—the radio came back before the damaged checkpoint was repaired. The radio was a symbol of existence. Media points—white caravans with screens—were positioned at every mosque. The same square where a man had been punished that morning might display a recruitment video that afternoon. The screen and the bloodstain occupied the same pavement.

The women's role went far beyond what the world assumed. An ISIS preacher in January 2015: "O men, open the way for women to join us. In need of fighter women." By March, women were setting up armed checkpoints in my neighborhood. In Sarjikhana, the women's *hisba* bit the bare hands of women who had failed to cover them. Eight foreign female volunteers arrived—two Kuwaiti, two Swedish, two Egyptian, two Tunisian—some not older than seventeen. Forty-three women trained at Mosul University in English, internet skills, preaching, rhetoric, and media production. The building that had trained hotel managers now housed the women who policed the caliphate's moral order.

People call them monsters. I will not. A monster is a creature without choice. To call these men and women monsters is to say they could not help what they did. That is a lie, and the lie serves them, because it removes the thing that makes their acts punishable: the choice.

I compiled intelligence files on thirty-eight of them. I will not publish their names. But I will describe how they lived inside the city they governed—because the living is where the truth sits. The killing is what the world already knows. The living is what the world refuses to see.

The shift change happened on Thursdays and Tuesdays. Each fighter received leave every fifteen days. Those who worked in the judiciary, the education bureau, and the real estate office kept regular hours. They ate at the restaurants on Thaqafa Street—the cultural district, the street where the bookshops had been. The foreign fighters—Chechens, Tunisians, men from the Gulf—treated the restaurants as though they were on holiday. They had moved into the furnished houses of families given seventy-two hours to leave with nothing. A German fighter married a local girl and was living in the Andalus neighborhood, in a home of displaced Christians. He cooked in a kitchen that still smelled of the spices the Christian woman had stored in jars she had labeled in Syriac.

I knew one of them. Two doors from a friend's house. He had been a taxi driver before the fall. After the fall, he appeared in uniform. He was responsible for interrogation. We still sat together sometimes in the evenings. He told me about the women they had killed. He used the word "cleaned." Then he asked whether I had eaten, and whether my mother was well.

A livestock trader—forty-eight years old, two wives, nine children—was appointed judge in the Sharia court, sentencing former police officers to death. The distance between the courthouse where he sentenced men and the bakery where he bought bread for his children was four minutes by car.

A petty criminal—illiterate, accusations of violence—joined the intelligence service. He was given a weapon, a salary, and the authority to arrest and kill. The authority came with a title. The title came with a department. The department came with a filing system. The filing system made him legitimate. The machine did not ask who you had been. It asked who you were willing to become.

The Education Bureau was rewriting the curricula inside the central library of Mosul University—headed by a German citizen of Egyptian origin from the al-Zarqawi network, a man known as Dhu'l-Qarnayn. By February 2015, the campus had become a military installation—residence halls housing fighters, laboratories converted to weapons workshops. The Sudair tourist village on the outskirts, where families had picnicked, became a training camp. The buildings were the same. The forest was the same. The picnic tables were still there. The weapons were new.

That distance—four minutes, the same afternoon, the same man—is what the word "monster" conceals. Monsters do not buy bread. Monsters do not ask about school. These men did all of those things, on the same days, with the same hands.

I do not hate them. Hatred requires a reduction of the other person to a category, and the work I did for eighteen months was the refusal to reduce anything to a category. I documented them with the precision of a man who understood that the record is the only thing that survives the regime that produced it. Accuracy requires seeing them as what they were—the taxi drivers and seminary students and livestock traders and petty criminals who made choices, who had full control of their actions, who bought bread on the way home from the courthouse, and who will one day answer for what they did between the bread and the sentence.

The regime that destroyed libraries and burned manuscripts was simultaneously producing a bureaucratic archive of extraordinary density. Every fine was receipted. Every tax was recorded. Every property transfer was filed. Every execution was logged. The same mentality that required every woman's sleeve to be measured required every confiscated property to be documented. The flogging and the filing were the same impulse—the need for total control, made visible.

I know this because I have seen the documents. Not the documents I produced. The documents ISIS produced about itself.

The entire provincial administration of Wilayat Nineveh had been built inside a single multi-tab spreadsheet. The header reads: "Departments and Centers of Wilayat Nineveh." Two branches of administration descend from it, each with named offices: Administration, Vehicle Workshop, Diwan al-Jund, Office of Those Who Left, General Administration on one side; Real Estate, Communications, Artillery, Camps, Medical Services, Special Forces School, Military Police, Booby-trapping, New Arrivals on the other. Each office has its own spreadsheet tab—visible at the bottom of the screen, the way any accountant's workbook shows its tabs. In the upper corner, the ISIS map showing its claimed territories from Khorasan to the Maghreb. The caliphate was a spreadsheet.

The General Police produced monthly statistical reports categorizing every case processed. The categories were arrayed in an organizational chart: Fights. Thefts. Debts. Cigarettes and Hookah. Hit-and-run Accidents. Murder. Homosexuality. Adultery. Night Patrol. Other Cases. A theft and an accusation of homosexuality occupied the same size box, the same color, the same position in the hierarchy. The administrative system had flattened the distinction between a debt dispute and a capital crime into the same monthly report, filed in the same office.

The police maintained comprehensive inventories—*jurudat shamila*—for every physical asset. A document dated Rajab 1437, bearing the ISIS flag and the header "Caliphate on the Prophetic Method," listed categories: database, weapons, receipts, generators, office equipment, furniture, vehicles, equipment. Fuel tracked by type. Each category had its own tab. This was the inventory system. The fighter I would later see in the archives—the man writing by hand under bombardment—was filling out this form. The form existed before the bombs. The form survived the bombs. The form was the system.

A budget spreadsheet tracked obligations in color-coded columns. Line items included: workers' food, martyrs' condolences, prisoners' food, disabled fighters' support, marriage of virgins, marriage of previously married women, rentals, manufacturing. Dollar exchange rate: 1,295. Gasoline: 1.54 per liter. Diesel: 0.46. Monthly tabs from one through twelve—a full fiscal year. The budget that allocated funds for forced marriages also allocated funds for motorcycle fuel, in the same row, processed by the same department. The marriage and the motorcycle were administrative equivalents.

The Islamic Police maintained a personnel management system built as a digital application. The organization that banned mobile phones for the civilian population had built a mobile app for its own personnel management.

One of these organizational charts was designed against a background of flowers. Pink and white blossoms, green grass, blue sky. Someone in the Islamic Police's administrative office had chosen this template. Someone had selected the flowers. The same department that processed flogging sentences and tracked executions had decorated its personnel chart with wildflowers. I do not know what to do with that detail except to record it. The flowers are the thesis of this chapter compressed into a single image: the office and the whip, together, in the same document, produced by the same hand. The flowers and the death sentences. The blue sky and the inventory of weapons.

Years after the liberation, working with UNITAD* among the thousands of documents recovered from the ruins, one stopped me.

It was handwritten. An ISIS fighter had been conducting an inventory of his post. But the post was being bombed. Coalition aircraft were striking the position. There was no electricity. The fighter could not use his laptop. So he switched to handwriting and continued the inventory by hand, recording the contents of the facility while the facility was being destroyed around him.

The bombs were falling and he was filing.

I have one of these documents in my possession. Two pages of lined notebook paper—the kind you buy in any stationery shop in Mosul for five hundred dinars. Handwritten in Arabic. The opening line: Bismillah al-Rahman al-Rahim. A field report from the Islamic Police of Wilayat Nineveh, addressed to the Amir of the Islamic Police. Ordinary handwriting. Ordinary ink. Ordinary paper. And at the bottom of the second page, stamped in blue ink: the circular seal of the Islamic State, the Islamic Police, Wilayat Nineveh, al-Marbu'a district. Signed by the Deputy of the Imam: Abu Saif al-Din. Dated.

A police report. Filed by the caliphate. On paper you could buy in any shop in the city. Stamped with the seal of a state that governed through

* The United Nations Investigative team to promote accountability for crimes committed by Daesh/ISIS.

paperwork and governed through pain, simultaneously, on the same street, in the same week, with the same hand that held the pen and the same hand that held the whip.

Not masked men in the desert. An office. Using the vocabulary of God. Staffed by the neighbors. Decorated with flowers. Stamped in blue ink on lined paper. Filing until the end.

THE INTELLIGENCE CITY

The people became robots. That is the phrase I wrote in my notes, and reading it now, I wish I had a better one, but I do not, because it was exactly right. By November 2014, Mosul had become a city in which every person was simultaneously watched and watching, in which ordinary social life had been reorganized so that other people became, without anyone choosing to make them so, an involuntary grid of accountability. You were not just afraid of ISIS. You were afraid of someone asking where you were. Your family. Your friends. The neighbor who might mention, without malice, that he had not seen you at the mosque.

ISIS required attendance at Friday prayers—the central communal prayer of the Islamic week—and absences were noted, sometimes reported. You had two options: attend and perform devotion or stay away and risk being noticed by whoever might mention where you had not been. The occupation did not need to station a fighter on every corner. It needed only the population's understanding that someone, somewhere, might be paying attention. After that, the population managed itself. People moved through the city like mechanisms. They prayed when required. They did not ask questions, even of themselves.

The deepest confirmation of this came from a source I had not expected: ISIS itself. In their own newspaper—*Al-Naba*, the weekly publication they distributed across the caliphate—they published an article addressed to the population under their rule, asking a question that revealed more than they intended. The article was titled, in effect: Is it fear of God that makes you obey, or fear of the *hisba*?

They described Muslims who sinned in private while maintaining perfect compliance in public. Who hid their cigarettes and their music and their unshortened trousers from the morality patrols but not from the God they claimed to worship. The article posed this as a theological failing—a crisis of faith among the population. What it actually documented, with the inadvertent honesty of the true believer, was the total failure of the project. The entire apparatus of enforcement—the patrols, the fines, the lashings, the checkpoints, the informant networks—had produced obedience without belief. The city was performing. Two million people wearing costumes, reciting lines, walking through the choreography of an imposed piety that had not touched the interior of a single unwilling soul.

Even the occupiers could see the difference between a conquered city and a converted one. They published the evidence in their own newspaper. They just could not understand what it meant.

I had confirmed by September that ISIS had adopted the same intelligence methods used by the Mukhabarat—the notorious secret police that had operated under Saddam Hussein's regime for decades, building a vast informant network that made neighbor fear neighbor across every city in Iraq. Recruiting cabdrivers, local shopkeepers, ordinary civilians to report on conversations overheard at checkpoints, on men who arrived at the wrong hour from the wrong direction. The method was not original. What was original was the speed of its reimposition. Three hundred children had been recruited and trained over a single month to carry out suicide missions, assassinations, and infiltration of Iraqi and Kurdish forces. Four ISIS members had been killed in solo operations inside the city in September alone—one shot at Bab al-Toub, one sniped in al-Noor, one killed in a hit-and-run in Humaydat, one assassinated by a man disguised in a niqab. The city was fighting back in scattered acts that ISIS could not fully control, and the organization was responding with tighter information management—the same cycle of resistance and repression I had been studying from inside both systems at once.

Mosul had lived under surveillance before. The Mukhabarat had operated for so long that most Iraqis over thirty carried in their bodies the habits of a surveilled population: the lowered voice, the glance before speaking, the instinct to say nothing specific in a public place. The city's body knew how to behave under scrutiny even before the new rules were announced. This was part of why compliance spread so quickly: not because people supported ISIS, but because the reflexes of managed fear were already practiced, already fluent. A new regime does not always need to build a new system. Sometimes the old system is waiting, intact, for someone to sit at the controls. What made the ISIS version different was the overlay of ideology. Under Saddam, surveillance had been political: to locate dissent, to protect the regime. Under ISIS, the informants were not merely watching for opposition—they were watching for sin, for deviation, for any evidence that the population had not fully submitted to a total vision of how life should be lived. The difference was the difference between a state that demands your silence and one that demands your soul. Both are unbearable. The second leaves no interior space at all.

I could receive information by then that would have been intolerable six months earlier and process it as data—a location, a number, a name to be verified and filed. The change had crept over me like a second skin, a layer of distance between what I witnessed and what I felt about witnessing it. I noticed it the way you notice, one morning, that a sound you used to hear—a bird outside the window, a neighbor's radio—has stopped, and you cannot remember when it stopped, only that the silence has been there for some time.

One could see the logic of this system most clearly in the letters on the doors.

By mid-October, Arabic letters had begun appearing on homes and properties across the city. The letter *nūn*—N, standing for Nazarene, the historical term for Christian—marked Christian homes, designating their contents as property of the caliphate. Most of those homes were already empty; the Christian community had been expelled in July, given seventy-two hours to leave or convert. The letter was not for them. It was for whoever came after—the displaced families, the administrators, the filing system that needed a category for what had been taken. The letter *ra*—R, for *Rafidha*, the slur ISIS used for Shia Muslims—marked Shia properties. The letter *ta*—T, for *tahqeeq*, investigation—appeared on the homes of Sunni Muslims whose owners had left the city. Why did they leave? The letter was the question. The letter *meem*—M, for *matloub*, wanted—appeared on the properties of government employees, professors, and doctors. My colleagues. People whose institutional affiliations made them suspect in the eyes of a regime that regarded the Iraqi state as an enemy. And the letter *jim*—J, for *jard*, counting—was applied to all properties without exception.

Five letters. An alphabet of administrative control painted on the surface of the city, converting a million private interiors into searchable categories. I had been building my own classification—the spreadsheet on my hard drive, each entry organized by date, neighborhood, perpetrator, ethnicity and affiliation of the victim. Now I understood that ISIS was building the same thing from the other direction. I was reading the city to preserve it. They were reading the city to govern it. The difference between us was not method. It was purpose.

The air strikes that autumn—carried out by a US-led coalition targeting ISIS positions across Iraq and Syria—forced the organization deeper into the city's residential tissue. On October 19, I noted that the strikes had pushed ISIS to relocate their headquarters deeper into the city center and neighborhoods, making it extremely difficult to distinguish an ISIS property from a civilian home. When the sky looks for you, you hide inside the people who cannot get away from you. The compounds that had been visible in the first months were dispersed into ordinary houses in Sumer, al-Wahda, al-Mohandisin, al-Majahah, Rifai, and the July 17 neighborhood. The families could not refuse.

Not all ISIS members were visible as ISIS. Through sources and direct observation, I assembled a picture of the organization's internal structure that no one outside the city possessed. Each member was granted three days of leave per week, returning to his family before resuming duties. Strict rules governed their contact with civilians—they were ordered to avoid it except in urgent situations and to reveal nothing to anyone, including their own families. Certain special units were prohibited from removing their face coverings under any circumstances, prohibited from growing beards or carrying electronic devices or wearing the official ISIS uniform. Through speakers, ISIS asked the city to donate blood for thirty-five injured fighters at al-Jumhuriya and Ibn Sina hospitals. I personally witnessed two pickup trucks loaded with the corpses of dead fighters moving through the streets. The organization was bleeding, and the population could see the trucks.

Al-Khasfa sat at the far end of this system. A deep natural sinkhole near al-Adthba village south of the city, it had been used before—by the previous Iraqi army administration, and now by ISIS—as a mass grave. An ISIS member told me that on one day alone, more than thirty women had been thrown into the valley under accusations of prostitution. Some had been thrown in alive. The accurate number of bodies was unknown, but it could well be over a thousand. The insurance building taught one kind of fear: You will be seen to die. Al-Khasfa taught another: You will not be seen at all.

The effect on the organization could be measured precisely. On October 18, ISIS held a military parade—the real one. Dozens of vehicles carrying armed men with heavy weaponry marched through half the city. On November 11—twenty-four days after Al-Kindi—ISIS announced another parade. What appeared was twelve KIA model cars and one pickup truck: young boys and teenagers in dirty, worn-out clothes carrying Kalashnikov rifles. One flag per vehicle. The attempt failed. The distance between those two parades was the distance Al-Kindi had opened inside the regime.

I reported what I saw. I also wrote: "I could not be more happy today." Reading that now, I see the optimism of a man who had observed something real. I also see a man who needed to believe it. Without the need, I could not have continued. Without the observation, the need would have been self-deception.

After Al-Kindi, the violence turned inward. ISIS feared a security breach and began investigating its own ranks, focusing on non-Iraqi members. The killing became more frequent, more organized—no longer only punishment but display, a message about what happens to informers, demonstrated on the bodies of men whose names had passed through a process the population would never see. I stood at the back of the crowds. I memorized names. The crowd was not the origin of the punishment. The crowd was its theater. What had preceded it—the gathering of a name, its entry into a category, the decision about when to make it public—had happened in rooms and on lists the city would never see. I was trying to reach them.

Five days before Al-Kindi, I had posted after a delay and written something new: Several reasons were behind my delays in posting, including nearly falling for a bait set up specifically for me. Someone had designed a trap aimed at Mosul Eye—not a general security measure but a constructed situation intended to draw the person behind the blog into exposure. The bait failed. I recognized it in time. But someone was not merely looking for an informant in general. Someone was looking for me.

I was afraid of misbehaving. That is the phrase I used in my notes and it requires explanation. To misbehave, for me, meant to emit any signal—a glance held too long, a question with the wrong inflection, a route walked one time too many—that might cause someone to look at me a second time. Mosul Eye was being read widely enough by then that when I walked through the city I sometimes heard people talking about the blog. ISIS knew it too. Its English-speaking Twitter accounts attacked Mosul Eye daily. They tried to construct a profile of who I was from the pattern of what I published—which neighborhoods I described, which details I included, what I could have known and from what vantage point.

After Al-Kindi and the bait, the stakes of publication had changed. Information I sent out could come back as an air strike. I began judging not only whether something was true, but how many people could plausibly have known it. How quickly a source might infer that the information had reached me. Whether immediate publication was worth the risk of exposing the channel.

On a street I had always used to visit my uncle, my brother Ahmad and I noticed fighters who had not been there before. Numerous, comfortable in the buildings, at ease in the way men are at ease only on ground they consider their own. I watched for several days. It was a car bomb factory, filled with foreign fighters. I reported it online. Within four hours, the site was struck. After that, sometimes a true fact had to stay in my notes because its route back to me was too narrow to survive publication.

During those months, offers arrived from another direction. The Kurds approached me. The Americans. Others who claimed to be journalists, but whose questions had a different shape. Each time the proposition was the same: Work with us. I refused. Every time. I could have easily accepted a position with a foreign agency—in practical terms it would have simplified everything. But the moment I became someone's source, what I was keeping would no longer be mine. I told them what I told everyone: I am not a spy and I am not a journalist. The information is published. It is public. It is free.

I knew something else too. If Omar died, Mosul Eye would go silent, and the silence would identify the body. The two identities were linked by the thread of continuity: As long as one was alive, the other posted. My life and my anonymity were the same thing.

Before the occupation, Adam, Samuel, Abraham, and I would walk on late nights along Forest Street, a promenade running beside the Tigris—the river that divides Mosul into its eastern and western banks. Adam had a small car and would drive us over Al-Shuhada Bridge into the oldest part of the city: al-Shahwan, a neighborhood of narrow lanes and ancient stone houses where an Ottoman hammam still stood near the *qalah*, the old citadel wall. Saint Joseph's church sat on the left as the street narrowed toward the boat makers and the fish market. The air off the Tigris on those nights was clean. After midnight there were no more cars and we walked the old bridge on foot. Adam always made the same joke at the parking garage on the way back.

Under occupation, those streets became tools. ISIS had moved through each neighborhood along lines that already existed: family connections, local familiarity, the social geography people carried without thinking. Through a neighborhood intermediary I had known before the fall—not himself ISIS, but standing where ordinary social life and the militant world still touched—I began moving through circles joined by family or proximity. One conversation opening another room.

Inside those rooms, men spoke differently. They spoke boastfully, lazily, with the ease of men who believed the company was safe. They spoke about promotions, salaries, fears that circulated among fighters who outwardly seemed certain of themselves. I listened as a man who was interested, not as a man who was working.

One of those men was Abraham. A taxi driver, two doors down from Adam's family. I had known him since roughly 2009—through daily proximity, the same tea seller, the same late-night crossing at Alshohada Bridge. He was fair-haired with a dark beard, particular about its trim. He cared about finding the right perfume. He had a large ego and beneath it a genuine warmth—he needed to feel that he mattered to the people around him.

In 2008, a Shia militia detained him. He spent nine months in custody. Something set during those months and then waited. ISIS arrived and the hardness found a direction. For several weeks after the fall he was gone. When I saw him again he was responsible for interrogation.

He came because the habit of neighborhood continued even after everything it had contained was destroyed. I let it continue because it was useful.

I was using that. I knew precisely what I was doing. He was an ISIS member responsible for interrogation—a man who had given his loyalty to an organization killing people I knew, destroying a city I loved. The habit of neighborhood was now a channel. Everything he said in those evenings was material: organizational structure, names, locations, the internal tensions he described without understanding he was describing them. I absorbed it and recorded it. The corrosion was not guilt. Guilt implies a choice that could have been made differently. What I felt was something colder: the recognition that I had become exactly what the work required, and that what the work required was a man who could sit with an enemy and give him the experience of being trusted while systematically extracting what he carried. The historian who valued friendship was now its counterfeit.

One afternoon, Abraham used the word "historian" for me, with a respect that contained something condescending, the title belonging to someone old, at a safe distance from events. He said I should try to be soft when I wrote about the Islamic State. I said: No one writes history. You write your own history through your acts. I knew immediately I had said more than was safe. I told him I was joking. He turned a blind eye to it.

He spoke of the women in the city the way a man speaks when he has confused cruelty with righteousness. He called them dirty. He said they were being cleaned. One day in the street he described the joy of it. His word, not mine. I did not respond. I thought about putting his location online. The thought arrived, clear and specific, and I let it pass.

Then one evening he told me something that stopped the air in my chest. He had mentioned my name to someone, and the reply came back: the secular one?

Under this regime, that word was not an opinion. It was a category of the condemned. Someone in Mosul had remembered me by it. Abraham told me this casually. He did not understand what he had handed me.

I did not sleep that night. For a week I could not sleep. Every sound outside the house—a car engine, a voice, the particular rhythm of boots on pavement—became the arrival I was expecting. Before the "secular one," the danger had been general—I was one anonymous person in a city of over a million, protected by the sheer improbability that anyone would connect a history teacher with a blog being read around the world. After it, the danger was specific. My name had entered the system. Not connected to Mosul Eye—not yet. But present in the mouth of a woman rewriting the curriculum for the regime, spoken to a man who worked for the regime, in a building controlled by the regime. And the danger had arrived through the relationship I was using for intelligence. The same channel that gave me access to the organization's workings had carried my name into the system that could end me.

It occurred to me, during that week of sleeplessness, that no one had asked me how I was since the fall. Not in the way the question is meant when someone actually wants the answer. My friends asked how things were going, meaning the situation. My mother asked whether I had eaten. But the question itself—"How are you, Omar?"—had vanished from my life as completely as the electricity or the sound of church bells. I did not hold this against anyone. I noticed its absence the way I had begun to notice other absences: not as a complaint, but as a measurement of how far the world had moved from what it used to be.

Adam and Samuel helped me through that week. Not by knowing what I was doing—they did not know about Mosul Eye—but by keeping the surface of ordinary life available when the ground beneath it had shifted. They started laughing, telling jokes. They said Omar is a good man, and this is in the past. They deflected without knowing what they were deflecting. That is what friendship does under occupation: It holds the ordinary in place when everything underneath is moving.

At some point, the conversations with Abraham began angling toward my conversion—toward the idea that I should join ISIS. Not a direct challenge at first, a circling. He would suggest that my objections came from misunderstanding rather than disagreement. I was afraid of the moment I would have to answer plainly. A yes would mean ISIS. A no would invite the scrutiny that ends a person's options. I learned to redirect: a joke, a question to Adam, a shift in the room before the pressure arrived. I preferred not to be alone with him—I said things I should not have, and it was easier to pull back when others were present.

He disappeared in 2015. I heard he was killed on a front where the organization was losing ground. He was an ISIS interrogator who had trusted me enough to speak without guarding his words. I used that trust for the duration it was useful. Whether what I published contributed to the circumstances of his death, I cannot say and have not tried to determine. He was an enemy. The work required me to treat him as an opening. I did. That is the record.

Not everything in those months was isolation. On certain evenings, I went to Junaid's house.

Junaid was an archaeologist—a man who had spent his career studying the physical past of a region whose physical past was being dynamited, bulldozed, and looted around him. His house was in one of the older neighborhoods on the east bank, a ten-minute walk from the river if you took the back streets. The room where we gathered was a long sitting room with thin cushions along three walls, the fabric worn smooth by years of use, a low wooden table in the center stacked with tea glasses, and a brass tray. The walls were bare except for a single framed photograph of an archaeological site—Nimrud, I think, though the glass was dusty and the light always dim because Junaid kept the curtains drawn even before the occupation. The room smelled of cardamom and cigarette smoke that had seeped into the plaster over the decades. A small kerosene heater sat in the corner, and by November, we needed it. Outside, a narrow hallway led to the kitchen where Junaid's wife prepared tea and plates of food without ever entering the room while we were there—the hospitality was total, but its source was invisible, which is the custom.

One of ISIS's informants sat on the street corner outside. We knew he was there. He knew we gathered. The question was what he understood the gatherings to be—a group of neighborhood men passing an evening, or something that required reporting. The cover was the ordinariness of the setting: men in a sitting room, tea on the table, the same kind of gathering that happened in a hundred houses across the city every night. The content of the conversation was invisible from the street.

Between seven and twelve of us would come on a given evening—artists, scholars, historians, archaeologists, men who had spent their professional lives working with ideas the regime outside the walls had declared illegal. Ahmad, my older brother, came when he could. He would sit near the heater and listen more than he spoke, but when he did speak it was to bring the room back to something practical—the price of fuel, the welfare of someone's family. He had the older brother's gift of making concern feel like observation. One evening, when the conversation drifted into whether art could survive the destruction of its objects, Ahmad said quietly that he thought it could, because his children still drew pictures even though no one had told them to. The room went silent for a moment.

We talked about Abraham—not the Abraham of ISIS's sermons, flattened into a justification for conquest, but the Abraham of the historical tradition: a figure claimed by three faiths, whose meaning had been debated for centuries by scholars who understood that debate itself was devotion. We talked about the origins of art—whether the need to make images was older than the prohibitions against images. We talked about the fate of nations that had tried to erase the cultures they conquered. The answer, every time, was no.

One evening an archaeologist described a site he had been excavating before the fall, and as he spoke about the layers—Assyrian, Hellenistic, Islamic, Ottoman—the room understood he was not talking about archaeology. He was talking about the city's identity as something that could not be reduced to a single layer. ISIS wanted Mosul to be one thing. It had always been many things.

Those evenings were oxygen. They were the hours in which the mind could move freely, in which language served thought rather than concealment, in which the version of myself that existed before the occupation could breathe.

The walk home was the more dangerous part, because the curfew narrowed the window in which a man could be on the street without explanation. One of the men who came to those evenings was killed in an air strike on his way home. The strike was not aimed at him. His death did not end the meetings. It entered them.

In November I turned to writing about women. The occupation was reconfiguring every dimension of their existence, and the men who documented ISIS were leaving out what was most total about its rule. I began with a statement of intention: I do not intend to discuss where religions and culture take their stance on women's rights. I do, however, intend to defend—with all my might—the most victimized from ISIS.

In one of the neighborhoods near the old city, I met an elderly woman who had lived long enough, she said, to be granted wisdom in a time of madness. She told me: "Over the years I have lost every feminine sense a woman can lose. I was married at twelve years of age and widowed during my twenties. I gave birth to three sons and only one remains alive today and he is physically challenged. The first son was taken by God, and then God sent his men to crucify my second son while crippling my third. Today a man growing a beard to hide his face demands that I wear black. Is the blackness of my heart not enough? What about the black circles around my eyes? Have they not stolen my face? I gave in to his orders nonetheless, for what use is there to reveal my face if God cannot see my heart? I hid the face which had disappeared long ago."

A young woman told me: "I love dancing to the sound of the wind. But today I am living in an eternal funeral. I no longer hear music in the wind. I am exhausted." Another said: "My father is now pleased that I am compelled to wear a burqa, as if I possess the beauty of Joseph the Dreamer. Where have I wronged?"

I published those voices because the testimony of women under occupation is the most easily erased—by the occupation itself, by the men who document it, and by the histories that follow.

On December 16, ISIS prohibited female students from attending university classes because their attire was considered un-Islamic—despite the fact that the students were already wearing the long gown and the burqa. The only acceptable attire was the one-piece long black burqa. The institution that had educated me was being emptied not only of its curriculum but of its students, and the emptying was being done through the regulation of women's bodies. The women had already complied with every previous demand, and the demand had been raised regardless. This is how administrative control operates: not by stating the final rule at the beginning but by moving the line forward in increments, so that compliance becomes the mechanism of further restriction.

I visited Fadel—a name I have changed—a shopkeeper in his thirties near the old city. He began talking before I could ask a question. He said he used to go to the mosque because he wanted to. Now he went because he had to, and while he prayed, he thought about his shop and whether someone was stealing from it. He had seen a man he once knew—cheap enough to sell his own mother, in Fadel's words—now wearing the long beard and the black uniform and carrying a pistol. "If these people are true Islam," Fadel said, "then I have no need for this Islam." Then he asked God's forgiveness.

His mother, in her sixties, interrupted with the fatalism of a woman who had survived enough regimes to know that regimes do not survive: "Whatever God has written will come to pass. Every oppressor will find someone more oppressive than himself."

Later I sat with four friends in another house, listening more than speaking. One said the only difference between ISIS and Saddam's regime was the slogan—both used bright words and cared nothing for the citizen. Another said the fundamental problem was God, that He had failed to designate a clear representative on earth. A third was optimistic: ISIS could not build a state with criminals and riffraff. When they turned to me I told them I did not agree that ISIS was merely a popular whim. I said I saw in it the deep expression of contemporary religion turned to violence, a form of conflict that might continue for years. Fadel's final word: "All I care about in this life is how to raise my children and live with dignity and safety." He was a model for a very large proportion of the population of Mosul—not the fighters, not the resisters, but the people trapped between forces that did not care whether they survived.

In al-Meydan—one of the old city neighborhoods I knew well—I walked during December with the particular hunger for the city that comes over me in the evenings. I stopped at the Chaldean church of Saint Joseph, one of the ancient Christian houses of worship that had stood for centuries as testament to the religious plurality ISIS was erasing. Before the occupation I had met a Christian family there—the old woman with white hair who tended the church, the small girl who had guided me through the ancient interior. They were gone. I stood at the door and looked in. The building was still there. What it had been for was not.

On November 24 I recorded a twelve-minute video inside the city—footage of daily life under the occupation. A video contains geography, angles that reveal where the camera was held, ambient sound that can be analyzed. I recorded it because the written word was no longer sufficient.

That same November I wrote a short self-portrait for the blog—the only moment in this period when I stepped outside the field report. I called the post "Something about me":

> I am currently living a life that only existed in my wildest dreams. Every move I make, word I say, action I take, is rethought over and over again. The security—and secrecy—measures I must adopt have driven me to read books about the criteria and characteristics of intelligence officers and secret agents. I have even read papers about the mechanisms of mice to combat obstacles, how to run and disappear; all to get a clear perspective on how to deal with any person or situation I might face. I have studied psychological warfare, verbal deception, and even played the insane/stupid/idiotic one in order to lead on those before me. I have taken on several characters and acts. I have observed many films and attempted to carry out parts of their narrative. I am doing all I hate, and all I despise. You do not know me, but I have always been the dreamer. I never forget putting a new fresh rose in the vase at my window every morning or watering my plants, nor do I abandon my habit of speaking softly to a few girls I pass on my way every day. I sit with my friends and dream of a civil nation. And out of the blue, all my dreams, hopes, aspirations… evaporate. I spend my days, alone, on the roof top monitoring, observing. I refuse leaving my city behind. At the same time, I am wanted for justice by two parts of the conflict—the justice of

> ISIS, and the justice of the sectarian hangmen: ISIS want my head because I refuse to join them, the sectarians want my head because I refuse to leave my home. And what do I want? A kitten to play with while reading a book and listening to some classical music, and a Cuban cigar.

A reader wrote back the next day: "Dear Friend, my heart goes out to you. Please be wise: go and leave the city for now."

I did not go.

The voice in that post is divided in a way that had not yet become visible to me: a man who speaks of fresh roses and psychological warfare in the same paragraph, who has taken on several characters and attempted to carry out parts of their narrative. That last detail I had never admitted before, and reading it now, I see a man who was learning to live inside fiction while insisting on fact. The division was not a literary device. It was what was happening to me. The two men I was becoming—the dreamer and the one who transmitted coordinates—were speaking through the same voice, and the voice could no longer hold them both without the seam showing.

At night, I came back to the family home and closed my door. My mother was asleep somewhere in the same house. She had no idea what I was doing. Every night, while she slept, I was at my laptop—using the same electricity, breathing the same air—writing things that ISIS would have killed me for. Possibly killed her for.

I put music on. I love Itzhak Perlman, and I would listen to him with the lights off and the curtain drawn, the computer screen the only illumination, the tip of a forbidden cigarette glowing beside it. The cigarette and the music were both illegal—ISIS had banned tobacco and all forms of music. Together they constituted the only minutes in the day when I was not performing for anyone—not for ISIS, not for the checkpoints, not for the readers of Mosul Eye. Then I wrote. First, as Mosul Eye—the field reports, the verified accounts, the coordinates, for the world to read. Then, in encrypted entries, the fuller record: what I had seen but could not yet publish, what I knew but could not yet prove, what I had heard in rooms I had entered under the cover of old friendship. Finally, when I had exhausted the factual, I sometimes shut down the computer and wrote on paper as Omar.

By December, I also wrote as Maouris Milton—a literary persona distinct from Mosul Eye, addressed not to the outside world but to the people of Mosul and Iraq. His page had to be closed for security reasons and reopened through Mosul Eye. In one of his December letters I find now: "I still fear the shadow that follows me everywhere, and when I run faster from it I realize I am running from my own shadow. Do I fear my own shadow? Is this fear legitimate?"

By December, I could count the occupation's cost in numbers I had spent months verifying: 1,300,000 refugees from the city. 480 civilians killed by ISIS in Mosul alone. Seventy suicide bombings on the outskirts. Forty suicide bombers under the age of fifteen. 1,700 estimated killed across Nineveh province. 1,900 in ISIS prisons. Eight million dollars extracted, not counting half a billion in seized bank assets. Three hundred and seventy civilian homes destroyed. Each number represented a decision about when something was verified enough to publish, whose name was too dangerous to attach, how to describe what I had witnessed without leading anyone back to the witness. The hard drive that held those numbers was a map of my vulnerability. If found, it would reveal who had told me what.

I walked long distances through the city at night during those weeks, searching for something I could not name—some remainder of myself that the months of disguise had not yet consumed. I walked without purpose through the pitch darkness of a city under curfew. Mosul at night is a city few of its own people know. It sleeps on top of the most ferocious historical phenomena—sleeps deeply, but is always ready to wake without warning and throw off whatever is crouching on its chest. This complicated, simple city confounds me more each day.

One night, I reached a spot where I had once been beaten by security forces under the previous government—a different regime, a different set of men with weapons, the same city. I stood on the exact place where they had put me down. I searched the ground for the mark where the rifle butt had struck the pavement after missing my head. I touched the surface, feeling for the crevice. I stood there for a long time. Then I continued walking and said to myself: If that blow had not missed, would I be remembering this moment now?

On my way back, I encountered an ISIS checkpoint. A boy—he could not have been older than sixteen—called me over. "Where did you come from?" I remembered in that moment a poem by Elia Abu Madi, a Lebanese poet of the early twentieth century whose verse "The Talismans" I had memorized as a student. I answered him: "I came, I know not from where, but I came. And I beheld before me a road, and I walked. And I shall continue walking, whether I will it or not. How did I come? How did I see my road? I do not know."

He stared at me. "Old man," he said—the word in our dialect is hajji, a term of respect for elders—"where did you come from?"

I said: "I passed from that road. I want to cross to the other."

He said: "Go."

I went home. I grew out my hair and beard again. I put the shortened trousers back on—the ankle-length style ISIS mandated as a sign of proper Islamic dress. And for the remainder of my time in Mosul, I smoked and listened to music in my room with the curtains drawn and the lights off.

My computer screen and the tip of my cigarette glowed as I wrote in the dark.

THE CONCEALED REGIME

By January, my body had begun keeping its own account of what the months had cost. I was losing weight. My stomach refused food at irregular intervals—not hunger, not illness, but a tightening that arrived without warning and left when it chose. The headache behind my eyes had become a companion I no longer tried to remove. I slept in fragments. I would wake at two or three in the morning with the hard drive's location on my mind—had I moved it? Was it still where I left it? Sometimes I got up in the dark and moved it again, from the place I put it before sleep to another hiding place in the same house, because the calculation I had not finished before sleep continued without me and arrived at a different conclusion. Then I went back to bed and lay in the dark until the light came and my mother began making tea downstairs.

I am writing about these months from a distance of years, and what strikes me now, reading the notes I kept at the time, is not the violence but something else: the ordinary structure of the days surrounding it. My daily records from January and February 2015 read, on many mornings, exactly like records kept by a careful administrator. Date, location, observation, source. It is only when I look at the material that surrounds the observations—the house I was in, the people who did not know what I was carrying—that the real shape of those months becomes visible. The violence was real and total. But the harder thing to describe is what the days looked like from inside them: the tea my mother made downstairs, the route I chose to the market, the face I held at a checkpoint. The methodical continuation of a life that had divided itself into halves that no longer touched. One half belonged to the household, to the daily rituals my family maintained without knowing what else the house contained. The other half moved through the city in character, gathering what it could, transmitting what it dared, and returning each evening to the same rooms where the first half waited, innocent of everything.

A specific morning: I woke before the call to prayer. The headache was there. I dressed in the clothes the occupation required—the shortened trousers, the beard I maintained at the right length, the kind of shirt a man wears when he is going to the market and not when he is going to gather intelligence about a military occupation. I drank the tea my mother had made. She looked at me the way she always looked at me in the morning—with the attention of a mother who has learned, over months, not to ask the questions she wants to ask. I chose my route to the market—not the shortest path but the one that passed two checkpoints rather than three, that kept me on streets where I had been seen often enough to be unremarkable. The notebook was in the inside pocket of my jacket. At the first checkpoint I handed over my identity card and stood still while the man behind the barrier looked at my face, looked at the card, looked at my face again. My breathing did not change. My expression did not change. He handed the card back. I continued walking. The notebook in my pocket carried the names of men who had been killed by the organization whose checkpoint I had just passed through.

By the first days of January, the organization that had arrived in Mosul the previous June with open convoys and flags hung from the highest buildings learned that visibility was a liability. On January 15, I wrote in my daily record: "Da'ish has been recruiting reinforcements to fortify its headquarters in Mosul and ordered its members to take undisclosed houses and leave the known and exposed buildings." The families in the neighborhoods where they settled—Sumer, al-Wahda, al-Mohandisin, al-Majahah, Rifai—could not refuse. A domestic street and a military zone had become, without anyone formally announcing it, the same thing.

The air strikes—carried out by a US-led coalition that had been targeting ISIS positions across Iraq and Syria since the previous autumn—forced the regime deeper into the city's residential tissue. What looked from outside like retreat was, from where I stood, ISIS learning that its best cover was the population it occupied. When the sky looks for you, you hide inside the people who cannot get away from you.

A source inside the organization told me in early January that the local *hisba*—the morality enforcement units ISIS used to police dress, prayer attendance, and daily conduct—had been restructured. New units were brought in from Diyala province in eastern Iraq, composed of foreigners and Syrians, to replace the Mosul-born fighters after leadership concluded there had been security breaches among the locals. ISIS grew to distrust the city's own connections, the family ties and neighborhood loyalties that made local members unreliable. On January 8, what began as arrests for public smoking was officially announced as the uncovering of a thirty-person spy cell with cameras concealed in the front of a car. The announcement was made publicly, as a warning. I could not verify how much of that accusation was accurate and how much was the regime's need to explain its own vulnerability through the category of conspiracy. A man arrested for smoking could become a man accused of espionage within the space of a single interrogation session. I read this and felt, not for the first time, the logic closing around a category that included me.

My mother made tea every morning. My brothers sometimes watched ISIS's television station in the evenings—state broadcasting, rebranded, full of Quranic recitation and military announcements. We lived in the same house, ate at the same table, moved through the same rooms. None of them knew what I was doing. The hard drive existed in the house as a presence whose nature was entirely invisible to the people I most needed to protect.

I do not know what the tea cost her, or what it cost me not to tell her why I needed it as much as I did.

There were moments when the two halves of the house nearly touched. I would be upstairs at the laptop, entering the day's dead into the encrypted file, and I would hear my brothers downstairs arguing about what to watch on the propaganda channel. The sound of their voices—ordinary, domestic, the voices of men who did not know what was happening one floor above them—reached me through the ceiling like sound from another country. Sometimes I closed the laptop and went downstairs and sat with them, watching what they were watching, saying what anyone would say. The transition required nothing visible. That was the frightening part. I could cross from one life to the other without any external sign that a crossing had occurred.

On January 10, I sat through a Friday sermon that I have not been able to set down.

I arrived at the mosque the way I always arrived—early enough not to be noticed for lateness, not so early that I would be conspicuous. The men around me were men I had seen for years, the faces of a neighborhood that had prayed in this building long before ISIS arrived and would, if the city survived, pray here long after. I took my place near the back. The sermon had not yet begun.

The preacher that morning was an ISIS-appointed imam—not the man who had led this congregation before the fall. He began with the standard recitations, the familiar cadences of a Friday sermon that in ordinary times would have spoken of God's mercy, of patience, of the obligations of the faithful. Then the language changed. He began describing the residents of Mosul who had not joined or fought alongside ISIS. He called them monkeys. The word was not a metaphor. It was not rhetorical excess delivered in the heat of exhortation. It was a classification. He said it from the pulpit with the calm of a man reading from a text he had been given, and the text had been distributed to preachers across the city's mosques that same morning—the same word, the same warning, the same Friday. He said that the coming days would bring collective punishment for those he called defeatists, hypocrites, and traitors. He said this to a room full of men who had been ordered to attend, men who could not leave, men who sat in rows on the floor with their faces held in the expression the occupation required—attentive, still, offering nothing.

I sat among them. I wore the same expression. The word hung in the air above a congregation that had prayed in this city for centuries, that raised its children to the sound of these same calls, that understood the mosque as a place where the pressures of life were briefly set aside in the presence of something larger. That morning the mosque was a delivery mechanism. What it was delivering was a threat aimed at the entire population, dressed in the language of faith.

I walked home afterward through streets that looked the same as they had that morning. The sun was the same. The checkpoints were in the same positions. The men I passed were walking at the same pace they had been walking before the sermon. Nothing had visibly changed. But I could feel the sermon sitting inside me the way a stone sits in water—it does not dissolve, it does not float, it is simply there, altering the weight of everything around it. The occupation had entered the mosques not the way an army enters a building but the way a language enters a mind—by replacing what was there before with something that sounds almost the same but means something different.

The financial system had grown more organized than improvised. By January, I had confirmed that a revenue schedule had been running for months: three thousand dinars—roughly three dollars at the exchange rates of the time—monthly from each single-story household in Mosul, five thousand from two-story houses, 10 percent from every barrel of oil produced by the city's small fuel operators, and separate collections from doctors, street vendors, shopkeepers, and every fixed or mobile business. Everyone in the city had been assigned a sequence number. Every two weeks, a department reviewed the books. On March 7, the enforcement mechanism made itself visible: 132 shop owners were arrested in a single morning for nonpayment, the forces of what ISIS called "economic security" deployed across the city with lists of names in their possession. Lists of names, carried into markets. That is not extortion in the ordinary sense. That is fiscal administration by a state that had declared itself sovereign.

ISIS also levied a 3 percent charge on the salary transfers to Mosul University's teaching staff—payments routed through the central government in Baghdad, which had not yet fully cut them off. When the company handling those transfers refused to continue without authorization, the salaries stopped. The faculty had already been teaching under rewritten curricula. Now they were doing it without pay. On February 8, I noted the transformation of Mosul University into a military location, its residence halls housing large numbers of fighters. The university had been founded in 1967 on the eastern bank of the Tigris, and for nearly fifty years had been the place where the city's historians, doctors, and engineers were trained. I had sat in those seminar rooms, walked those corridors, argued history in those spaces. By March 1, ISIS completed the preparation of new curricula for all colleges—humanitarian and scientific—written inside the central library building by Mosul University's own faculty, under the supervision of observers sent by ISIS. The institution was producing its own academic replacement from within. A historian understands that the contest over what the next generation will be taught is a contest over what the city will remember of itself.

The looting in the occupation's first days had been chaotic—men carrying things away in the confusion of the fall. What was happening now was different. In February, I tracked the transfer of equipment from the textile factory and the cement plant at al-Kisk, on the city's western outskirts, to Syria, moved piecemeal in a way that suggested planning over weeks. Medical equipment from hospitals followed the same route. That same month, a man purchased the Church of al-Tahira—a Syriac Orthodox cathedral that stood in the city since the seventh century—and the Chaldean church, purchased them as properties, their contents included, and burned a library estimated to hold forty thousand books. He was selling the stolen items from a location in the Mosul al-Jadida district. The city was being stripped of what could be moved and of what could be remembered. I tracked the transfers in my daily reports, entering the dates and locations the way I entered everything—as data, as evidence, as the material from which a future prosecution or a future history might eventually be built.

On January 9, a physician I will call Dr. Hafiz told me what she had witnessed at Mosul's hospitals. Yazidi girls—members of an ancient ethno-religious minority from the Sinjar region whom ISIS had enslaved en masse the previous summer—were being brought in by ISIS fighters requesting mandatory abortions and sterilizations. She described a girl of seventeen who had been raped repeatedly by multiple men and was in a state of nervous collapse. The girl refused the procedure. The number of such cases Dr. Hafiz could confirm at that point was between fifty and sixty. At least twelve girls younger than fifteen had died of injuries from the violence.

I wrote it down that evening in the same compressed register I used for everything—date, location, number, source. I am not sure I have ever found the right language for what it takes to apply that method to that material. I wrote it down because if I did not, it would disappear into the silence ISIS was building around everything it did to Yazidi women. Disappearance was the point of the silence. I closed the file and went downstairs. My mother was still in the kitchen. I sat with her for a while without speaking.

On January 12, I recorded that coalition aircraft had dropped leaflets over Mosul urging residents to help identify ISIS positions. I picked one up from the street. It was printed in Arabic, addressed to the people of the city, and asked them to transmit information outward through whatever channels they had. The leaflet was simultaneously a message of hope and a mechanism for increasing danger—it told the population that someone outside was still thinking about them, but it also told ISIS that the coalition was trying to activate the city as an intelligence resource, which would intensify the searches and the executions of anyone found with unauthorized communications. I put it in my pocket and kept walking.

The distrust was not only of the population. Inside ISIS itself, by January, there were signs of fracture. More than four hundred fighters—Mosul residents and men from surrounding areas who had joined the organization—deserted when ordered to transfer to fronts in Syria, Anbar, and Salah al-Din provinces. At least twenty-two fled to Turkey. One, I was told, had sold his weapon to fund the journey. By March I was recording that fighters on the front lines were openly complaining that tribal elders connected to ISIS leadership arranged safe postings for their relatives while sending unconnected foreigners to the worst fighting. The ideology that had declared the abolition of tribal identity as one of its theological foundations was reproducing tribal favoritism inside its own command structure.

In February, I watched a woman slap an ISIS member across the face in a market because he had ordered her daughter to change her veil. The crowd gathered. He could not respond, not in front of that crowd. A few days later, during a small ISIS vehicle procession—four cars, slogans, the usual performance—people on the street barely looked up. One man, standing still, said under his breath: "Your state is fleeting." I wrote it down. By then the population was reading something I was also reading: The organization's visible numbers in the city had fallen enough that women became, as I noted on February 13, "particularly comfortable about the subject of strict niqab"—testing the limits of enforcement in ways they had not dared in the previous months. A woman's hand moving across a man's face, a sentence spoken low enough that only the people around the speaker could hear: small refusals, legible only to those who knew what the previous months had looked like.

That same month the possibility of leaving ended. Since ISIS had taken the city the previous June, movement out of Mosul was possible under various conditions—documentation, guarantors, deposits. What came in February was categorical. Twelve families trying to leave via the Sinjar road were stopped and returned for investigation. Then the rule was formalized: Anyone wishing to leave for educational purposes had to deposit two thousand dollars, surrender the title deed to their property or vehicle, and return within ten days or lose both. I was in a market when I heard the news. I did not stop walking. But something inside the body received the information before the mind could process it—a tightening in the chest, a momentary difficulty breathing, the physical sensation of a door closing that I had not known I was still counting on. I had stayed by choice when staying was possible. Now staying was compulsory, and the difference between those two conditions was the difference between conviction and captivity. The notebook I carried through the city had always been a risk I could theoretically end by leaving. That option was closed.

February produced, inside the same few weeks, two observations that belonged together without resolving each other: The grip was showing its first cracks, and it had just been tightened to seal the exits. The woman who slapped the fighter and the twelve families returned at the Sinjar road existed in the same city, in the same month, under the same occupation. One was the evidence of resistance. The other was the evidence of the cage.

At night, when my mother was asleep, I returned to the desk and the three registers I had been moving between for months—the public reports for Mosul Eye, the encrypted file that held what could not yet be published, and the private writing where I kept what neither of the other two could hold. Some nights, instead of the field reports, I wrote as Maouris Milton.

I decided something I had not fully decided before: The front of the foreign agencies was done—I had refused them. The front of the Iraqi government was done—they treated us as suspects. Now there was only ISIS. My fight was against ISIS and for Mosul. If the coalition wanted to act on what I had gathered, the information was public. But the deeper work—the work of preserving what the city meant against the version ISIS was building—was mine.

This was different from writing as Mosul Eye. The blog required compression, precision, the stripped register of the field report. Maouris Milton required something else. He was the voice through which I could address the city in a register the field reports could not hold—speaking to the people of Mosul not as someone transmitting intelligence but as a man thinking aloud about what was happening to them and what they might become after it was over. People inside Mosul were reading those posts and writing back. A girl in her twenties contacted Maouris—I told her to be careful of her location, to publish about multiple locations so she could not be traced. People from other Iraqi cities who had been attacking the people of Mosul online began, through those conversations, to shift toward defense. They became friends of Maouris Milton. They started defending the people of Mosul.

In one of those nights, I wrote as Maouris: "Tens of questions cross my mind as I wander the streets of this grieving city. Some I know the answer to, others I wish not to know. I still fear the shadow that follows me everywhere, and when I run faster from it I realize I am running from my own shadow." The Mosul Eye voice would not have written that sentence. But the man inside the reports needed to, and Maouris Milton was the space where that need could breathe. Sometimes Mosul Eye would quote Maouris Milton—the field reporter citing the poet, as though they were two different people. They were. That was the point. The information kept people informed. The meaning kept them alive.

By the end of February, I had been documenting the occupation for nine months. Each month added something the previous month had not contained—a new category of extraction, a new form of punishment, a new layer of administrative control.

On March 1, for the first time in my neighborhood, I saw four women carrying Kalashnikovs, walking the street, stopping and setting up a checkpoint for women. By March, it was simply there, in the morning light, on a street I had walked since childhood.

The executions in Mosul by March had developed their own geography. There was the open area in front of the national insurance company in the city center. There were the parks near the mosques where, after Friday prayers, crowds were gathered to witness what ISIS prepared for them. There were the buildings from which people were thrown. In the last week of February, in the Dorkaliya district, a large number of people had been gathered to watch the cutting off of the hands of five people accused of theft—five amputations, carried out one after another in front of the crowd. What had been exceptional was becoming administrative. The amputation was no longer an event. It was a line item.

The court records I received from a source inside the Sharia judiciary in the first weeks of March carried their own authority. They came from inside the judicial apparatus itself, and I recorded their attribution exactly: "This information is from the court of the judiciary of Da'ash in Mosul." Then the numbers. Thirty-two people sentenced to death in a single session. Twelve executed within twenty-four hours on homosexuality charges. Thirty-one amputation sentences for theft in one week. Three hundred and twenty-one people arrested for selling cigarettes in the same period. On March 3, eleven people thrown from a building in the Bab al-Toub area. On March 5, fourteen executed for alleged spying for the Kurdish Peshmerga—the military forces of the Kurdistan region, which controlled territory along Mosul's eastern and northern borders. On March 8, a young man killed in front of a crowd in the Zanjili district—I recorded him as perhaps fourteen years old. That same day, twelve arrested for selling cigarettes at the Prophet Younis market, three flogged in the street. I kept the file open. I kept entering the dates. The method had not changed. But there is a point in any sustained effort at recording where the recorder and the recorded begin to press against each other in a way the beginning had not prepared for. Something was thinning. I did not examine it. I entered the next date, the next location, the next charge.

The two men I had been living as for nine months were closer than they had been at the start. The one who moved through the checkpoints and composed the reports could still function. But the person underneath—the one who had put a rose in a vase at his window every morning before the occupation, the one who listened to Perlman in the dark, the one who had studied the history of this city because he loved it—that person was running out of the material from which endurance is made. I did not recognize this at the time. I recognize it now.

Then it was the child's hand.

A friend and I had arranged to meet on a side street near the square that morning to exchange CDs—the only reliable way to move music through the city, because the internet connection was too slow and too monitored for large files, and music was forbidden. We had been doing this for months: classical music, passed hand to hand inside a bag on a street corner, both of us dressed in the shortened trousers and the beards the occupation required. He arrived. We made the exchange. Then one of us noticed the crowd gathering at the end of the street. The crowd had been assembled in the usual way—an announcement, a location, the understood obligation to attend. I moved toward it, because that was what I did. I was standing near the back, where I always stood. The light that morning was the flat gray light of a Mosul winter, the kind that erases shadows and makes the buildings and the faces and the square itself look as though they have been flattened into a single surface. There was no sound from the crowd. Not silence—silence would have been a response. This was the absence of response, the acoustic quality of a group of people who have learned that the only safe expression is no expression at all.

A boy accused of stealing had been brought before the crowd. The executor told him that his hand was a gift of repentance to God. Then he cut it off, calmly, in full public view, before the crowd that had been gathered to witness it. I had attended executions. I watched men die in squares I could name on a map. I documented atrocities for nine months with enough procedural distance to keep the record intact. I do not know what it was about this specific act—the language of the man, the calmness of it, the word "gift," the child's face—that crossed whatever line remained. But something did cross it.

I put down my notebook. I did not open it that evening.

THE LETTERS FROM MOSUL
THE CAPTIVE

After the child's hand, after the notebook closed and the evening passed in silence beside my mother at the kitchen table, the operative's mechanism stalled. For days, I could not write the field reports. I could not open the encrypted file. The part of me that had maintained the method for ten months—the dates, the locations, the charges, the names—had reached a surface it could not pass through. What remained was the other part: the part that had always needed music, and language, and the company of a mind that understood what those things were for. The only writing I could do was the letters to the German orientalist.

If it were not for music, I would have gone mad. If it were not for my mother's face, I would have killed myself.

Two sentences. Two things. The piano concerto playing in a room where music was punishable by flogging, and the face of a woman sleeping downstairs who did not know that her son was carrying, in the same house, the most dangerous archive in the city. Those were the walls between me and the end of myself. I wrote it in Arabic, at midnight, on the 352nd day of the occupation, in a letter addressed to a man I called the German orientalist who was, at that moment, the only person on earth to whom I could say what those two sentences say. Not because he could rescue me. Not because he had any power to change the conditions in which I lived. But because he was a scholar who loved the things I loved, and in all of Mosul, in all the careful architecture of concealment I had built around myself, there was no one left to whom I could speak in the voice that was disappearing.

Before Mosul fell, I was a historian. I do not mean that as a general description. I mean it as the center of my identity—the thing around which everything else in my life was organized. I had completed my M.A. at the University of Mosul on Abd al-Rahman al-Jabarti's chronicle of Napoleon's occupation of Egypt—a work of witness written by an Egyptian scholar during a foreign invasion two centuries before mine. I was reading, corresponding, building the relationships that a young scholar needs if he is going to do serious work. I was in contact with orientalists and historians across the world—the Israeli scholar Michael Lecker; the late Samuel Moreh, whom I had helped get a work into print; and the German orientalist who spoke many languages, including Arabic, and who had found in Sufism—the mystical tradition within Islam that seeks God through inner experience rather than outward law—something that answered a question his own tradition had not fully resolved.

These were not casual acquaintances. They were the network of a mind that was trying to become something—a historian of Mosul, a scholar of the Ottoman period. When ISIS took the city, that network did not disappear. But by the spring of 2015, Mosul Eye was consuming me. The blog, the encrypted file, the sources, the routes, the concealment, the face I wore in the street, the daily recording of the dead—all of it had expanded to fill every waking hour and most of the sleeping ones. The operative had grown so large inside me that the historian was disappearing. The man who had read al-Jabarti and corresponded with Lecker and helped Moreh—that man was being eaten alive by the man who counted the dead and maintained the most dangerous archive in the city. I could feel it happening. The shrinking of the part of me that thought about history, about ideas, about the long arcs of civilizations. The part that read for pleasure. The part that wrote in Arabic for the joy of writing well in Arabic.

The letters to the German orientalist were my refusal to let that part die.

I wrote to him because he was the right person—not because he could help me escape or publish my reports, but because he was a scholar who loved the things I loved and who spoke the language I needed to speak them in. His Arabic was real Arabic—not the functional Arabic of a diplomat but the Arabic of a man who had studied it because the tradition it carried mattered to him. He loved Sufism—the poetry that emerges when a person tries to say what cannot be said about the encounter between the finite and the infinite. In a city where Islam had been reduced to a machinery of punishment and control, where the Friday sermons called the congregation monkeys and the morality police measured the length of men's trousers, writing to a man who had found in Islam the tradition of Rumi and Ibn Arabi was itself a kind of restoration.

I wrote in Arabic because the German orientalist spoke Arabic and loved receiving it. And I signed each letter from al-Mawsil al-Asira—Mosul the Captive. I dated them by the day of the occupation—the 348th, the 349th, the 350th—because counting the days of captivity was itself a refusal to accept the permanence of what had been imposed.

On May 4, a Monday, I went out walking with friends. We walked from four in the afternoon until half past nine at night—through the markets, the old quarters, along the Tigris—searching for something resembling peace of mind, because the worries of life here were many and painful and exhausting. That night, at 11:54, I sat down and began writing to the German orientalist everything I had seen.

An ISIS fighter, an older man who had lost his hand in combat, walking through the street with his small son beside him. The child was carrying a pistol nearly as large as his own arm, and the father was watching him and laughing. What will this child do when he grows up? I wrote. He will spill blood like his father. An elderly man who could barely stand, seized by *hisba* officers because they had caught him smoking. A group of Central Asian fighters—Azerbaijani or Kazakh, by appearance—walking the street as though the city were a house they had inherited from their ancestors, laughing in a language no one around them understood. Three women in full niqab carrying Kalashnikov rifles, one of them with the gun on her shoulder, a pistol in one hand, and a white handbag on the other.

On one of the propaganda screens, a video of a child executing a prisoner. The production was cinematic. The child loading his weapon. The prisoner in the orange suit. The sentence on the screen: condemned to death for apostasy. The child fires. The crowd watches with the eyes of people who are learning to watch without expression.

The street is dark. There is no spirit in it. Emptied of all light and life.

And then I saw what made me happiest that day.

A gasoline seller on the street—a man with a small station where he sold fuel from gallon cans. He was holding a book in his hand, and he was reading.

I stopped in front of him. I stared. I asked: What are you reading? The cover was torn. He said: Ali al-Wardi. When I looked more closely, I recognized it—*Social Aspects of Modern Iraqi History*, the most famous work of Iraqi social analysis. I said: Will you allow me to thank you? He said: For what would you thank me? I said: because you have restored hope to my soul. By God, I was on the verge of despair. He laughed. I asked him what his work had been before selling gasoline. He said: I was a physics teacher in a secondary school.

Can you imagine, the German orientalist—what it means for a physics teacher to work selling gasoline? In the street, under the sun? I said to him: By God's truth, give me your hand so I may kiss it. He said: God forgive you, my son. Praise God in all circumstances.

Years later, his face is as clear to me as it was that evening. I do not know his name. I do not know what happened to him.

The first thing I did when I came home that night was kiss my mother's head. She had been waiting, frightened by the shelling. I was afraid for you, she said. Thank God you are safe, my son.

Then I went upstairs and closed the door to my room and turned on the music.

Music was my only refuge. I played Michel Camilo—"On Fire," performed by Katia and Marielle Labèque. Then Khachaturian's *Piano Concerto*, Alicia de Larrocha with the London Philharmonic. The room was small. The hard drive was in its place. The city outside was dark and ruled by men who would have flogged me for what I was listening to. The music entered the room in a frequency the regime did not govern.

I told the German orientalist: I hope greatly that you will tell your friends that there is a human being in Mosul who loves music and whose life resembles the strings of a violin. And one day I will build an opera house in Mosul, and I will invite the most famous musicians to play melodies of eternity and tranquility and peace. I will build myself a room inside the opera house, and I will live there for the rest of my life.

I love life, my dear friend. I am writing all of this while crying now. Not because I want to die, but because I am afraid I will die before my eyes see my city at peace.

I will tell you something, friend. If my death comes, I want to die while I am listening to music. I want a white flower in my right hand and a white piece of paper in my left, so that when I meet God I can tell Him: I came to You with this white flower and this white paper. Look at what those who killed me did. You created me white, and they stained Your creation with blood.

I asked him to listen to Josef Hassid playing Achron's *Hebrew Melody*, and to Itzhak Perlman. After ISIS occupied Mosul, I wrote, I stayed a full twenty-four hours listening to Perlman without stopping. I was crying with the strikes of the violin. Will my city return? Will I live to see flowers growing again in the land of peace, the city of al-Hadba'?

On May 7, I described a flogging. A young man of twenty, his crime that he had not closed his shop during prayer time. Sixty lashes, full force. He began screaming after the fifteenth. By the twentieth he fell silent—I believe he could no longer feel his back. The executioner screamed God is great with every stroke, and the crowd repeated it. Take this, enemy of God. After sixty lashes the young man asked permission to sit down. The executioner said: If you sit I will give you the same again. The young man said: Do what you wish, I cannot endure standing. He collapsed face-first, unconscious. The executioner struck him thirty more times on the ground. Ninety lashes. The crowd chanting. The executioner counting.

I was standing there and I cried like a child. I felt the pain of every lash the young man received. I wanted to stop them. My friend held me back and said: They will kill you. I said: Let them do it, so I can be free of this darkness.

That night I wrote the longest letter. The crying had broken something open, and the words came not as report, not as record, but as the sound a person makes when the container finally cracks.

On May 9, I went to the university to try to obtain my M.A. certificate. The campus was empty except for a few people and, inside the grounds, a donkey and three cows grazing on the lawn. The University of Mosul—where I had studied history, where I defended my thesis on al-Jabarti, where the Faculty of Arts shaped the mind that was now recording the occupation of its own city—and cows were grazing inside it. A member of ISIS was at the faculty. I asked about the certificate. He said: You people of Mosul are always looking for worldly things. Go and fight and obtain a certificate in the way of God. I said: and why don't you go and become a martyr yourself? He threatened to call the *hisba*—the morality police who enforced religious law in the streets and could deliver a man to prison or worse on any pretext. I left. I was on the verge of striking him, but I restrained myself. I walked out of the faculty building and across the lawn where the cows were still grazing and I could feel the adrenaline in my hands and the back of my neck. I had just told an ISIS member to go and become a martyr. The words had left my mouth before the part of me that managed risk could stop them. On the street outside the campus, I stood still for a moment and understood what I had done: I let the anger speak in a place where anger could be reported, and the reporting could lead to everything I was carrying.

That same day I told my mother about my decision to leave. She wept and asked me not to go. I said: If I stay here I will die, I cannot endure it any longer.

She said: Take my liver and my heart to live on, but do not leave.

I cried with her. Then I lied to her and said: I will not leave.

Take my liver and my heart to live on. That is the sentence I carry from that day. She was offering me her organs, offering me the inside of her body, as though the thing that could keep me alive was the literal substance of the woman who had made me. Seven months later I left.

On May 13, I went to the market at dawn with my mother. I had not slept. I did not go because I needed to buy anything. I went because I wanted to memorize the city before I left it.

I wanted to preserve the smell of the streets and the faces of the people who passed through them. I wanted to remember the old man in the fish market, who had sat with me on his ancient wooden seat and told me his stories about his youth, about what it was like to sit overlooking the bank of the gentle Tigris and listen to the birds. All of it memories I wanted to store before they became the memories of a man who was no longer there to refresh them.

For the first time in months, I noticed the flowers at a stall near the entrance to the market, and the noticing hurt more than the numbness had. Color existed. It had been there the whole time. I had not been able to see it.

Cities are not merely stones, I wrote to the German orientalist. Cities are spirit and life. That is why I love my city. I search in the spirit of the stones for everything that connects me to it.

By May 12, I was ill—stomach pain from the unpurified water, sleeplessness, physical weakness that had been building since January and was now settling into my limbs as though the body were deciding, independently of the will, to begin its own withdrawal. I tried to describe to the German orientalist what I was living inside:

> I feel fear and safety and anxiety and terror and joy and sorrow and darkness and light and mixed emotions I cannot understand. All these feelings invade my mind and my soul and my heart. I do not see colors. I do not smell scents. I do not know the taste of things. I feel the sky and the earth with all their limits have closed in on my chest, and the walls—the walls of my room—are standing on my chest. I feel everything around me wants to kill me. A raging chaos. I feel the air is very hot, scorching air that penetrates my chest and tears it to shreds and scatters my being. I

> feel everything around me is a volcano of anger about to explode in my face. My hands were shaking when I wrote this. I could see the tremor in the script—the Arabic letters unsteady in a way they had never been, the pen moving through a hand that had lost its authority over its own fingers. I had not eaten that day. My stomach had closed itself against food the way a door closes against weather, and the body that had carried me through ten months of checkpoints and crowds and midnight sessions at the laptop was announcing, in the only language it had, that it was approaching a limit the mind had not yet acknowledged.

In the second letter, dated May 6, I opened with a formal Arabic salutation so elaborate it belonged to a different century—layered with blessings and honorifics: Dear brother, greetings filled with esteem and reverence, from Mosul the Good, city of plains and mountains, rivers and generous trees, watered by the pure Tigris. May God free it from every ungrateful tyrant. This was the register in which part of me still lived—the part that had studied Ottoman correspondence, that belonged to a tradition of learned Arabic prose ISIS could not reach because it existed in a dimension of language they did not control.

In the third letter, I quoted the Quran and wrote an analysis of how ISIS enforced compliance through religious ignorance. There is a saying among the people here, I told the German orientalist: Put it on the head of a scholar and come out of it safely. Meaning: Do not tire yourself thinking. The men of religion are the people of authority. Take their opinion and rest.

On May 23, I was reading *Martin Luther and Islam* by Adam Francisco. Perhaps in the coming days everything will change, I wrote, even the shape of the world as we know it. I was lying in a room in an occupied city, physically ill, planning an escape I was not sure would work, and I was thinking about civilizational frameworks.

On May 25, I walked through the city in the early morning and saw trucks dumping rubble from houses destroyed by coalition air strikes.

Children were searching through it for clothing—a jacket, a pair of trousers. The clothes of the dead.

I picked up a stone and spoke to it silently. This stone is the last witness to those innocents who perished. Stones are the truest witnesses. The rubble had a tongue. Here the girl was playing. Here the mother placed her hand. Here a young boy passed, laughing.

I went home and turned on the music. Richard Strauss—*Also sprach Zarathustra*. You Germans know the meaning of war well, I told the German orientalist, and you know how to give a person the meaning of life. Strauss can convince me that I am a child who resembles an old woman who cannot manage to die.

I will hold on to life with all the strength I have, and with all my passion for colors and flowers and birds, despite the tragedy and the pain and the fear and the loss of hope. But there is a thin white thread of light. It will be a path for the darkness to disperse one day.

That same month, my grandmother died. I did not grieve her the way I should have. I could not locate the grief inside the larger numbness that had become the condition of every day. She had been born in 1928, in Mosul, when the city still carried the last traces of the Ottoman world—the woman who said to me when I was ten years old, with the certainty of someone who remembered a world that no longer existed, "We are Ottomans." She was the oldest thread connecting me to the Mosul that existed before the borders were drawn, before the republic, before the wars, before ISIS. She died during the occupation, in the city she had never left, and the link between the historian and the oldest version of his own origins was severed. I could not grieve her properly. Grief requires space, and the space inside me had been occupied for ten months by the work and the fear and the daily discipline of not breaking. I noted her death the way I noted everything. I did not open the grief. I do not think I have opened it yet.

On May 24, I planted new flowers in the garden. A climbing plant had begun growing on my balcony, which overlooked the street and resembled the prow of a ship. I tended the soil with my hands and felt, for a moment, the simple animal fact of being alive—fingers in dirt, green things reaching toward light in a city where so much had been cut down. On the twenty-sixth, I told the German orientalist I could not take his letters with me when I left—the risk was too great. I would leave them in the house. In the same letter, I reported that ISIS had published a decree exempting musical instruments from the protection of property—there is no hand-cutting for the theft of musical instruments, or pork, or alcohol, or similar things. Perhaps I will steal a musical instrument, I wrote. What do you think?

On May 28—the last letter—I could barely write. I am angry, sad, depressed. All the doors are closing in my face. Every driver said ISIS would cut off his head. The Satanic State is like a person who loves dogs and puts them in a cage and enjoys watching them suffer and beat against the bars. That is what we are. We are dogs in a cage, and whenever we bark, they laugh.

I drew you something, I told the German orientalist. I tried to express what I feel. Please forgive me. I have no ability to write today.

When I eventually left Mosul, months later, I would not be able to take the letters with me. The bag would hold the hard drive, the orange notebook, a book from Amazon. The letters stayed in the house, among my mother's things. I do not know whether they survived the battle that came later—the nine months of fighting that destroyed the western half of the city. I do not know whether the paper on which I wrote to the German orientalist from Mosul the Captive still exists, or whether it was consumed by the same fire that consumed the al-Nuri mosque and the leaning minaret and thousands of houses and the bodies of the people who were still inside them.

Years later, I met him in person. First in Istanbul, then in Berlin. The man I had been writing to at midnight from the captive city was standing in front of me in a room that was not dark and in a city that was not occupied. We spoke. We spoke in Arabic. The language was the same language. The world around it was entirely different.

I had been writing to him as though he were a witness across centuries rather than a man across an ocean. In person he was quieter than I had imagined, and he spoke Arabic with the care of someone who had learned it through love rather than necessity. I found I did not know how to begin. In Mosul I had said everything—the floggings, the music, the decision by the river, the fear, the counting of the days. Now I was in a room in Berlin with the man whose name on a screen had kept the historian alive, and I had no words. We sat with coffee. He asked about the letters. I told him I had left them in the house when I crossed, that I did not know whether they survived the battle. He was quiet for a long time. Then he said: Wherever they are, they were received.

For days, I could not write the field reports. I could not open the encrypted file. The part of me that had maintained the method for ten months had reached a surface it could not pass through. What remained was the other part: the part that had always needed music, and language, and the company of a mind that understood what those things were for.

If it were not for music, I would have gone mad. If it were not for my mother's face, I would have killed myself. I wrote that to a man in Germany who had taken the name of a prophet because he had found in Islam what the men who ruled my city had buried under blood. I meant every word. I still do.

THE NARROWING

I opened the notebook again in April. Not the morning after the child's hand—weeks had passed since then, weeks in which the only writing I could do was the letters to the German orientalist, weeks in which the part of me the work was consuming had found, in those letters, the only space where it could still breathe. But the city did not wait for me to recover. The occupation continued and I was still inside it and the notebook was still where I left it, closed, beside the laptop. I picked it up and opened it to the next blank page and wrote the date.

That is all. There was no reckoning, no dramatic resolution, no moment of clarity in which the purpose of the work reasserted itself against the image of a boy's hand being described as a gift. I wrote the date because it was a fact, and facts were what I recorded, and the morning had come, and the city was still occupied, and I was still inside it. If I could explain the resumption more honestly than that I would. The truth is that the work had become so deeply embedded in the structure of my days—the routes, the listening, the writing, the hiding, the transmission—that stopping it would have required a second transformation as violent as the one that started it. I did not have that second transformation in me. I had only the first, still running, still demanding its daily tribute of attention and concealment and risk. So I opened the notebook and continued.

But the person who continued was not the same person who had put the notebook down.

The city that April was being prepared for a battle that had not yet arrived. On the third of the month, an armed group carried out an assassination against a senior ISIS commander called Abu Khattab near his house in the Saddam district—a residential neighborhood on the eastern bank of the Tigris, named during the Ba'athist era—four men in a Hyundai taxi, a quick operation that killed the man directly and sent the organization into furious response. Checkpoints went up across the city within the hour. Houses were raided in the area around the church. I heard about it first through the change in the street: the particular quality of sudden military movement, vehicles accelerating where vehicles had not been minutes before, the sound of a city contracting around a wound. The perpetrators were never found. The information I gathered pointed toward an armed resistance cell operating inside Mosul—something I heard whispers of before but had not been able to confirm through a second route. I recorded what I could verify and kept the rest in the encrypted file, where attribution could be preserved without the narrowness of the source path leading anyone back to a living person.

On April 7, four days after the assassination of Abu Khattab, I did something I had not planned and cannot fully explain.

It was Easter.

The Christians of Mosul had been gone for nine months. Every family expelled, every church seized or converted, every cross pulled down, every door that had been marked with the letter *nūn* now belonging to someone else or to no one. The quarter was emptied. The bells were silent. The city that held Christian and Muslim life together for fourteen centuries was surgically halved, and the half that was missing was the half that had prayed in the churches I had known since I was a boy.

I went to the Church of the Immaculate, in the Shifaa district.

I did not go alone. I will not say who came with me. What I will say is that we did not discuss it at length. The idea formed and we went, the way a person goes to visit the house of someone who has died—not because the visit will change anything, but because absence from it would be a failure of something the body understands better than the mind.

The Church of the Immaculate had already survived more than the occupation. It had been bombarded in 1743, during the siege of Nadir Shah, when the Persian army brought 300,000 men and hundreds of heavy cannon against the walls of Mosul and the city held. In that siege, the people of Mosul—Muslims, Christians, Yazidis—fought together under Husayn Pasha al-Jalili, and the church took damage alongside the mosques and the houses and the walls themselves. The city survived because it fought as one city, not as a collection of sects. That was 270 years before ISIS arrived with its letter *nūn* and its deportation orders and its three bureaucracies for managing the theft of Christian property. After the siege, the church was repaired. After al-Qaeda occupied it and detonated explosives inside it years before ISIS, the windows were sealed with rubble and the building closed. It endured. It was still standing. I wanted to see what ISIS had done to what had already survived so much.

We managed to get inside.

ISIS had crushed every cross. Every statue of the Virgin Mary that stood at the top of the church—gone, smashed, the fragments cleared away or ground into the floor. The interior was empty of any furniture, any icon, any object that identified the building as a place where people had gathered to pray. The southern and eastern gates had been demolished. The trees in the churchyard were still standing—the regime had not yet thought to destroy what could not be converted or sold. The building itself remained, the walls holding the shape of a church the way a skeleton holds the shape of a body after everything else has been taken. The name of the church on the exterior wall was partially destroyed—not entirely, as though whoever had done it had lost interest or been interrupted or decided that erasing a name was less satisfying than the larger project of erasing what the name referred to.

I walked through it slowly. The space where the congregation had sat. The space where the altar had been. I had not been a member of this church. I am a Muslim. But I grew up in a city where the church bells and the call to prayer occupied the same air, where Christian neighbors and Muslim neighbors shared the same streets, where the presence of the churches was not an exception to the city but part of what the city was. Standing inside the emptied church on the day the Christians of the world were celebrating the resurrection, I understood that what had been done to this building was not a military act or even a theological act. It was an amputation. Part of the city's body had been cut away, and the wound was here, in this silent nave, on this April morning, with nobody left to pray in it.

I came to pray for them. That was my main reason—not the damage assessment, not the documentation, though I did both. I came because it was Easter and the Christians of Mosul could not be in their church, and someone from Mosul should be. A Muslim, standing where the altar had been, asking for peace on behalf of the people who had been driven from this room and from this city and from the life they had built here across seventeen centuries. I do not know whether the prayer was heard. I know it was made. I know the building was standing around me while I made it, and the trees were still in the churchyard, and the city outside was occupied by men who would have killed me for being inside a church and praying for Christians to return.

We wanted to light a candle at the altar. That was the impulse—to leave one small flame in the darkness, one gesture that the church had not been entirely abandoned. But we stopped ourselves. The fear was specific: A lit candle might be seen, or its evidence found, and the discovery could trigger the demolition of the building itself and a hunt through the surrounding streets. The church had survived Nadir Shah's cannons and al-Qaeda's explosives. I was not willing to be the reason it did not survive a candle.

We left the way we had come. I walked home through streets that did not know what I had just done. The notebook was in my pocket. I wrote the date and the location and what I had seen. I did not write what I had felt. Some things belong to the record, and some things belong to the man who carries it, and standing in an empty church on Easter, praying for people who could not pray there themselves, belonged to the second category.

The assassination mattered not only for what it revealed about resistance but for what it produced in response. ISIS began broadcasting scenes of destruction in Tikrit—the city roughly three hundred kilometers to the south that had recently been retaken by Iraqi government forces and Shia paramilitaries—on screens and in sermons throughout Mosul, warning that any force sent to liberate the city would commit the same massacres against the population. The images were real. Make the population fear liberation more than occupation: That was the logic, and it worked. In the markets that week I watched families converting their savings into gold and foreign currency, small enough to carry in the event of flight. Merchants were unloading their shops. The streets were emptier than they had been since the first days of the fall.

By April 8, I could see what anyone walking through the city could see: Roughly 70 percent of the fighters at the checkpoints and headquarters were teenagers, boys between thirteen and eighteen. Some of them were too small for the weapons they carried—the Kalashnikov barrel reaching past the shoulder of a boy who had not yet finished growing, the weight of it pulling his frame to one side as he stood at a barrier in the midday heat. At a checkpoint near the Muthanna district I handed my papers to a boy who could not have been older than fifteen. His hands were dirty. His beard had not come in. He looked at the card, looked at me, looked at the card again, and waved me through with a motion that was trying to be authority and was mostly exhaustion. The European foreign fighters whose faces I had learned to recognize in the early months had largely disappeared. Several field commanders I had tracked were gone—transferred to Syria, according to a source who had reason to know. Asian fighters had increased in number, replacing the Europeans in a rotation I could now follow by the accents at the checkpoints and the faces outside the headquarters I passed on my way to the market.

On April 9, the governor of Mosul—the wali, ISIS's appointed administrator of the city, a man known for severe extremism even within the organization's own ranks—announced that he would search every house and shop in the city to find anyone sending information to outside media. There would be a campaign to confiscate weapons and disarm the population entirely. The announcement was broadcast in mosques and carried through the streets by men with loudspeakers.

I heard the announcement while walking. I kept walking at the pace I always kept. The pace itself was a discipline I had practiced for months—neither too fast, which could suggest a man with something to reach before someone else reached him, nor too slow, which could suggest a man lingering where a man should not linger. I turned the corner into the street that led toward our house and walked the rest of the way with the governor's words moving through me in the form they always took when danger became specific: not fear exactly, but a rapid internal inventory. The hard drive. The notebook. The laptop. The internet café where my friend still gave me access. The routes by which messages left the city. The names in the encrypted file that would convict me of everything the governor just described. I had been living with this possibility for ten months. The difference now was that it had been spoken aloud as policy, given a timetable, attached to the authority of the governor himself. I moved the hard drive that night to a location I had prepared for it outside the house. Then I moved it back before morning, because the location outside the house had its own risks that I had not thought through carefully enough in the dark. That kind of calculation—moving danger from one place to another, each place carrying a different species of risk—had become the texture of my nights.

The presidential compound was emptied in mid-April. ISIS removed furniture, equipment, and weapons from the monumental sites it had occupied since the fall and moved its headquarters into residential neighborhoods, into houses inside narrow alleys, among families who could not refuse them. The old compound was opened to the public—a gesture meant to appear confident, almost generous. But the regime was not leaving its positions out of strength. It was learning to hide inside the population it occupied. From the air, the compound was a target. From inside a neighborhood, the organization became indistinguishable from the civilians around it. I understood this with a precision that carried its own danger: The more clearly I could read the regime's movements, the more the reading itself became evidence of a kind of attention that ordinary civilians were not supposed to possess.

I tracked the movement because the movement was the story. On April 15—the same day that the headquarters relocated—eight men were executed in the Muthanna district. A quarrel between civilians had led someone to report them for apostasy, and that was enough. The report became an accusation, the accusation became a sentence, and the sentence was carried out the same day. Eight men killed because a neighbor's grievance found the regime's machinery available. That afternoon, four houses belonging to displaced Sunni Arab families—not Christians, not Shia, but Sunni families who had simply left—were confiscated in Al Arabi on the grounds that their owners had abandoned the land of the caliphate. And then the bodies arrived. Eighteen dead ISIS fighters were brought to the hospitals from the battles near Baiji to the south. They were all children—boys between fourteen and sixteen years old. Twelve more came from the fighting near Kwer to the east. In the wards where they were received, the staff processed them without speaking about what they saw: the faces that had not finished becoming adult faces, the uniforms that did not fit, the injuries that belonged to a battlefield inflicted on bodies that belonged to a schoolyard. I recorded the number. The distance I maintained in my prose was not the distance I felt. The prose required steadiness. What I felt required management.

A week later, on April 22, three women were shot in al-Hermat al-Thania on charges of adultery. They were not stoned—the method ISIS used in some cases to stage doctrinal spectacle—but shot, which carried its own message: efficiency over theater, the act completed quickly, the bodies left where they dropped. No one was permitted to approach them. They lay in the street for hours in the heat of late April—three women in the clothing they had been wearing when they were brought to the site, in a neighborhood where other women were still walking home from the market, where children were still in the houses along the same road. The prohibition against approaching was enforced. Neighbors who might have covered the bodies could not. The bodies remained, visible to anyone who passed, until they were eventually transferred to the Republican Hospital—the city's largest public hospital, on the eastern bank of the Tigris, which had become, under the occupation, both a medical facility and a way station for the regime's dead. That is what a public execution of women means in a residential neighborhood: not a distant event, not a headline, but three bodies on a street that people use, left there long enough that the street itself becomes the punishment's instrument.

I wrote the date, the location, the charge, the method. By now the hand moved across the page with a fluency that replaced the hesitation of the early months. The hesitation did not disappear. It had been absorbed into the motion itself—a steadiness that looked, from the outside, like competence, and that felt, from the inside, like a numbness I could not afford to examine while the work continued. To examine it would have meant stopping to ask what the recording was doing to the person recording, and that question had no answer that would have helped me record the next entry.

Then came the tunnels. I confirmed through a source with direct knowledge that ISIS had been digging passages beneath the Al Arabi and Al-Hadbaa districts—two densely built residential neighborhoods on the western side of the city—for months. The tunnels were three meters high and two meters wide, dug by workers and prisoners forced into the labor. Fake water pipes and dummy launchers were being placed in visible areas while real weapons were hidden elsewhere. The city aboveground was the city everyone could see. The city belowground was being prepared for a war that would use the population as cover and the streets as killing fields. I published what could be published without exposing the route of the knowledge. The rest I carried in the file, where a confirmed fact that the public record could not yet safely contain pressed against the silence around it.

The orphanage had been in my reports since the beginning.

In the first weeks of the occupation, when the city was still learning the shape of what had taken it, I contacted Dar al-Bara'im—the orphanage for parentless children in Mosul—and was told the children were fine but that they were asking me to visit. By September. I was reporting that the orphanage was suffering from a possible food crisis, and that I could not organize help because ISIS prohibited any public gatherings. In July, ISIS placed children from Tel Afar inside—boys and girls, aged between three and fourteen—after killing their parents. Among them was a boy the staff described as an extremely talented artist whose drawings caught the attention of his teachers. His siblings were with him. The children had been brought from the edges of the occupation—from Tel Afar, from Sinjar, from places where ISIS had killed their families and then delivered the survivors to an institution in the city it controlled, as though the act of housing them canceled the act of orphaning them.

By February, ISIS had begun taking children out. Three were removed for what the staff were told was training to join the ranks of the mujahideen: two brothers from Tel Afar, twelve and ten years old, and a Yazidi boy from Sinjar, thirteen. These children had been brought by ISIS from the beginning of the occupation. Now they were being converted from victims into instruments.

By April, the number had reached twelve. Children between seven and thirteen years old, all Shia and Yazidi, were being taken to the tourist village of Sudair in the forests east of Mosul for continuous military training—physical fitness, weapons, religious lectures. They returned to the orphanage on Thursdays. Later that month, I confirmed that six Yazidi children kidnapped from Sinjar and trained by ISIS were sent into their first battle, near the village of Vlafil, against the Peshmerga. Two of them were killed. They were fourteen years old.

I decided to go inside.

I will not name the person who helped me. What I will say is that I could not have entered alone. ISIS had taken full control of the orphanage and placed it under security—not the casual presence of a fighter at the door, but the organized watch of an institution the regime considered its property. The children inside were assets. The building was governed accordingly.

I entered by pretending to be staff. The details of how this was arranged belong to the person who arranged them, and I will leave them there. What matters is that I got inside, and what I saw when I did.

The orphanage looked like a prison.

That is not a comparison chosen for effect. It is the most precise description I can give. The building that was supposed to house children who had lost everything—children whose parents had been killed by the same organization that now controlled their daily lives—had the atmosphere, the discipline, and the surveillance of a detention facility. What had been a place of care was reorganized around the logic of control. The children were not being raised. They were being held.

I conducted an inventory. Names. Ages. Origins. Where each child had come from, how they had arrived, what had been done to them since. This was the method—the same method I applied to everything, the historian's reflex that kept me functional through the occupation. Date, location, number, source. But writing the names of children in that register, children who looked at me without knowing why I was there or what I was recording, required the separation I have described before—between the man holding the pen and whatever the man holding the pen still was underneath the method.

Some of the children had been given new names. A Yazidi boy from Sinjar—whose family, I would later learn, believed he was dead—had been renamed Abdullah. The name erased everything: his parents, his village, his people, his faith, his origin. Abdullah is one of the most common Muslim names. It means servant of God. They had taken a Yazidi child whose family had been destroyed in the genocide of August 2014, placed him in an institution under their control, and replaced his identity with a name that made him theirs. The boy who had been someone's son in Sinjar was now Abdullah in Mosul, and the distance between those two names was the distance between a life and its erasure.

I wrote down what I could verify. I noted the names they had been given and, where I could establish it, the origins they had arrived with. Then I left the way I had come—through the arrangement that let me in, back into the street, back into the character I wore in the city, back into the daily movement of a man who was not supposed to know what he had just seen.

I added the inventory to the encrypted file. The names of the children joined the names of the dead, the coordinates of the hidden headquarters, the testimony of the Yazidi girls, the record of the amputations and the executions and the confiscations—all of it carried in the same archive, on the same hard drive, in the same house where my mother made tea every morning without knowing what was stored above her head. By this point, ISIS was no longer content merely to discipline the city. It was harvesting the city's future.

By May and into June, the city's daily texture had changed in ways that were harder to name than executions or confiscations. The commercial streets that once stayed open until late at night—the Muthanna district, the Beautiful Lady market, the area around the cultural group building—were emptying by early evening. After nine o'clock the city resembled curfew, though no curfew had been formally declared; people simply stopped going out, the way a body stops using a limb that has been hurt too many times. I felt the change in my own routes. Streets I had used for gathering information in the early evening were no longer populated enough to give me cover. A man walking alone on an empty street is a man who can be remembered. I adjusted, the way I had been adjusting for a year, but each adjustment narrowed the space inside which the work could be done.

Water came only a few hours a day. Electricity was unreliable. Fuel prices had risen beyond what many families could afford. The salaries that the central government in Baghdad continued sending to civil servants in Mosul—one of the few remaining threads connecting the occupied city to the state that still formally claimed it—were being seized by ISIS before they reached the employees. The fighters' own salaries had been cut—reduced by 40 percent across all ranks that spring, according to a decision from the organization's financial authority—prompting desertions and resentment inside the ranks even as the population outside them continued to be taxed. The *hisba*, the morality police, shifted from doctrinal enforcement toward revenue collection—inventing fines for dress violations, for errors during prayer, for infractions so minor that they could only be explained as pretexts for extraction. The city was not merely being punished. It was being invoiced. And the invoicing entered the house: my mother calculating how long the cooking gas would last, my brothers wondering when the next salary seizure would come, the small daily mathematics of a household trying to survive inside a system designed to drain it.

In this atmosphere, ISIS turned its suspicion more sharply inward. The repentance registries that had been assembled in the first weeks of the occupation—the lists of former soldiers and police who had come forward, given their names, and received stamped documents promising their safety—had already been used for targeted arrests and executions through the previous year. Now the campaign widened. On a single day in April, thirty bodies of former police officers were delivered to the forensic department after execution. Their families received the remains only after paying fees to the morgue workers. The stamped documents had become death warrants with a delay built into them—the delay measured not in days but in the organization's assessment of when the city had grown quiet enough to process the names without provoking resistance. I recorded the number. I had known some of those men—not closely, but in Mosul, a city where neighborhoods held their people for generations, knowing someone did not require intimacy. It required only presence in the same streets over enough years.

The house searches, when they came, were as thorough as the governor had promised. Women accompanied the inspectors to search the women. Every room was entered. Identity papers were checked against files the inspectors carried with them. Mobile phones and computers were examined. In our neighborhood, the search teams moved through the streets with the unhurried precision of men following a list. I was in the house when I heard them—not the knock but the sound before the knock: voices in the street, the particular rhythm of a group moving from door to door. The hard drive was not in the room where I normally kept it. It was in a place I had prepared, a place I will not describe because the method of hiding may still matter to someone else in some future occupation of some future city. What I can describe is the quality of the waiting. It was not the sharp fear of a single moment. It was the sustained attention of a man who has calculated the distance between himself and destruction and knows that the distance is the width of one discovery. They came to our door. They entered. They searched. They left. My mother offered them water before they moved to the next house. That is the kind of detail that belongs in the record—the ordinary courtesy of a woman whose son was carrying, in the same house, evidence that would have ended them both.

In July, they arrested my cousin.

He had nothing to do with Mosul Eye. He was not a source, not an intermediary, not a man who carried information. He was my cousin—a relative, a man connected to me by kinship in a city where kinship was the primary social architecture, where everyone knew which families were related to which other families, where a name led to a neighborhood and a neighborhood led to a house and a house led to the people inside it. ISIS had been investigating Facebook pages it suspected of being connected to Mosul Eye. They arrested several people, among them my cousin, because something in the pattern of connections had pointed toward him, or toward someone near him, or toward someone near me. I did not know the exact logic of the arrest. I knew only that the suspicion had moved through kinship lines and arrived at a man whose only connection to my work was that he shared my blood.

After that, the archive was no longer simply a danger to me. It was a danger distributed through the lives of people who had no idea what I was carrying. My mother sleeping downstairs while the hard drive sat in the room above her. My brothers who watched television in the evening while I sat among them with the day's dead recorded in a file they had never seen. My cousin in a cell somewhere in the city, arrested because of a proximity he had not chosen and a project he did not know existed. The concealment I had practiced for a year was not protecting only me. It was failing to protect the people around me, and the failure was built into the structure of the work itself. I could not tell them what I was doing without endangering them with knowledge. I could not stop doing it without abandoning the record. And the record, by now, was not a choice. It was the thing I had become.

I do not know exactly when the weight of those months crossed into something I should call by its real name. There was no single day. There was a gradual narrowing—of sleep, of feeling, of the distance between the man who moved through the city in character and the man who came home and opened the files. The two had been separating for a year. By the summer of 2015, they had moved so far apart that what lay between them was no longer a gap I could manage through discipline. It was an emptiness. I do not mean sadness. I mean the absence of the thing that sadness requires, which is the capacity to feel that something has been lost. What I felt was closer to a withdrawal of the self from its own experience—as though the person who walked through the city and the person who recorded the city had consumed the person who lived in it. My body was registering what my mind refused to name. I was losing weight I could not afford to lose. The headaches that had started months earlier no longer came and went; they settled behind my eyes and stayed. My hands, when I wrote, sometimes trembled in a way that had nothing to do with the temperature. The stomach that had once been merely reluctant now refused food for whole days, accepting only tea and bread, sometimes not even that.

On July 28, I wrote on the blog: I lost all hope in anything, I lost the feeling of sense in what I'm doing, even I lost the meaning to be alive. Reading that sentence now, years later, I recognize the voice. It is mine. But it is the voice of a man who has passed through a door I can no longer fully reenter—a man who could still use the word hope because he had only just finished losing it, who could still name the meaning to be alive because the phrase had only just become untrue. The face of the city was dark. It was not the city I had always wanted to live in. I was in a very long tunnel, and it was dark and there was no end. You cannot continue and you cannot stop.

For many reasons. That is how I put it later, when someone asked me directly whether I had decided to die. Yes, I decided to die. First, there was no one I could talk to. There was no one to whom I could express what was happening inside me. I felt alone, tired, empty of any feelings—the kind of feelings I used to have. Love, hate, being angry, crying, laughing—basic human feelings. I felt myself empty of all this. I had stopped believing I was alive in any sense that mattered. That is not a phrase chosen for dramatic effect. It was the thought that ran through me during the long afternoons when the city was emptying and the light was the hard white light of an Iraqi summer and I walked through it wearing the correct beard and the correct trousers and carrying the notebook in which the day's facts would be recorded by a man who had ceased to feel that recording them was keeping him alive.

What came next was not a plan. It was a collapse that chose its own form.

I shaved my beard. Under ISIS rule, men were required to grow their beards and keep them uncut—a visible mark of submission that every man in the city wore and that every checkpoint could verify at a glance. Shaving was not merely a violation of the dress code. It was an act that made you immediately visible, immediately suspect, immediately a man who had chosen to announce that he no longer cared about the consequences of being seen. I shaved the beard and I cut my hair. I put on a red sweater—red, against the enforced darkness of a city dressed in black and dust and obedience. And I went to the river.

I went to the Tigris because I love the river. That is the first reason and the truest one. The Tigris is the only truthful witness of the whole history of Mosul—the river that has run through the center of the city since before the city existed, dividing it into its eastern and western halves, carrying the silt of every civilization that has risen and fallen along its banks. Moslawis call it the immortal river. I sat down near the Mosul Hotel, in a place where Nineveh—the Assyrian capital whose ruins face the old city across the water, the site of a civilization that rose and fell 2,500 years before ISIS arrived—lay in front of me, and the old city of Mosul rose behind me.

Such a combination of history. I felt myself in a place where I was living among the immortal people—among the elements of Mosul that had outlasted every conqueror and every occupation and every attempt to rewrite what the city was. I called it my last tea party. I had my tea. I smoked a cigarette in the open, in daylight, in an occupied city where smoking was a punishable offense. I played music in the car.

I was ready to die at that moment.

I did not want to kill myself by my own hand. That distinction matters, though from the outside it may not look like one. I was violating every rule ISIS had placed on the city—the beard, the hair, the clothing, the cigarette, the music—and I was doing it in the open, deliberately, to attract them to come to me. That was the only way I wanted to die: not as a man who had surrendered, but as a man who had refused. I wanted to do something against them first. And if I was going to be destroyed by what I had been carrying, I wanted the destruction to happen in a place that deserved to witness it—by the immortal river, between Nineveh and the old city. I wanted to die among the things that had always survived.

Samuel sat with me. He understood, though I do not know how much he understood. He had brought his car. The music was still playing. The tobacco was bad—Syrian, locally made—but I enjoyed the cigarette and the tea, sitting between the ruins and the river, waiting for a death that did not arrive.

I sat there for a long time. The river moved the way it has always moved, indifferent to what has been done along its banks for three thousand years. The cigarette burned down. The tea cooled. Nobody came. ISIS did not come, and I felt that I was invisible, that nobody could see me. The city was too consumed with its own survival to attend to one more violation among the thousands that moved through it daily.

When my death did not come, I did not immediately understand what had changed. For a while, I simply sat with the fact of still being alive, the way you sit with an unexpected answer to a question you had stopped expecting anyone to answer. The readiness drained out of me slowly—not replaced by relief, not replaced by anything I could name, but leaving behind it something that felt less like the wish to live than the body's quiet, stubborn refusal to let the mind finish what it had started. The river kept moving. The ruins did not speak. And in the space where the death wish had been, something else began to reassemble itself—not hope, which was still a word without purchase, but a kind of attention that had turned back toward the world. I noticed the color of the water. I noticed the heat on my arms. I noticed that I was still breathing. These were not revelations. They were the ordinary facts of a body that had outlasted its own decision to stop.

What I can say is that I felt I had been given a new life. That I had been told—not by a voice, not by a sign, but by the simple fact of still being alive in a place where I had expected not to be—that I did not have to die to join the glory of Nineveh. That I had to continue. From that point I understood the reason why I was alive. I understood the meaning of my life in a way I had not understood it during the months when the work had been consuming me faster than I could replenish whatever it was the work consumed.

I do not want to make this sound like a revelation. It was not clean. It was not a story with a beginning and an ending and a lesson drawn neatly from the middle. It was a man sitting by a river in a red sweater who expected to die and did not die and who now had to decide what to do with the fact that the city was still occupied and the files were still in the house and the notebook was still waiting and the morning would come and the work would still be there. I finished the tea. I went home. I did not tell my mother where I had been or what I had done with my face.

I grew the beard back.

Something had shifted in its foundations. I cannot call it recovery—the word implies a return to something prior, and there was no prior state left to return to. But after the river I became more protective of myself, more careful, and more committed to the city than the months of exhaustion had left me. The river returned me to the work with a clarity the work itself had nearly destroyed. The man who came back from the Tigris was carrying the same files and moving through the same streets, but the quality of the carrying changed. I knew now that the work could break the person doing it, and that the person doing it could arrive at the edge of the break and continue—not because of courage or conviction but because the alternative was something the body refused even when the mind had briefly stopped caring.

Mosul Eye continued to publish. The field reports continued. The encrypted file continued to grow. But I also began, in this period, to think about multiplication. If I was the only voice, and the voice was attached to a body that had nearly broken, then the entire record depended on a single point of failure. The Tigris had given me arithmetic: one voice, one body, one archive, one failure away from silence.

Through Maouris Milton—a literary persona I had created alongside Mosul Eye, the voice through which I could address the city in a register the field reports could not hold—I called on the people of Mosul to resist. Not with weapons, but with information, with witness, with the refusal to let the city disappear into silence. I asked young people especially to describe what they saw, to document what was happening in their neighborhoods. I gave practical instructions: Change some details before publishing. Do not tie yourself to a single neighborhood. Do not write in a way that reveals that only one person in one place could know what you are describing. What I had learned through necessity, I was now trying to teach as method.

No one responded.

I put out the call through Maouris Milton, and the city—a city of more than a million people living under a regime that was grinding them down daily—returned silence. I did not blame them. The silence was itself a product of the system I was trying to fight: When punishment is public and comprehensive, when informants may be sitting in your own street, when the act of typing a sentence on a phone can end in a prison cell or a square, the rational response to a call for resistance is to say nothing. I understood that. But understanding it did not change what it felt like to sit alone with a screen that held nothing but the call I had sent and the silence that had answered it.

Then one person answered.

She was nineteen. She did not give me her name. She wrote simply that she wanted to know how to protect herself online and that she was responding to my call. Out of an entire city, one voice. I did not let her publish immediately. The first thing I needed to know was whether she understood what she was entering—whether she understood it as well as I did, which meant understanding that a single sentence, carelessly placed, could end a life. I asked her to describe what she saw—not for publication, but so I could study where her own words might betray her. A person often reveals herself in syntax before she does in facts: the way she locates an incident, the way she refers to a street, the assumptions she carries about what others around her know. These patterns can point back to a writer more efficiently than a name. I needed to teach her to see those patterns in her own language before she could safely use that language in public.

She chose the name Rachel Corrie—after the young American woman killed in Gaza in 2003 while trying to protect Palestinian homes from Israeli military demolition. In the Arab world, the name carried a specific meaning: a woman from outside who had chosen to place her body between power and the people power was destroying. That a nineteen-year-old girl in occupied Mosul chose that name for herself told me something about who she was before I knew anything else about her.

I trained her. That is the precise word. I coached her on what to write and what to withhold, how to disperse herself across locations in her text so that no single neighborhood could be traced back to her, how to handle the information that arrived through the ordinary channels of a young woman's life in the city—the markets, the mosques, the conversations between women that men never heard, the things that happened behind the doors that the male fighters of ISIS could not always enter. The occupation had been reconfiguring women's existence more totally than any other dimension of the city's life—accusations of adultery, detention, the policing of dress, the armed female checkpoints, the fate of Yazidi women hanging over every female body as warning and possibility. When she was ready, I introduced her publicly. Rachel Corrie became the female voice against ISIS from inside Mosul. Teaching her what I knew—transferring the method that had nearly broken me into the hands of someone I could not see and could not protect beyond the quality of the training itself—was one of the most unsettling things the work required of me. I was now responsible not only for my own survival inside the method but for hers.

Her arrival changed something I had not anticipated. Others saw that a woman had spoken and survived it—survived it so far—and some of them began to speak too. People from outside Mosul who had been attacking the city's population, blaming them for what had happened, calling them complicit, encountered these voices and some of them shifted. The silence that ISIS had tried to impose was developing fractures, small ones, each one a risk, each one a proof that the city had not been fully consumed. But each new voice was also a new responsibility. What had begun as solitary witness was becoming mentorship under danger, and protecting other people's courage was harder than protecting my own.

ISIS understood the problem. A blog appeared called Mosul Mahabba—the name means Mosul Love—produced by an ISIS fighter in an attempt to simulate independence while functioning as propaganda. The organization had grasped that it was no longer enough to punish bodies and collect taxes. It also needed to compete in the field of narrative—to produce counterfeit authenticity from the side of power. Every regime that has tried to hold a city by force has eventually had to contest the story being told about it. ISIS had reached that stage.

By the end of the summer, the public messages I wrote had changed their register. Not because I had decided to change them but because the city required something different. On August 11, I wrote: The entire world is silent and turned a blind eye towards what's going on in Mosul. Mosul has become a forgotten city.

The word "forgotten" carried more weight than any description of violence I had published. It named the condition that made the violence possible—a city that the world had agreed not to see. Three times the people of Mosul had heard that liberation was approaching. Three times nothing had come. The Iraqi government announced operations that dissolved into nothing. The coalition promised progress that remained invisible on the ground. Hope became unstable—spoken too cheaply it turned into another cruelty, withheld entirely it ceded the city to despair. The people had begun to feel they were alone. They had been promised too many times. The city was sinking into the particular kind of despair that grows when suffering continues and announcements dissolve into nothing.

I wrote, in a post I still remember composing word by word because I understood what each word might do to a person reading it inside that city: that ISIS was using every possible means to collect taxes from the Moslawis; that daily executions and amputations of the innocent continued; that arrests, detention, torture, and prison violations continued; and that with all of this ISIS was still trying to paint a utopian image of life under its rule. Then I addressed the city directly—my brothers and sisters, my sons and daughters—and wrote: Freedom is very near. Just bear this ordeal a little more.

I wrote that because hope could only be spoken responsibly if the machinery of suffering was named first. That was the law of this phase: The world must be told the horror, and the city must be told it has not disappeared, and neither statement can be false. The difficulty was that the person writing both statements was himself inside the horror and himself uncertain whether the hope was true. I wrote it anyway, because a city that loses the belief that its suffering is known begins to die in a way that has nothing to do with bombs.

I was still inside Mosul. I was still carrying the archive. I was still, each night, at the desk. The red sweater was in a drawer somewhere in the house. I had grown the beard back to its required length. My mother still made tea in the mornings. The notebook was still open. The work was not finished, and neither, it turned out, was I.

But the narrowing had not stopped. The exits from the city were closing. By the end of the summer, anyone wishing to leave for any reason had to deposit two thousand dollars, surrender property deeds, and return within ten days or lose everything. Sermons had declared departure itself a form of apostasy—a renunciation of the caliphate's claim to divine authority, punishable as a crime against God. The roads were watched. The smugglers who could still move people out of the city—through the desert routes toward Syria or along the roads toward Kurdish-controlled territory to the north and east—were more expensive and more dangerous. The city that had driven hundreds of thousands out in the first months of the occupation was now sealing the rest inside—holding them as cover, as revenue, as audience for the punishments that continued in the squares and from the buildings and along the roads that led nowhere anyone could safely go. I had stayed by choice; now staying was compulsory.

I was among the sealed. The notebook was among the sealed. The archive, the files, the names of the dead, the coordinates of the hidden headquarters, the testimony about the Yazidi girls, the voice of the old woman who had asked whether God could see her heart, the record of the child's hand described as a gift—all of it was inside the city with me, and the city was closing.

The question of how to leave began forming in a part of me I was not ready to examine. I did not yet call it a plan. I called it nothing, because naming it would have made it real, and making it real would have meant confronting everything that leaving would mean: that the man who stayed when everyone else fled would now become the man who left. That the record, which depended on presence, would have to survive distance. That the city I tried to keep alive through documentation would continue to suffer without the witness who insisted on remaining inside it.

I was not ready for those questions. But the city was narrowing around me, and the questions were forming whether I was ready for them or not.

THE CROSSING

The decision came as a result of a series of events, and none of them was the last one. That is the truth of how a person leaves a city he refused to leave. There is no final moment. There is an accumulation that one morning becomes a weight the body can no longer redistribute, and the question that had been forming in a part of the mind the mind was not yet ready to examine becomes the only question left.

The house next door to ours—separated from my room by a single thin wall—was occupied by a senior ISIS leader and his family. The house behind us held another. On the same street there were three ISIS commanders with their households, and at the end of the street a weapons depot the organization had established inside a residential building. Their checkpoints sat directly in front of our house, because our house was on the main road. Every night when I heard aircraft overhead I lay in my bed and performed the calculation I had been performing for months—the distance between the wall of my room and the wall of the room where the Syrian leader slept, the probable radius of a missile strike, the margin between a hit on his house and the destruction of mine. The calculation was not abstract. It was architectural. One thin wall.

I had accepted the price from the beginning. If I were alone, I would have continued. That is not bravery. It is the specific arithmetic of a man who has already calculated his own death and found it acceptable against the work. But I was not alone. My mother was in the house. My brothers were in the house. The hard drive was in the house, and the hard drive, if discovered, would not convict only me. It would convict the address, the family, the name. I had to run away with the proof that would protect

Mosul for years to come, and to at least be loyal to the people who were killed in the city. And I did not want to become another casualty of the monsters. I think I deserve life, deserve to be alive.

South toward Baghdad was impossible—the Shia-dominated government and its associated militias had decided that anyone who remained in Mosul during the occupation was an ISIS affiliate or sympathizer, and a man from the city traveling south would be treated accordingly. North toward Kurdistan was closed—the border between ISIS-controlled territory and the Kurdish autonomous region was a combat front. East was surrounded by the Iraqi army. The only corridor that remained open ran west, through ISIS-held territory in Syria, and from there to the Turkish border. It was not a direction I chose. It was the direction that was left.

I knew a smuggler through a mutual acquaintance. I went to Abu Ali's house one evening, knowing that his two brothers were ISIS fighters—men whose membership in the organization was essential to the business model, because they provided the cover story and the stamps needed to pass through checkpoints. Abu Ali said he had a trip the next morning. He promised to get me to the Turkish border. I told him I would be ready.

I filled the small bag before going to bed. The yellow one-terabyte hard drive with my evidence against the Islamic State—the encrypted files, the daily reports, the names, the dates, the coordinates, the photographs, the testimonies I had gathered from sources inside the regime and from ordinary people whose voices would have been lost without the recording. An orange notebook half-filled with my notes on Ottoman history, with a hand-drawn map of Mosul on the cover—the research I had been working on before the fall, the scholarship that belonged to the person I had been before the occupation made me into someone else. And a keepsake: a copy of *Father Bombo's Pilgrimage to Mecca*, an obscure American satirical novel from 1770 that I had ordered through a new shop in Mosul that was the only place in town to order from abroad online—the first book from Amazon ever delivered to the city, which had arrived in 2011 when such deliveries were still possible and Mosul was still a city where a man could order a book and expect it to reach his door.

Three objects. The archive, the scholarship, and the memory of a city that had once been open enough to receive a package from the outside world.

I passed another sleepless night. I left behind years of handwritten journals—hidden inside books, in the wood of a bookshelf, among my mother's clothing. I said nothing about the manuscripts I had rescued from a church before it was pillaged—manuscripts from Mosul's Christian heritage that were now in the hands of an archaeologist friend whose name I will not write here. Everything that could not fit in the bag stayed in the house, distributed across hiding places I had learned to maintain the way a man maintains the rooms of a building he expects to return to—except that I did not expect to return.

Before dawn, I woke my mother in her bedroom on the ground floor.

"I'm leaving."

"Where?" she asked.

"I am leaving."

That was all I could say. Anything more could endanger her—not only emotionally but practically, because a mother who knows where her son has gone is a mother who can be made to say where her son has gone, and the men who would ask her were not men who asked gently. Since ISIS arrived, I lived a life about which she was totally unaware, putting her and the rest of my family in unwitting danger with every keystroke. I was two men, and one of them had been condemned to death. Now, at least, she would never have to watch the capture and killing of Mosul Eye.

Her eyes burned the back of my neck as I stepped outside.

The Chevrolet was waiting in the street—the long model that people in Mosul called the Obama, for reasons the city never explained to itself. Abu Ali was behind the wheel. The morning was still dark—the particular cold of a Mosul winter. For the first time since the arrival of ISIS, I had no desire to take notes. Everything I would need was inside the hard drive. Everything else—the city, the house, my mother, the streets I had walked for eighteen months under a name that was mine and a purpose that was hidden—would have to survive without me or not survive at all. I got into the car and closed the door.

We drove first to a mosque that ISIS had turned into a transit station, where Abu Ali obtained the paperwork needed for the western route. If they asked, we were going to Tel Afar to visit family. It took half an hour and five thousand dinars. Then we pulled out onto the road.

As we left the station, an ISIS fighter flagged us down by the side of the road, stranded by a broken-down car. He needed a ride to Tel Afar—a town roughly seventy kilometers west of Mosul, the same Turkmen town whose Shia community had been massacred in the first months of the occupation. Abu Ali agreed. I moved to the back seat and sat silently thumbing the Quran that Abu Ali kept in the glove compartment, hoping the fighter would take me for a shy and pious scholar of Islam. He would be only partly wrong. The hard drive sat in the bag between my feet while a man who served the regime that would have killed me for what it contained rode in the front seat, watching the road.

We rolled slowly toward a checkpoint at the al-Hul bridge, surrounded by families headed to market, sheep, goats, other cars. Most of them would be turned back to Mosul by the ISIS guards, who would seize their identity cards and note them as potential escapees in a database. Some were arrested. We passed through. An ISIS fighter in the car was a better travel document than anything Abu Ali could have purchased.

At Tel Afar the fighter got out. Abu Ali told me to hide my passport. I shoved it deep under the back seat. Then I climbed into the front, and Abu Ali drove on, crossing into Syria. For forty minutes we bumped along empty back roads, dust billowing behind us. The smuggler stopped at an oil station to collect fuel—part of his own commerce, oil being one of the currencies that moved between Iraq and Syria through these routes. At the border, near a town called Umm al-Dhiban—Mother of Wolves—on the Iraqi side, I saw men exchanging goods in the open, the commerce of a stateless economy operating under the flag of a state that had declared itself divine. Then the landscape shifted and we were in Syria.

Abu Ali could not drive toward Hasaka—the nearest major town in northeastern Syria—because the roads were held by Kurdish fighters who were at war with ISIS. He went through Shaddadi instead. In Arabic, the name means something very difficult, and the town carried the meaning of its name.

Before the Syrian civil war, Shaddadi had been a small oil town in the flatlands south of Hasaka, the kind of place travelers passed through rather than stopped. By 2015, it had become something else—a town run entirely by the most extreme elements of the organization, a place where what passed for restraint even in Mosul did not apply. I had spent eighteen months documenting what ISIS did in my city. I had recorded executions, confiscations, forced conversions, the systematic machinery of an occupation that used violence the way other governments use memoranda. But Mosul was a city of nearly two million people, a city with history and institutions and a population whose sheer size imposed certain limits on what the regime could do in the open. Shaddadi had no such constraints. It was a town small enough that ISIS could practice the full expression of its ideology without the logistical compromises a major city required.

Approaching a small cluster of buildings, Abu Ali drew to a stop in front of what looked like an abandoned school. In front of it was a man nailed to a cross.

He was mounted in the manner described in the scriptures—arms extended, nails through the hands, the body suspended above the ground. A piece of paper bearing his name was attached to his chest: Sulyman Ayoub. The charge was apostasy—the accusation that a Muslim had abandoned his faith, one of the offenses ISIS punished with the most theatrical severity. The word for death was written beneath it in Arabic. But the man was not dead. He was moving—the small involuntary shifts of a living person in agony. Below him, dogs were feeding on his legs. Not strays circling at a distance but animals that had been allowed to reach the body and were eating from it while the man lived.

The street around the cross was open and ordinary—a road, buildings, the flat light of a Syrian winter afternoon—and the man was alive on the cross and the dogs were eating him and the town continued around this as though it were furniture. I had heard of crucifixion under ISIS. I had not seen it in Mosul. The distance between hearing and seeing is the distance between a word and the thing the word describes, and that distance closed in Shaddadi and has not reopened.

A few minutes later we passed two men locked in a metal cage in the middle of the street—exhibited like animals, barely alive, their bodies folded into the enclosure. Then an oncoming pickup truck passed us with two more men crucified in the flatbed, mounted on crosses that had been loaded into the vehicle and driven through the town so that the punishment could be displayed in motion, brought to the people rather than waiting for the people to come to it. The streets were nearly empty. An ISIS fighter from somewhere in Asia passed alone, his rifle slung over his back.

I sat in the front seat of Abu Ali's car with the bag between my feet and I said nothing. There was nothing to say. In eighteen months, I had learned the specific silence of a man who sees something and stores it without visible reaction—the discipline of the face, which in Mosul had kept me alive and which on this road through Shaddadi was all I had left. But behind the silence something was happening that I could not have explained at the time and can only describe now as recognition. Not of the scene itself, which was new and specific and worse than anything I had witnessed in person. Recognition of my own condition.

In my first months under ISIS, when I had begun recording and transmitting what I saw, I thought of my work in the terms available to me—as documentation, as journalism, as the duty of a historian in extraordinary circumstances. And it was those things. But sitting in a car on a road in Syria with the most dangerous archive in Iraq between my feet, watching a man die on a cross while the town continued around him, I understood something I had not understood before. I understood what I had become.

There is a film by Roman Polanski called *The Pianist*. It tells the story of Władysław Szpilman, a Polish musician who survived the destruction of the Warsaw ghetto—the sealed district where the Nazis confined the Jews of

Warsaw before deporting them to the death camps. Szpilman was a pianist for Polish Radio. When the ghetto fell, he survived by hiding in the ruins of the city, a man who lived by being nowhere, belonging to nothing, visible to no one, sustained by nothing except the fact that he had not yet been found. He could not play the piano. He could not make music. The thing that defined him—his art, his skill, the practice that gave his life meaning—had to be carried in silence because the act of playing would have revealed his presence and killed him. The piano was there. The music was inside him. But between the music and the world there was a wall of danger that could not be breached, and so the pianist became a man who carried his art the way a fugitive carries a weapon—hidden, potent, unusable, and essential.

Abu Ali drove on. The road continued. The bag stayed between my feet. The town of Shaddadi fell behind us, and I said nothing, because there was nothing to say that the silence did not already contain.

A little after midday, Abu Ali pulled into Raqqa and stopped the car in front of a restaurant called Kebab al-Zahra. Raqqa was the administrative capital of the caliphate—the Syrian city where ISIS had established its central government, its courts, its ministries, and its propaganda apparatus. It was the seat of the organization's declared state, the place from which it governed territory spanning two countries, and it was also a city where people ate lunch.

"Let's have lunch," Abu Ali said.

Lunch was the last thing I wanted. Leaving behind the hard drive—even for the time it would take to walk from the car to a table and back—was unthinkable. The Mosul Eye blog entries, the encrypted files, my browser history, the names and coordinates and testimonies were in that bag, and that bag was tantamount to death if anyone opened it. Abu Ali insisted. I grabbed the backpack and went inside. He ordered a kebab. I was not hungry. I sat with the bag on my lap in a restaurant in the capital of the caliphate, surrounded by people eating lunch in a city that ISIS governed the way other cities are governed by mayors and councils, and tried to keep my face in the expression I had spent eighteen months learning to hold in places where the wrong expression could be the last one.

Then Abu Ali said: "I'm leaving."

My voice rose. "What?"

"Don't worry. They'll come to pick you up." He waved me toward a small group of families standing near two vans outside the restaurant. Then he left. Abu Ali drove away, and from inside the restaurant, my backpack secure against my chest, I watched him go. My dark green passport was still jammed under the back seat of his car.

Near the restaurant, sitting alone in the middle of the street, was an ISIS fighter. He was very young and very fat, sitting on the ground with a weapon beside him, and I did not understand why he was there or what he was guarding. The road was otherwise empty. I was cargo between handlers, standing in the open in the capital of the caliphate, and the only thing separating me from the regime I had been documenting for eighteen months was the assumption that a man standing outside a kebab restaurant near a group of families was a man with legitimate business.

One of the Syrian smugglers introduced himself. His name was Mustafa—though everyone called him Steff, the local abbreviation. He spoke in the dialect of eastern Syria, the flat vowels and clipped consonants of the territory between the Euphrates and the Turkish border. Twelve of us were loaded into one van, another six into a second. Five were from Tikrit, the rest from Mosul. Steff drove us to his house in a village near the border and said we could not move until dark.

We waited. The hours passed in the particular quality of suspended time that belongs to people who have left one country and not yet arrived in another. Men, children, one very old woman. We all listened as Steff explained what was about to happen—our lives depending on advice from a man we had met only hours before. Women held their children. No one spoke much. The room smelled of bodies and cold tea and the staleness of a place that has held too many people passing through and none of them staying.

At the farm, I recorded a video on my phone. There was a cow standing behind me in the yard, the ordinary animal life of a Syrian village continuing around the extraordinary fact of what we were about to do. I held the phone and said what I was thinking, because I did not know whether I would have another chance to say it: Behind me is death, and in front of me is freedom, yet there is no guarantee I will know which path I will take. I recorded it with the cow behind me and the dark coming on. Then I put the phone away. When night came, Steff moved us to the border.

The border between Syria and Turkey at that crossing point was a trench and a fence. The trench was three meters deep, cut into the earth along the line where one country ended and another began. Above it, a chain-link fence, and beyond that, Turkish gendarmerie—border police—patrolling on foot and in vehicles, their flashlights visible at intervals as they moved along the rim. Steff explained the method. We would descend into the trench and wait until the patrol passed. When the guards moved out of sight, we would climb the wall of earth, scale the fence, and run across the open ground on the Turkish side until we reached a vehicle that would be waiting. The trench was narrow enough that I could touch both walls if I extended my arms, and deep enough that standing inside it I could see nothing of the landscape above except a strip of night sky. Tens of people descended—men, women, children—crouching in the dirt, pressing against the cold walls, waiting for a gap in the patrol that would last long enough for a human body to climb three meters of earth and breach a fence before anyone with a rifle decided to stop it.

The trench cannot be climbed alone. That is the first thing to understand about what happened next. The wall is too high, the earth too loose, the angle too steep for a single person to pull themselves out without help. You need two people—one below pushing, one above pulling. You go in pairs. One lifts the other, then the one on top reaches down and pulls the one below. If the second person does not reach down, the first person stays in the trench.

The patrol passed. Steff said: Now.

People began climbing. We were among the last. There was a man beside me—I did not know his name, but I would later learn he was from my own neighborhood in Mosul, a man who had been waiting at the border for two days before I arrived. He was heavy. His body could not do what the trench demanded. He asked me to help him climb. I told him: Do not leave me behind. You have to help me after. He said yes. I could have gone first—I was lighter, I was capable of the climb, the logical sequence was for me to go up and then reach down for him. But he was heavier, and if I went up first I was not sure I could pull him. If I left him there, no one else was coming. We were the last two people in the trench. I gave him my turn. I pushed him up from below, my hands against his weight, his body struggling against the wall, the earth crumbling under his feet and falling into my face. He made it to the surface.

He reached his hand down for me. I grabbed it. He tried to pull. Once, twice, he grabbed and could not hold. His grip slipped. He dropped me.

"I'm sorry," he said, and disappeared over the other side.

I fell back to the bottom of the trench. In that same moment the Turkish police appeared along the rim. The man ran. I do not blame him for running—in the calculation of the border, the man who stops is the man who is caught, and being caught means being sent back to the country you just climbed out of. He ran and the police caught him and arrested him. He was from my neighborhood. He had waited two days. He had promised to help me, and his body had not been able to keep the promise.

I was alone at the bottom of the trench.

I was exactly in the middle between death and life. If I went back, I went back to ISIS, to Syria, to the crucified man named Sulyman Ayoub and the caged men and the roads that led nowhere anyone could safely go. If I raised my head above the rim, the Turkish gendarmerie would see me and either arrest me or shoot. I could not go forward and I could not go back. I was lying in the dark earth between two countries, in December, and neither the life I had left nor the life I was trying to reach could be accessed from where I was.

I lay there for twenty or thirty minutes. Time in the trench was not the time of clocks. It was the time of the body—heartbeat, breath, the cold entering through the ground, the sound of movement somewhere above that could be patrol or wind or other people lying in the dark the way I was lying in the dark.

I saw my whole life. That is the phrase people use, and I can confirm it is not a metaphor. It came as a film—compressed, accelerated, stripped of everything except the faces and the moments that had brought me to this specific piece of earth. I saw the faces of the people I had known. I remembered my life—not in order, not as narrative, but as images arriving without sequence: the university, the river, the streets, my mother's kitchen, the notebooks, the nights at the laptop, the checkpoints I had passed through wearing the correct face, the crowds I had stood in while men were killed, the red sweater by the Tigris, the child's hand in the square. All of it compressed into the space between one breath and the next in the trench where I lay.

I asked myself the question the trench demanded: Was it worth doing this? Why did I believe writing history could save Mosul? How would my mother ever accept my death? Why did I even leave?

I did not answer the question. The trench does not give you time for answers. It gives you time for the question, and the question is enough to fill every second of the minutes during which you do not know whether the next thing that happens will be a hand reaching down or a flashlight finding your face.

"Yo!"

Steff found me there, huddled in the trench. He spoke in his local dialect—the same eastern Syrian vowels I had heard that afternoon in the village. He said: Do not worry. I will help you. He had come back when he did not have to come back. He had already moved the rest of the group. He could have considered his job done. Instead, he returned and waited with me until the patrol moved again. Then he said: I found a better place. We moved along the trench in the dark, crouching, until we reached a section where the climb was possible. He went up first and reached down.

He said: Give me your hand.

I was holding the bag. The yellow hard drive, the orange notebook with the map of Mosul on its cover, the copy of *Father Bombo's Pilgrimage to*

Mecca. Everything was in that bag. Everything was also in my head. The bag was too heavy to carry while climbing, and the trench was too deep for a man to hold both his own weight and the weight of what he had been carrying for a year and a half. Everything is in the bag. Everything is in the brain. You do not trust anything in this moment. You have to make a very difficult decision.

I threw the bag up to him. He caught it.

Then he pulled me out.

He said: When you run, do not look behind you. Even if they shoot, do not stop. If you stop, they will arrest you and send you back. If you do not stop, they will let you cross. This is the most they do.

I ran. The bag was in my hand. The ground was flat and dark, and I could not see what was ahead of me. I heard nothing behind me—no shot, no voice, no sound except my own breathing and my feet on the earth. I did not look back. I did not stop. After five minutes, I saw the vehicle—a truck used for transporting frozen food, parked in the dark with its engine running. The people who had crossed before me were already inside, crouched among the cold metal walls of a cargo space designed for perishable goods, not human beings. The driver said: You can stop now. You are safe.

I stopped. I was in Turkey.

Near the border, at a small building where Steff went to arrange the final paperwork, boys were selling cookies, snacks, and Turkish SIM cards. I watched as cars and vans filled with people like us pulled up, and one smuggler after another went inside. Only after watching others do the same did I dare leave the group to buy a SIM card. Inside the shop, ISIS fighters were doing the same thing—buying Turkish SIM cards for their own communications. I stood beside them at the counter. They did not know who I was. I bought the card and walked out.

The frozen food truck drove us through the night along the route north from Tel Abyad. The road north from Tel Abyad was the same route Abraham was said to have walked, centuries before borders existed and before anyone had thought to cut a trench between one country and another. I did not think about Abraham in the trench. I am thinking about him now. A man escaping fire. A man landing in water. A man whose survival became a sacred site. The parallel is not mine to claim. But the road was the same road.

They dropped us in the middle of Urfa—a city in southeastern Turkey that had become one of the main destinations for people fleeing the wars in Syria and Iraq—at three in the morning. They left us at Ayn Zeliha, Abraham's sacred pool, the site where tradition says the patriarch landed after Nimrod's fire was turned to water, where the old stone walls with their pointed arches are lit at night and reflected in the dark surface of the pond, where carp have been swimming for centuries because the fish, like the water, are said to be holy. Steff said: No one will ask you what you are doing here. You are free to go.

I called my mother.

I am safe.

I lied. I was not safe in any sense except that ISIS was no longer on the other side of the wall. I had no passport—it was still jammed under the back seat of Abu Ali's car. I would ask Adam in Mosul to retrieve it and send it to Turkey, but three months would pass before I learned the truth: My family did not want to send it. They thought I would go to Europe. Turkey was closer. They wanted me near. I was three months without documents in a country where Turkish police periodically searched the apartments of Iraqi residents looking for people who were exactly what I was—undocumented, unregistered, and present.

A Syrian man who worked in a small restaurant near the park saw that I had arrived from the direction of the border and did not ask questions. He gave me food. Then he walked me to his mother's house—a tiny place, half of it a courtyard, the other half a staircase. She woke up and let me in without a word. She said I could lock the door from the inside if I did not feel safe. In the morning I woke to a cup of milk and a biscuit she had placed beside me while I slept. I never asked their names. They never asked mine. In a region where war had made suspicion the default condition between strangers, a woman opened her door in the middle of the night and placed breakfast beside a man she had never met. That is the other story. It is always the other story, running beneath the one about the cruelty and the fear—the one about the people who help anyway, who do not ask for reasons or identification, who simply see a person at the door and let him in.

I moved between cities the way a man moves through rooms he does not own. From Urfa I tried Zonguldak—a city on the Black Sea coast, where a distant relative of my mother lived. Fourteen hours on a bus, not knowing whether police would board and check papers at any stop along the route. The relative was not awake when I arrived at seven in the morning. The woman who had agreed to rent me a flat changed her mind. I moved to Kütahya—in central Anatolia, another fourteen hours by bus, a city famous for its ceramics, which I noticed with the part of my mind that had not yet stopped observing the surface of things. After three nights a friend said it was impossible to find a flat without documents. I tried Konya—the city of Rumi, the thirteenth-century Sufi poet whose work I had read in quieter years. I did not stay. I moved to Yalova, on the far shore of the Sea of Marmara. I arrived at two in the morning. A man said I could stay. I started paying rent. I cooked. I established myself in a room with a large screen on the wall, my laptop, the map always open, the light always off.

Through all of it I never lost connection with Mosul. The sources I had cultivated during eighteen months inside the city were still there, still sending information, still taking risks I could no longer share physically but could still manage from a distance. I verified what they told me against satellite imagery—an application that updated every few days with high-resolution photographs of the city. I could see the smoke from the air strikes. I could check the condition of my family's neighborhood. The method had changed. I was no longer walking the streets, no longer passing through checkpoints, no longer wearing the face I had learned to hold. But the obligation had not changed. The city was still occupied. The people were still inside it. The record still had to be kept.

I often think about the trench. Not because it was the most dangerous moment—there had been moments in Mosul that were more dangerous in the strict arithmetic of proximity to death. The house search. The cousin's arrest. The weeks after Al-Kindi. The Tigris. Any of those moments could have ended everything. The trench was not worse. But it was the moment when the two lives I had been living—the visible life and the hidden one, the man and the record—were compressed into a single body lying in the dirt between two countries, holding a bag that contained everything and belonging to nothing. And it was the moment when the question I had been carrying for eighteen months—is the work worth the life?—stopped being a question I could defer. In the trench, there was no later. There was only the bag, the earth, the dark, the strip of sky overhead, and the man above me who either would or would not reach down.

Steff reached down. A Syrian smuggler whose real name I never learned, who came back when he did not have to, who found another place along the wall when the first place had failed, who called out Yo! into the dark until he found me. I do not know what happened to him afterward. I do not know whether the trench is still there or whether the crossing has been sealed. I know only that in the earth between Syria and Turkey, a man I did not know reached down for a man he did not know, and that is how the archive crossed the border.

The bag made it. The hard drive made it. The orange notebook made it. The book made it. The record of eighteen months—the names of the dead, the dates, the locations, the charges, the coordinates, the hidden files, the public posts, the encrypted entries that contained what the public posts could not safely hold—all of it crossed the border in a bag thrown upward from a trench by a man who did not know whether the hands reaching down would hold.

My mother was still in Mosul. My brothers were still in Mosul. The city was still occupied. The journals I had hidden in the bookshelf and among her clothing were still in the house. Rachel Corrie was still inside, publishing under the name of a dead American woman who had placed her body between power and the people power was destroying. I have not heard from her since. I do not know what happened to her after I crossed.

I was outside. The notebook was open.

It had only changed its address.

THE DISTANCE

The screen showed Mosul from above. Updated every three to five days, the satellite imagery rendered the city as a pattern of rooftops and streets and open ground—the same city I had walked through for eighteen months, flattened into a view no one inside it would ever see. I could zoom into my family's house. I could study the roof, the courtyard, the street where I had turned left each morning on my way to the market. I could see the smoke from air strikes over neighborhoods I had documented from the ground. What I could not see was what I had always seen from the street: the faces, the checkpoints, the bodies after an execution, the expression on a man's face when he passed a *hisba* patrol—the religious police who enforced the regime's codes of dress and conduct and prayer—and did not know whether he would be stopped. The satellite showed the city's surface. The sources told me what was happening beneath it. My work was now the reconciliation of these two views that could never, together, complete the picture—the eye in the sky and the voices from inside—into something as close to reliable as the distance permitted.

The application I used was adapted from a Department of Defense site designed for tracking military operations. I ran it on a laptop connected to a large wall-mounted screen. Every time I opened it, I checked my family's house first. Always first. The rooftops intact, the street visible, the courtyard where my mother had served tea on summer evenings reduced to a cluster of pixels. I could not see whether anyone was home.

Before Yalova there had been other cities. In the weeks after the crossing I moved from place to place—Urfa near the Syrian border, where the streets were full of Arabic and the refugee population was large enough that one more Iraqi attracted no attention; Zonguldak on the Black Sea coast, where a relative of my mother's had promised to help me find a flat but the woman renting it changed her mind; Kütahya in the interior, fourteen hours by bus, where the landlord said after three nights that it was impossible to rent without papers; Konya, the city of Rumi, where I sat in the poet's mausoleum and felt the silence of a man who had found a way to speak about what cannot be spoken, and wished I could stay but could not. Each city was a different version of the same problem: how to exist without documents in a country that was not mine, while continuing to run a clandestine project aimed at a city a thousand kilometers to the southeast. Through all of it I never lost connection with Mosul. The work continued from bus stations, borrowed rooms, cafés where I sat with the laptop angled away from the other tables. The work was me. It did not stop because the city changed.

I arrived in Yalova on a bus from Istanbul, in the early evening, in January. The town sat on the southern shore of the Sea of Marmara—a place built for summer holidays, emptied by winter, its waterfront promenade quiet in the dark. The bus had taken the ferry route across the water, and for the hour of the crossing I had stood on the deck watching the lights of Istanbul recede and the dark coast of the southern shore approach. The air was cold and smelled of salt and diesel and nothing at all like the Tigris. I found the door. I climbed the stairs. I entered the room that would become, for the next several months, the new center of the operation I had been running since June 2014.

The room was small and sparsely furnished—a bed, a desk, a kitchen counter, a window onto the street. I set the bag down and plugged in the laptop and opened the satellite application before I did anything else. I checked the area around my family's house. The rooftops were intact. I closed the laptop and stood in the room and listened to the silence of a place where no one knew who I was or what I was carrying. The silence was different from the silence in Mosul. In Mosul, silence was dangerous—it meant something had happened or was about to happen. Here, silence was simply the absence of sound. I did not yet know what to do with that absence.

I developed a routine because routine was the only structure available. I woke before dawn—the habit from Mosul, where the call to prayer had organized the first hour, followed me into a country where no one required me to pray. I made Turkish coffee in the small kitchen, brewed in a specific cup I bought near the Yalova waterfront—Ottoman-patterned, the blue and gold geometric design reminding me of something between Mosul and the centuries before Mosul became what it had become. I carried the coffee to the desk. I turned on the large screen. The map appeared. I checked the family's house. I checked the neighborhoods where my sources operated. I checked the locations I had flagged in the previous days—a suspected headquarters here, a reported air strike there—looking for changes in the imagery that would confirm or contradict what the voices from inside had told me.

The sources reported at irregular hours. A message might arrive at three in the morning—someone who witnessed an execution and could not sleep and needed to transmit what they had seen before the details faded. Another might come at midday—a merchant who overheard a conversation at a checkpoint and waited until he was home to type it. I was available for all of them. The screen was always on. The light in the room was always off—partly because the screen was easier to read in darkness, partly because darkness had become the condition in which I worked best, the condition my body associated with the hours of writing and transmission.

The books on the desk accumulated: Montefiore, de Bellaigue, an Arabic history of the Jews of Mosul, a third edition of Bernard Lewis's *The Emergence of Modern Turkey*. A bronze Iraqi plate engraved with the Ishtar Gate and a lamassu—the winged, human-headed bull that had guarded the palaces of the Assyrian kings who built the first civilization on the plains east of Mosul, three thousand years before the men who destroyed their statues arrived. A prayer card of a man in a Capuchin robe, propped between the books because his face looked like the face of someone who carries what he carries without putting it down. These objects were the room's only personal markers—the evidence that the person who lived here had a history and a mind and was not merely a function of the screen on the wall.

I did not know who the man on the prayer card was when I found it. Somewhere in those months—I cannot fix the exact date—it appeared among the objects I was accumulating in the room, and I kept it because something in the photograph stopped me. An old man with a gray beard and heavy eyebrows, wearing a brown Capuchin robe, looking directly at the camera with an expression I can only describe as the face of a man who has seen suffering that cannot be spoken about and has chosen to carry it rather than explain it. I did not know the tradition. I did not know the name. I knew only that the look on his face corresponded to something I recognized in myself—not the religious context, not the theology, but the expression itself. The expression of a man who carries what he carries and does not put it down.

Years later, I learned that the man in the photograph was Padre Pio—the Italian Capuchin friar and mystic who was said to have borne on his body the wounds of Christ for fifty years, who heard confessions for hours each day, who lived in the same monastery in San Giovanni Rotondo in southern Italy from 1916 until his death in 1968. I knew none of this when I found the photograph in Turkey. I knew only that the face stayed with me the way certain faces do—not as information but as company. I propped the card between the books on the desk, and it remained there through the months of the screen and the satellite and the sources reporting at three in the morning and the police knocking and the Sea of Marmara in the evenings. It watched me work.

In 2025, nearly a decade after I found the photograph, I visited his tomb in San Giovanni Rotondo. I stood in front of it and thought about the man who had found this face in a Turkish apartment while hiding from three intelligence services and documenting an occupation by satellite and walking by the Sea of Marmara in the evenings with no documents and no legal name and no certainty that the next morning would not bring the knock that ended everything. I do not know why I kept that photograph. I know that I needed it.

When a source reported an air strike, I checked the satellite imagery three to five days later to verify the location and assess the damage. The delay was the cost of distance—in Mosul I could walk to the site within hours; from Yalova I had to wait for the satellite's next pass, trusting that the source was reliable enough to hold. When a source reported a new ISIS headquarters in a residential neighborhood, I cross-referenced it against the imagery to confirm the building and its proximity to civilian structures. When my mother told me on the phone that the shelling had been bad the previous night, I checked the area around the house. The rooftops were intact. I could not see whether she had slept.

In Mosul, I had been the body that moved through the checkpoints, the eyes that witnessed, the hands that wrote the notes and hid the files. In Turkey, I was the eye that verified from above, the voice that communicated through encrypted channels, the judgment that decided what was reliable enough to publish and what had to be held. The distance between the screen and the street was a gap I could never fully close. I saw the rooftops. My sources saw the blood.

Most evenings, I walked along the Marmara. It was the only space in those months that made no demands—no questions, no constructed identity, no face to hold. On some nights, I sat on the stone wall along the promenade with a stray Labrador that had found me and attached himself to my evenings—a large yellow dog with gentle eyes who appeared from somewhere along the waterfront each time I came and settled beside me as though we had an appointment. He leaned his weight against my leg, and I rested my hand on his broad warm skull, and for those minutes I was a man with a dog by the sea and nothing else. He was the closest thing to being asked how I was. He did not need an answer. Neither did anyone else, because no one was asking.

The guilt arrived on those evenings. Not during the work—during the work I was occupied, and occupation is its own anesthetic. But on the promenade, with the dog beside me and the water moving, the guilt found room. I was safe. My sources were not. The men and women who fed me information from inside Mosul—who walked the same streets I had walked, who passed the same checkpoints, who carried the same risk of exposure—were still there, still inside the closing city, still endangered by the same work I was now conducting from a seaside town where the worst that could happen to me on any given evening was that the dog would not come. I could not share their danger. I could only use what their danger produced. The distance was not geographic. It was moral.

Then I went back to the room. The sources had sent messages while I was gone. Mosul did not observe my walking hours.

During those months in Turkey, a channel opened that changed the nature of the work.

Through intermediaries—the precise chain I will not describe—I established contact with officers at the United States Central Command, the military headquarters responsible for operations across the Middle East, including the air campaign against ISIS. The channel was not formal. I was not an agent, not a recruited source, not a man on anyone's payroll or bound by anyone's instructions. I was a free source—a man who published independently and who also, through this separate connection, could transmit information that was too sensitive or too time-critical for the blog. Every intelligence agency that had approached me since 2014 had received the same answer: No. The work had to remain a scholar's project, answerable to no government. That principle did not change. What changed was that the quality of what my methods produced had created a demand I could not ignore.

I had spent eighteen months inside the city building what no external agency possessed: a network of sources embedded in the population, cross-referenced against my own direct observation, verified through methods developed under conditions that would have been impossible to replicate from the air or from a foreign capital. I knew the city's geography from having walked it daily under disguise. I knew the organization's internal structure from having sat in rooms where its members spoke freely because they did not know what I was. I knew the locations of command posts, weapons facilities, and training camps from sources who lived beside them.

What I began providing were target assessments on senior ISIS figures—their locations, their movements, the facilities they used. I provided intelligence on high-value sites that the coalition could not identify from the air: command centers hidden inside residential neighborhoods, weapons depots concealed beneath ordinary buildings, the car-bomb factories I had first discovered from the ground by noticing fighters who were too comfortable on a street where they should not have been comfortable. I developed methods to protect the civilian population still inside—methods designed to ensure that when the military operations everyone could see approaching finally came, the forces entering Mosul would know the difference between the population and the occupation.

The man who had refused every agency's offer to become a controlled asset had become, through the logic of his own methods, one of the most effective intelligence sources operating against ISIS in Mosul. Not because I had sought that role. Because each stage demanded the next. The documentation demanded verification. The verification demanded sources. The sources demanded methods. The methods produced intelligence. The intelligence demanded a channel. And the channel connected a man in a Turkish apartment, with no legal existence and no institutional backing, to the military command that would eventually plan the liberation of his city.

This channel would become, in the months ahead, the route through which hundreds of people were rescued from inside the battle of Mosul. But in those early months it was one more line of communication maintained from a dark room by a man trying to make the distance between himself and his city narrow enough to be consequential.

I never stopped working against them. I escalated.

I knew the financial architecture that sustained the occupation because I had documented it from inside—the zakat collections that functioned as a compulsory religious tax, the oil revenues from seized fields south of Mosul, the property confiscations, the salary seizures. What I had not fully understood from inside was the external dimension: the supply lines that fed the regime from across borders.

When ISIS seized Mosul in 2014, the conventional banking system collapsed. What remained were the *hawala* networks—an informal system of money transfer based on trust between brokers, older than any bank, used by millions of ordinary people to send funds across borders where the formal system was too slow or too broken. There were more than 1,600 exchange houses in Iraq alone. ISIS absorbed them. The regime made the operators an offer that was not an offer: Keep your business, but handle our money. The exchange houses became the financial circulatory system of the caliphate, with cash routes running from Istanbul through Kurdish towns to Mosul, from Amman through Baghdad to ISIS-controlled Anbar Province, from Gaziantep in southern Turkey to Raqqa in Syria.

One of the companies operating inside this network ran out of a storefront on a commercial street in Istanbul—Arabic and Turkish signage, the words "daily shipping to Iraq" printed in both languages, as ordinary as a laundry or a phone-repair shop. I had been watching the storefront for several days before I went in. The method was the same one I had used in Mosul: Observe first, enter second, ask questions that elicit answers without revealing why they matter.

I walked in on a Tuesday. The street was wet—heavy gray rain, an Istanbul winter. I presented myself as an Iraqi who needed to send money to family in Mosul, which was true. A man behind the counter explained the process. He confirmed they could transfer funds into the city. He described the routes. He named the intermediary cities. He answered everything. He was not guarding information. He was selling a service. And the service was a financial pipeline between ISIS-controlled territory and a NATO country, operating in the open, on a commercial street, while the most powerful military alliance in the world was spending billions trying to sever the same networks I had just walked into and recorded.

I walked out into the rain. The recording was in my pocket. The feeling was familiar—the particular lightness that follows a successful extraction of information, the adrenaline metabolizing into a quiet alertness as you move away from the site at a pace that is neither too fast nor too slow. I had felt it in Mosul, leaving rooms where men had spoken without knowing what I was. I felt it now on a wet street in Istanbul, doing the same work in a different country with the same body that had learned its methods under a regime that would have killed me for using them.

I exposed them. I will not describe the full details of how, because some of the methods and some of the people who helped are still matters I must protect. I had documented the regime from inside the city. Now I was documenting its supply lines from outside it.

The Turkish police came to the apartment building three times a month, sometimes more. Early morning. Two or three officers. A clipboard. Who lives here, how long? Show your papers. They were searching the flats of Iraqis, looking for people who were in the country illegally. People like me.

One morning they knocked. Adam was in Ankara. I was alone with the screen, the laptop, the hard drive containing eighteen months of clandestine intelligence from inside an ISIS-occupied city. I heard the knock. I turned off the screen. I opened the door.

I told them I was the cleaner.

One held the clipboard. The other stood slightly behind, looking past me into the apartment. I held the expression I had learned at checkpoints in Mosul—the expression that gives nothing, that belongs to a man who is exactly what he says he is. I had used it a hundred times with armed men who could have searched me, detained me, killed me. I used it now on two Turkish officers in the doorway of an apartment that contained enough evidence to end my life in any of the ways that the various organizations looking for me had in mind.

They asked whose apartment it was. I gave the name on the lease. They asked where the tenant was. Ankara, I said. They looked at the apartment behind me. They did not enter. They wrote something on the clipboard. They left.

I closed the door and stood in the silence that follows a lie that has worked. Not relief. The calculation of how many more times it could hold.

Then the danger changed form.

Information reached me through channels inside Iraq that Iraqi intelligence services had identified my Turkish phone number—the number through which I communicated with sources, received reports from inside the city, maintained the connection that kept Mosul Eye operational. Traced. A friend I trusted told me directly: We feel you are under threat by Turkish intelligence.

They had killed Syrian activists inside Gaziantep, a city near the Syrian border where refugees concentrated and where ISIS operatives moved freely among them. Targeted killings, professional, carried out in a country that was supposed to be beyond the regime's reach. Turkey was not beyond its reach.

It was no longer only ISIS. I was at risk of being arrested by the Turkish government itself—illegally present, no papers, no status, no protection. If the police came again with authority and searched properly, they would find a man who did not officially exist, living under someone else's name, in a room containing satellite imagery of an ISIS-occupied city and a hard drive holding the most detailed clandestine archive of the occupation that anyone had produced. When I tried to think about what would follow, I recalled the stories my uncle had told me as a child about prison under Saddam Hussein's regime. They take him walking and they send him back in a stretcher. I had been a child when I heard those words. They had stayed in my body—not in the mind but in the chest, in the legs, in the part of the nervous system that decides whether to run.

Turkey was no longer safe.

I lay awake running calculations that had no resolution. If I stayed, the Turkish police would eventually find me. If I ran, the sources inside Mosul would lose the person who knew their patterns and their risks. If I was arrested, the hard drive would be seized, and it contained not only the intelligence but the identities of the people who had provided it—people still inside, still walking through checkpoints, still alive only because their connection to Mosul Eye had not been traced. The hard drive was not only my vulnerability. It was theirs. And they did not know it existed.

The room in Yalova was no longer safe. The distance I had crossed was closing behind me, and this new country was narrowing the way the old city had narrowed—different walls, different pressures, but the same constriction, the same feeling that the space in which the work could continue was shrinking toward a point where continuation would become impossible.

I had to leave. Not because I wanted to. Because staying had become as dangerous as staying in Mosul had been in the months before the crossing—the same accumulation of signs, the same tightening of the possible, the same moment when the rational mind says: If you do not go now, you will not go. The original plan had been for the United States. For reasons I will not detail here, that was not possible at the time. What was possible was Paris. I was asked: *Would you like to fly to Paris instead?* I answered, *Yes, why not? Paris is okay too.* The arrangements were made. I could leave. In April 2016, I packed the laptop, the hard drive, the books, the Iraqi plate, and the prayer card of the man in the Capuchin robe.

The Labrador was not at the promenade that last evening. I walked the route anyway—the rocks, the water, the lights of Istanbul across the strait—and the walk felt like the walks I had taken through Mosul in the last days before the crossing: a man moving through a place he is about to leave, carrying the knowledge that the leaving will not end the connection but will change its nature forever. I left Turkey the way I had left Mosul: because the danger of remaining had overtaken the danger of going, and because the work—the sources, the screen, the archive, the obligation that had begun in June 2014—demanded a place where it could continue.

The work continued. The city it was trying to hold was about to be destroyed.

THE EYE ABOVE

The first thing I saw from the window of my room in Paris was a cemetery. Headstones in rows. Trees between the rows. The geometry of a country that had enough peace to bury its dead properly and tend the ground afterward. I stood at the window and thought: Perhaps this is a sign. A man who has not slept soundly in two years, and the first thing the city shows him is a place where people rest.

The air in Paris in April has a specific quality I was not prepared for. Cool and faintly damp, carrying something that might have been bread or stone or the particular cleanness of a city whose gutters are washed each morning. On the street below the hotel, a woman walked a dog. A man stood at the window of the café across the road and drank his coffee without looking up. The light on the cemetery wall was the soft gray of early spring in northern Europe—a light without urgency, without the white pressure of an Iraqi summer. I stood at the window and received it for perhaps thirty seconds. Then the graves below me stopped being the graves of Paris.

I stood at the window on the first night and thought about the graves in Mosul—the unmarked ones, the mass ones, the bodies left in streets after executions, the people who had disappeared into the machinery of the Islamic State and whose families did not know where they were buried or whether they were buried at all. In Paris the dead had addresses. In Mosul the dead had coordinates, if they were lucky, and nothing if they were not.

The room was small. I set up the laptop, connected to the wireless network, and opened the satellite application. The rooftops of Mosul were where I had left them. Smoke from a recent air strike over the western neighborhoods. My mother's house was intact. I checked. I always checked. The map was open. The light was off. I stayed there for more than a week, waking each morning to the cemetery through the window and the city on the screen, before I found an apartment and moved the operation there.

It was April 2016. My passage from Turkey had been arranged—Paris, not the United States, which had been the first destination discussed but which, for complicated reasons, could not receive me then. I had legal status for the first time since June 2014: documents with my name on them, the right to be where I was. I could smoke when I wanted. I could play music without closing the door. These were not small things. In Mosul, each of them had been forbidden or dangerous. In Turkey, each had been possible only in private and at risk. In Paris, they were ordinary. And the ordinariness was the thing I could not absorb, because I had forgotten what it felt like to live in a place where ordinary life was not a performance designed to conceal a dangerous archive.

A morning in the apartment: I woke before six. The first thing—before coffee, before the news, before the sounds of the Parisian street below the window had fully registered as sounds belonging to a city that was not Mosul—I opened the laptop and navigated to the satellite. The mother's house first. Always the mother's house first. The rooftop filled the screen, its familiar rectangle of concrete and the shadow of the water tank and the edge of the neighbor's wall. Intact. Then I widened the view: the neighborhood, the district, the western bank, the eastern bank. Smoke over al-Zanjili. A new dark mark in the Yarmouk district that had not been there three days ago. I switched to the encrypted channels. A source had reported overnight: an air strike on a residential building in al-Jadida, casualties unknown. Another source: ISIS had moved a weapons depot from the industrial district to a house in al-Rifai. I noted the coordinates. I cross-referenced against the satellite imagery. The house was visible—an ordinary residential structure, indistinguishable from the houses around it, except that I now knew what was inside it.

Then I closed the laptop and took the Métro to EHESS.

L'École des Hautes Études en Sciences Sociales—one of France's most distinguished research institutions for the humanities and social sciences—had its campus near the Raspail station. The commute was twenty-five minutes through the tunnels of a city whose underground was designed for commuters, not for war. I sat in the carriage with students and office workers and read the messages on my phone. The woman across from me was reading a novel—something with a blue cover, her face tilted into it with the absorbed calm of a person whose reading carried no risk. The man beside her was checking football results. I was reading a message from a source who had just confirmed the coordinates of the weapons depot in the al-Rifai neighborhood and who had signed off with the phrase "God protect us," which was not a formality but a prayer spoken by a man who knew that the information he had just sent could be traced back to him if any link in the chain between his phone and mine was compromised. The carriage stopped at Denfert-Rochereau. The woman turned a page. People got on. People got off. The source's prayer and the woman's novel occupied the same metal tube beneath the streets of Paris, and neither knew the other existed. I put the phone in my pocket and walked the rest of the way to the campus.

At EHESS, I entered the reading room the way a scholar enters a reading room—with books under my arm, a notebook, the posture of a man who is here to study. Around me sat other doctoral students and researchers, quiet, focused, surrounded by the Ottoman and Islamic sources that were the common language of this discipline. I opened Badriyya's Tawarikh al-Mawsil—the chronicle of Mosul covering 1855 to 1920, written by Behnam Hanna Badriyya, a Christian historian who had documented his city during a period of Ottoman decline and imperial transition. The pages were calm. The prose was measured. The city Badriyya described was a city of coexistence: Christians, Muslims, Yazidis, Shabak, governed by an administration that was imperfect but that recognized the city's plurality as a fact rather than a problem to be solved through expulsion.

The scholars at adjacent desks worked in the particular quiet of people who have chosen to spend their lives with old texts. They did not know that the man at the desk near the window was not only studying those traditions but was living inside their twenty-first-century consequence—that the city whose nineteenth-century chronicles he was reading was, at that moment, occupied by men who had declared those chronicles heretical and who were rewriting the university where the chronicles had been preserved.

While I read, my phone vibrated under the table. A message from a source inside Mosul. I read it below the desk, between pages of Badriyya. The source reported that ISIS had executed four men in the Bab al-Toub district that morning on charges of espionage. I noted the date and the location in the margin of my notebook, beside a note about Badriyya's description of a similar public punishment in Ottoman Mosul in 1893. The two entries sat side by side on the same page—the nineteenth century and the twenty-first, the Ottoman punishment and the ISIS punishment, the chronicler's distance and the witness's proximity. Three chroniclers of Mosul under pressure: Badriyya in the Ottoman twilight, al-Jabarti—the Egyptian historian whose unsparing account of Napoleon's occupation of Egypt had shaped my understanding of what a chronicler could be—as the model, and I, reading the chronicles of one while producing the chronicles of the other, the past and the present collapsed into a single reading room in Paris. I closed the phone. I returned to Badriyya. The reading room was quiet. The city on the phone was not.

The first time I saw Notre-Dame I was walking along the Seine in the late afternoon, still carrying the dislocation of those first weeks, and the cathedral appeared above the rooftops of the Île de la Cité the way certain buildings appear when you are not looking for them—not as a monument but as a fact. It had been there for eight hundred years. It had survived the Revolution, which stripped its saints from the facade and turned it into a

Temple of Reason. It had survived two world wars. It was still standing. I stood on the Pont de l'Archevêché and looked at it and thought about the al-Nuri mosque in Mosul—the mosque where Abu Bakr al-Baghdadi, the leader of the Islamic State, had declared the caliphate in July 2014, the mosque that held the leaning minaret of al-Hadba', the landmark that had defined the city's skyline for eight centuries. The same eight centuries. Notre-Dame and al-Hadba' were contemporaries. One was standing in the evening light of a city at peace. The other was standing in a city under occupation, and no one could promise the minaret would survive what was coming.

I went back late one night, weeks later, when the facade was lit and the tourists were fewer and the stone seemed older in the dark. I sat on the low wall by the river and I thought about God. Not in the way the Friday preachers in Mosul spoke about God—the God whose name was screamed during floggings, whose law was invoked to justify the execution of a boy, whose authority was claimed by men who cut off hands and threw bodies from rooftops. That God I knew. I had documented what was done in His name. What I thought about in front of Notre-Dame was a different question. Not whether God existed—that was a question for philosophers in warm rooms. The question was why. Why had a city of mosques and churches and shrines and libraries and a minaret that had stood for eight centuries been handed to men who used God's name the way a butcher uses a knife—as an instrument, as a tool of work, stripped of everything except function.

I did not arrive at an answer. I do not have one now. What I had, sitting by the river at night with the cathedral illuminated above me, was the question itself, and the question was enough to keep me sitting there for hours. In Mosul I had not had time for it. I had been too deep inside the thing the question was about. The distance of exile had given me the one thing the occupation could not: the space to ask why. And sometimes I prayed. Not in any formal way—not the prayer of the mosques in Mosul where prayer had been turned into a weapon, not the prayer of the cathedral before me which belonged to a faith that was not mine. A private prayer. The prayer of a man asking God, if God was listening, to preserve what could still be preserved. The minaret. The house. The mother. The people whose names were on the hard drive and whose lives were still inside the city. I did not know if the prayer reached anywhere. I knew that the act of praying, in front of a building that had been prayed in for eight hundred years, was itself a form of survival.

Liberté, égalité, fraternité. The words were carved into the facades of public buildings across Paris—schools, town halls, courthouses—so familiar to the people who walked past them that no one looked up. I looked up. I could not stop looking up. The rights they declared were real and their absence in Mosul was real and the difference between a city that protected speech and a city that killed for it was the difference between life and death. But the civilization that had declared these rights universal had watched Mosul fall, had debated its suffering, had dropped bombs and sent coordinates, but had not prevented the occupation or the silence or the two years during which the people of Mosul had lived without a single one of the rights carved into the stone above the doors of French schools.

I had admired Voltaire since before the fall. His courage. His precision. His refusal to let religious authority escape the scrutiny of reason. *Écrasez l'infâme*—crush the infamous thing—the phrase he used against the alliance of superstition, intolerance, and institutional cruelty. In Mosul I lived inside the infamous thing. ISIS was the *infâme* made literal. But Voltaire had written from relative safety—exile in Geneva or Ferney, with a printing press and a European reputation. And the Enlightenment he helped create did not prevent the world from producing ISIS. The rights of man were universal in principle and absent in practice in the city I fled. I admired Voltaire. I carried him. But from Mosul, even Voltaire was not enough.

The intelligence work continued from Paris, and in Paris it became more sophisticated. The methods evolved. I was combining overhead imagery with ground-level source reporting in ways that produced a picture of the city's military geography more detailed than what any single collection system could generate alone. I could see, from the satellite, that a building had been modified—new barriers, vehicles, construction activity. I could confirm, from a source on the ground, what the modification meant: a new command post, a weapons depot, a car-bomb workshop. The fusion of the two produced intelligence that was actionable in a way that either one alone was not.

Through the channel I established with CENTCOM—the United States Central Command, which oversaw the international coalition's military operations in Iraq—I proposed something that had been forming in my mind since the first coalition leaflets were dropped over Mosul in January 2015. The leaflets asked civilians to provide information. But they did not address the deeper problem: When liberation came, how would the liberating forces distinguish between the population and the occupation? The people of Mosul had been living under ISIS for two years. They were forced to comply with the regime's rules—the beards, the shortened trousers, the prayers, the appearances. From the outside, from the vantage of a soldier entering the city, a civilian who had been forced to look like a supporter and a supporter who had chosen to look like a civilian were indistinguishable. If the forces coming to liberate Mosul treated the population as collaborators, liberation would become another form of violence against the people it was supposed to save.

The campaign I proposed used the hashtag #Messages2Mosul. The idea was to collect personal messages from Iraqis—from displaced Moslawis, from people across the country—and have the coalition distribute them as flyers over the city. Not military instructions. Personal messages. A mother telling her daughter she was waiting. A friend saying he had not forgotten. The messages would serve two purposes: They would tell the population inside that they had not been abandoned, and they would signal to the approaching military forces that the people inside the city were civilians, not enemies—that the city they were about to enter was a city of families, not a city of fighters. The people inside had been silent for two years. The silence had to be broken before the guns arrived, or the silence would be read as complicity.

Now that I write about those days, I do not think I ever really saw Paris. I lived there. I walked its streets. I took the Métro from my apartment to the library and back. I sat in cafés and ate bread and watched the Seine from bridges and went to Notre-Dame at night and sat by the river and thought about al-Hadba'. But Paris was never the city I was looking at. Paris was the city in which I looked at Mosul.

The screen was always open. The sources were always sending. The map was always running. I walked through the Jardin du Luxembourg and thought about the parks in Mosul that ISIS had turned into training grounds. I passed the bookshops along the Seine and thought about the libraries that had been burned. I walked through neighborhoods where people ate dinner on terraces at ten in the evening and I thought about the curfew in Mosul where no one was outside after dark. Every ordinary gesture in Paris was the negative image of an ordinary gesture in Mosul. An open window there was a risk. A cigarette was a crime. A woman walking alone was unthinkable. I had left the city but the city had not left my way of seeing, and in Paris I saw everything twice—once as it was, and once as it would have been in Mosul.

I passed a florist on the way to EHESS one morning and stopped without knowing why. The colors in the window were the colors of the Mosul I carried—the roses and jasmine of the gardens before the fall, the flowers my mother placed on windowsills, the bright thread that had run through the city's ordinary beauty before that beauty was forbidden. Then I kept walking.

Paris gave me shelter. I must say that clearly, because it is true and gratitude is not something I withhold when it is deserved. Paris gave me legal status and physical safety and access to a tradition of thought that stretched from Voltaire through the Revolution to the reading rooms of EHESS. But Paris did not give me itself. I was too full of Mosul to receive another city. The space inside me where a new place might have entered was already occupied—occupied by the sources and the screen and the archive and the obligation and the nightly walk to the river where I sat and asked God why and received no answer and returned to the apartment and opened the laptop and checked whether my mother's house was still standing.

I did not tell my classmates at EHESS who I was. I did not tell the professors. I did not tell the people I met in reading rooms or at conferences. I was an Iraqi doctoral student working on Ottoman Mosul. That was true. It was not the whole truth. The whole truth was on the hard drive in my apartment and on the screen that was always open and in the encrypted channels through which I communicated with sources inside a city that the people around me knew only as a name in the news.

By the autumn of 2016, the signs were unmistakable. Military forces were moving into position around Mosul. The international coalition—led by the United States and supported by Iraqi government troops, Kurdish Peshmerga fighters, and various militia forces—was preparing what would be the largest military campaign in Iraq since 2003. On the satellite, I could see what the news programs could not: the specific movements, the staging areas, the buildup along the approaches from the east and the south. Tens of thousands of troops were being assembled to retake a city that still held more than a million civilians.

In the cafés where I sat with my laptop, the news segments played on screens above the bar while people ate their lunch and checked their phones. They watched with the distant interest of people for whom the battle would be a news story. For me, the screen above the bar and the screen on my laptop were showing the same city from opposite distances—one from the remove of a news studio, the other from the intimacy of a man who knew the coordinates of his mother's kitchen.

My mother was inside. My brothers were inside. Ahmad was inside, in north of Mosul's Old City—a neighborhood in the western half of the city, deep in the old urban fabric, the kind of place where the streets were narrow and the houses shared walls and the density that had made the neighborhood intimate in peacetime would make it lethal in war. Ahmad called me on a Thursday evening. He wanted to know what Paris looked like. He asked about my studies, whether the library was good, whether I had found a café I liked—the questions of a man who was interested in the life his brother was building, as though that life existed separately from the work I could not tell him about. I told him the library was good. I told him the bread was better than I expected. I did not tell him that I could see the coordinates of his neighborhood on the screen in front of me while we spoke.

He said he was fine. He said the children were fine—all four of them, the eldest ten, the youngest barely two. He said the little one had learned a new word that week and kept repeating it at the dinner table until everyone laughed. He said he would visit me in Paris when this was over. He said it with the calm of a man who has decided that the future will arrive and that he will be in it, and I did not argue with him because arguing with Ahmad's calm was like arguing with the Tigris—it listened politely and continued in the direction it had chosen. He was not going to leave. He had decided that, and the decision was as fixed as the walls of the house he lived in.

After we hung up, I sat for a long time in front of the screen. The tunnels I had reported in April 2015 were now part of the defensive architecture ISIS had built beneath the old city. The child soldiers I had documented were now fighters. The weapons depots I had mapped were now targets. The people whose names filled the encrypted file were in the path of what was coming. The intelligence I had been providing—the target assessments, the facility locations, the source reports—was about to be tested against the reality of a battle that would last months and destroy the western half of the city I spent two years trying to preserve. Everything I had gathered, every coordinate I had verified, every source I had protected—all of it was about to matter in a way that was no longer abstract. The battle would use the intelligence or it would not, and the people inside the city would live or die partly as a consequence of what I had transmitted and how accurately I had transmitted it.

That was different from documentation. It was consequence.

I had been fighting this war for more than two years—first from inside the city, then from a room in Turkey, now from an apartment in Paris. Each distance changed the texture of the work without changing its nature. The documentation, the verification, the intelligence, the obligation—these traveled with me through every crossing. Now they were about to enter their most consequential phase. The battle was coming. My mother was inside. Ahmad was inside, in the narrow streets of Zanjili, with four children and a calm that no argument could move. The screen was open. And somewhere in the gap between Ahmad's certainty and my knowledge, the thing I could not say to him—that I could see the shape of what was coming and that I was afraid for him in a way I could not put into words—sat like a stone in my chest, silent and heavy and impossible to set down.

THE BATTLE

On October 17, 2016, 864 days after ISIS seized Mosul, the battle to retake the city began. I was in Paris. I had a satellite application open on my laptop, the map centered on the eastern approaches where the first movements were visible—vehicle columns on the roads south of the city, smoke rising over villages to the northeast, the pale signature of artillery fire drifting across otherwise still terrain. The sources inside the city were already reporting: shelling on the Gogjali road, checkpoints reinforced, ISIS fighters repositioning heavy weapons into residential buildings. The information came in fragments, the way it always came—a message here, a phone call there, each piece carrying the voice of someone risking death to speak to the outside.

I sat at the desk in the apartment and did what I had been doing for months through the CENTCOM channel—transmitting target coordinates, facility assessments, the locations of ISIS command posts I had been tracking through the source network and verifying against the satellite imagery. The intelligence I had gathered over two years was now entering the operation in real time. The coordinates I sent from a desk in the sixth arrondissement were shaping decisions made by commanders in the field outside Mosul. The scholar's archive had become an instrument of war.

More than a hundred thousand troops converged from every direction. The Iraqi army's conventional divisions pushed from the south, through the staging areas at Qayyarah airbase—an installation sixty kilometers below Mosul that had been recaptured months earlier to serve as the operation's southern anchor. From the east came the Golden Division,

Iraq's elite counterterrorism forces—the most capable fighting units the Iraqi military possessed, trained by American Special Forces, the only units most commanders trusted to fight house to house. They pushed through the towns of Bartella and Bazwaya, through open ground where the suburbs began and where the first buried explosives waited in the roads. Kurdish Peshmerga forces advanced on the northern and north-eastern flanks toward the town of Bashiqa. Federal police entered from the southeast. And from the west and southwest, closing toward the city of Tel Afar and the desert roads connecting Mosul to the ISIS capital of Raqqa in Syria, came the Hashd al-Shaabi—the Popular Mobilization Forces, a constellation of Shia paramilitary groups, many of them funded, trained, and in some cases directly commanded by Iran.

Above all of them, the coalition air force. American, British, French, Australian—aircraft from a sixty-nation coalition providing the air power that the Iraqi military lacked. The operation had been named Qadimun Ya Naynawa—We Are Coming, Nineveh. The senior coalition commander, Lieutenant General Stephen Townsend, would later call it the most significant urban combat since World War II. Historians would compare it to Stalingrad, to Grozny, to Huế. None of those cities were my city. None of them contained my family, my archive, the streets I had walked with Abraham and Adam and Samuel on nights when the river air still smelled of fish markets and old stone. This battle was not a comparison. It was the thing itself.

The first days changed the air inside the city before any forces entered it. ISIS set fire to oil-filled trenches dug around the perimeter—long ditches filled with crude petroleum and ignited to produce columns of black smoke dense enough to blind the coalition's drones and surveillance aircraft. I could see the smoke on the satellite imagery: dark stains spreading across terrain I had mapped inch by inch over two years. South of the city, at the Al-Mishraq sulfur plant—one of the largest sulfur deposits in the world—fires sent toxic fumes across entire districts, hospitalizing hundreds of people in camps and villages downwind. Inside Mosul the population could hear the shelling. Not yet aimed at the city itself but at the villages being taken around it. And the sound was the sound of something approaching that could not be stopped.

I refreshed the satellite application. The imagery updated every three to five days, and between updates I relied on the sources, the phone calls, the encrypted messages that arrived at no predictable hour. A source reported an air strike on a neighborhood I knew, and I checked coordinates against the last available image. A source went silent, and I sat at the desk staring at the screen, not knowing whether the silence meant the connection had dropped, or the network had been disrupted, or the person had been killed. The distinction between those possibilities was the distinction between inconvenience and death, and the screen could not tell me which one it was.

There was a particular quality to the helplessness of watching from a satellite. I could see the rooftops but not the rooms beneath them. I could see a road but not the family crossing it. I could see a building and then, on the next update, the building was gone—a gray smudge where a structure had stood—and I did not know whether the people who lived there had left before the strike or had still been inside when it came. The satellite gave me the geography of destruction. It did not give me the human cost. For that I needed the sources, and the sources were people I could not protect.

Inside the city, the battle arrived first as sound and then as absence. Shelling distant on the first day—a dull percussion from the east and south. Closer on the second. By the third, accompanied by the black columns from the oil trenches, the sky over the eastern outskirts darkening in the middle of the afternoon. Schools did not open. Shops that had operated through the entire occupation closed. The streets emptied in a way they had not emptied even during the worst days of ISIS rule—not the managed emptiness of curfew but the instinctive emptiness of a population that could hear the machinery of its own liberation approaching and did not know what form that liberation would take when it arrived.

The sources reported that ISIS had begun executing people suspected of communicating with the advancing forces—men found with mobile phones, men accused of signaling positions, men whose only crime was possessing the means to speak to the outside. Forty people were killed in the first week for this crime alone. Forty people killed for possessing the means to speak. The paranoia of the occupation's final months fused with the paranoia of the battle's first days, and the city was caught in a trap whose geometry was merciless: an enemy that killed its people for communicating, and an army that could not reach them without destroying the ground they stood on. I was on the other side of that trap, receiving what the people inside it risked their lives to send, transmitting it outward through channels that could produce air strikes on the very positions where the killers were stationed. The same information that could save the population could, if traced, destroy the person who sent it.

On October 15, two days before the offensive began, I sent an urgent message through the CENTCOM channel warning that the Mosul battle plan had been leaked to ISIS. The information came through sources inside the city who confirmed that ISIS commanders were discussing specific axes of advance, timing, force dispositions—details that should not have been available to them. I wrote the warning in Arabic, transmitting through the encrypted channel I had built from a Turkish apartment and maintained from a Parisian one. Whether the warning changed anything I do not know. What I know is that the information I was providing—the target assessments, the facility coordinates, the source reports verified against satellite imagery—was reaching the command structure of an operation that was about to enter the city where my mother was making tea in the kitchen, where my brother Ahmad was sitting in his house with his wife and four children, where everything I had documented and everything I loved were sealed inside the same perimeter the battle was about to breach.

There is a difference between a battle to liberate a city and a battle against ISIS. A battle to liberate a city takes the population into account—the lives to be protected, the infrastructure to be preserved, the fabric to be restored. It accepts slower advances, targeted strikes, corridors for evacuation. A battle against ISIS treats the city as terrain on which the enemy is destroyed, and the people inside it as acceptable cost.

More than a million people remained inside Mosul when the battle began. Old women who had not left their houses in two years. Children born inside the occupation who had never known a world without checkpoints and mandatory prayers. Men who survived by performing obedience, by wearing the expression I knew because I had worn it myself—the expression that gives nothing, reveals nothing, offers nothing to the watcher that might be used against the wearer. Shopkeepers who reopened under ISIS because the alternative was starvation. Teachers who taught the regime's curriculum because the alternative was execution. Families who stayed because leaving meant crossing front lines in every direction and arriving as refugees in countries that did not want them.

The American Secretary of Defense, James Mattis, described the strategy against ISIS as one of annihilation. The word was his. More than a million people were sealed inside the city when the annihilation began.

Mosul sits on both banks of the Tigris, the river that has sustained the city since before recorded history. The eastern half—wider streets, more modern construction, residential blocks and boulevards that could accommodate armored vehicles—was where the forces would enter first. The western half was the old city: centuries of shared-wall construction, alleys too narrow for two people to walk abreast, a fabric so dense that a mortar round striking one house would bring down the houses on both sides. Every great mosque and church and market, and the leaning minaret of al-Hadba' that had stood for eight hundred years, visible from every part of the city—all on the western bank. ISIS spent two years turning the west into a fortress: tunnels between houses, car bombs positioned at intersections, snipers placed on minarets, the civilian population held inside as human shields. The full weight of what that meant belongs to the next chapter. What matters here is the eastern campaign—three months that would liberate half the city and seal the other half for what came after.

The Golden Division entered the city proper on November 1, pushing through Gogjali—the eastern gate of Mosul—under sniper fire, car bombs driven at speed from side streets, and mortar rounds that fell without warning. ISIS had prepared Gogjali as a killing ground: improvised explosive devices buried in the roads, suicide vehicles hidden in alleys, fighters in fortified positions who fired and withdrew through tunnels while the advance moved into terrain that appeared cleared and was not. The fighting for a single neighborhood lasted days. Fighters emerged from tunnels behind units that had already passed. The pattern would repeat across the entire three-month campaign: advance, clear, believe the ground was held, discover it was not.

From Gogjali the forces pushed into al-Zahra, al-Bakr, Kirkukli—clearing block by block, searching houses, detonating booby traps left in doorways and under floorboards. The Ninth Armored Division entered from the southeast through al-Intisar. Federal police from the south. The Sixteenth Division from the north. Each axis of advance contained civilians—families trying to flee through corridors the military kept open and ISIS kept mining, families unable to flee because they were elderly or injured or had children too young to run or simply did not know which direction was safe, because no direction was safe.

The advance slowed through November and December. Rain turned the unpaved roads on the outskirts to mud that immobilized vehicles. ISIS counterattacks came not as large offensives but as persistent, exhausting strikes: a suicide vehicle driven into a column at dawn, a tunnel opening behind a cleared position at night, snipers holding buildings for days because the rules of engagement made it difficult to call in an air strike on a structure that might contain civilians. The advance that had covered kilometers in the first weeks now measured its progress in city blocks. By mid-December the counterterrorism forces had captured roughly forty of the fifty-six eastern districts, but each one required days of clearing, and the fighters driven from one district reappeared through the tunnels beneath the next. The battle for east Mosul was supposed to take weeks. It took three months.

Tens of thousands fled in those first weeks, streaming eastward carrying blankets, documents, children. The displacement camps outside the city were overwhelmed within days. By November more than forty thousand had reached the Kurdistan Region of Iraq. By January, the displaced exceeded a million. The people who did not make it out stayed in their houses and waited, and the battle came to them as shelling that shook the walls and the uncertainty of not knowing whether the next explosion would strike the building next door or theirs.

I tracked it on the screen the way I had tracked the occupation—neighborhood by neighborhood, incident by incident, the same method applied to a different catastrophe. Neighborhoods I had known as places where families lived, where children walked to school, where tea sellers opened before dawn, became place names in a military progression. Al-Tahrir. Cleared. Al-Karama. Heavy resistance. Al-Bakr. Booby-trapped. Al-Salam. Counterattack repelled. The city I carried in my mind as a living place was being converted, district by district, into a sequence of tactical objectives, and each conversion meant shelling, and each shelling meant families in basements hearing the world above them come apart.

The intelligence continued flowing in both directions. Sources reported ISIS positions I wasn't able to confirm from the satellite. I cross-referenced and transmitted. Air strikes followed some of those transmissions. I knew this because the satellite updates showed the results—a building I had identified as a command post, now a collapsed heap of concrete; a compound I had flagged as a weapons depot, now a crater with scorch marks radiating outward across the surrounding streets. The information I spent two years gathering inside the city was producing consequences I could see from the screen in Paris. Some of those consequences were military necessities. Some of them destroyed the neighborhoods I had walked through, the streets where I had bought bread, the blocks where people I knew still lived. The distinction between the two was the distinction I had been living inside since the first coalition air strike struck a car-bomb factory near my uncle's house two years earlier. It did not resolve itself. It simply continued: each coordinate carrying the weight of both its purposes—the military objective and the human geography beneath it.

My mother called when she could. Short calls, the connection dropping when cell towers were hit or overloaded. She told me the shelling had been bad the night before. She told me they were staying. I told her to leave. She said they were fine. She raised her voice over what sounded like a wall collapsing somewhere nearby—not in the house, somewhere on the street, the dull implosion of masonry giving way. The call dropped. I called back. No answer. I sat at the desk staring at the satellite image of her neighborhood, the rooftops intact, the resolution too low to show whether a wall on a particular street had fallen. I could not see whether she was alive. She called back the next day, her voice the same, as though nothing had happened. They were staying.

Ahmad called in the evenings, when the shelling was quieter and the connection sometimes held for five or six minutes before dropping. His voice carried the calm that the occupation had built into him—the quiet patience of a man who had survived two and a half years under ISIS by holding steady, by managing the household, by keeping the family together in a city designed to pull families apart. He was not going to abandon that steadiness now. Not even with artillery falling on the neighborhoods around him.

One call I remember completely. It was late November, after the eastern offensive had been underway for five weeks. The connection was poor—a faint hiss underneath his voice, the kind of distortion that meant the signal was bouncing through damaged infrastructure. I could hear something in the background, a child's voice, one of the younger ones, and then the sound stopped, as though someone had closed a door. Ahmad told me about the children. The eldest, who was ten, had learned to identify the difference between outgoing and incoming rounds—a distinction no child should possess, but one that in Zanjili became a survival skill. The youngest had just started walking. The middle ones figured out which rooms in the house were safest when the shelling came—interior rooms, away from exterior walls, the lesson taught by the physics of fragmentation that every family in a war zone learns, and no family should have to.

He asked about my studies. He asked if I was eating. He said it the way he always said it—not as an afterthought but as a genuine concern, as though my eating habits in Paris were a problem of equivalent weight to the artillery falling on his district. He told me he wanted to visit when this was over. He said it simply, the way a man says something he intends to do, not the way a man says something he hopes for. He had plans. He would see Paris. He would sit with me somewhere in the city, in person, instead of through a phone that dropped every time a tower was hit. He wanted to know what it looked like. He wanted to know what my life was like on the other side of the screen. I described the river, the bridges, the cold. He said he did not mind cold. He said cold was better than what they had. Then the connection cut. I called back. The phone rang without answer. I called again twenty minutes later. He picked up. The shelling had started again, he said. He had moved the children to the interior room. He was fine. Everyone was fine.

I told him to leave. I told him what I could see on the satellite—the forces closing from the south and southwest, the pattern of the advance, the neighborhoods that would be next. I told him that his area was going to become a battle zone. He listened. He did not argue. He said they were fine. He said the house would hold. Then he asked me again about Paris, and I understood that arguing with Ahmad's calm was not going to change the outcome—that the man who had oriented our family through every crisis since our father's long absences, the man who had been more father to me than brother, who had taught me to ride a bicycle by refusing to accept that I could not, who ran a curtain-making shop and raised four children and held everything together with a patience I could not match—that this man had decided to stay, and the decision was as fixed as the walls of the house he was sitting in.

Of Adam and Samuel, I knew less. The war severed the threads of ordinary communication. Adam left Mosul before the battle began—I heard this through a mutual contact, though I did not know where he had gone or whether he was safe. Samuel, I had not heard from in months. The silence could mean anything. In the Mosul of that period, silence was the most common sound, and it carried every possible meaning at once. I have not heard from Samuel since the battle ended. I do not know if he survived.

In the middle of all of this—the satellite, the sources, the shelling reports, Ahmad's calm, the silence where Samuel used to be—a message arrived from a CNN correspondent named Moni Basu. She told me that Itzhak Perlman wanted to speak with me.

I read the message twice. Itzhak Perlman. The violinist whose music I had listened to for twenty-four hours straight on the day Mosul fell, weeping in a room that was about to become a prison. The man whose recordings I played in dimmed light in the house while ISIS controlled the streets outside, the volume low enough that no one beyond the walls could hear, because music was punishable by flogging and the punishment was not theoretical—I had watched it administered. This news, I wrote back, is one of the most thrilling I have ever received in my life.

I remembered a night in mid-2015. I had made myself tea and was sitting in the dark, getting ready to write a detailed report about what was happening in the city—the kind of report that required me to hold in my mind, simultaneously, the names and the dates and the locations and the charges, to verify each one before publishing, to be the machine the work demanded. And in very dimmed light I started to play his music. Stravinsky first, then Brahms. The sound filled the room the way water fills a container—completely, without gaps, pressing against the walls. On the other side of those walls, ISIS members were planning operations. I knew this because I had documented who lived in the surrounding houses, who came and went, what the patterns of movement meant. On one side of the wall, they were plotting to kill. On the other side I was hiding, listening to Perlman, and planning for life—how to maintain it, how to preserve the record of it, how to save the people who were living it. A single fine wall was all that covered me from their eyes.

I remembered the CDs. During the most dangerous months of the occupation, my closest friend and I had exchanged discs filled with music—smuggled, copied, passed between us at the kind of risk that would sound absurd in any city where music was not a crime. Once, in the middle of that exchange, during one of the most critical moments, I asked him: Does it include Perlman's music? He looked at me and said: If he's not here, then it's not worth the risk. We both laughed. We both meant it.

On November 29, 2016, six weeks into the battle, I sat down and wrote Perlman a letter. The battle was on the satellite screen behind me. I wrote it by hand, on lined paper, in English, because I wanted the words to carry the weight of a hand that had spent two years writing reports about the dead and was now writing to the man whose music had kept the writer alive. I told him about the city—that it had once been the home of a wonderful composer, Othman Al-Mosulli, that the eternal river Tigris was flowing through it since the dawn of civilization. I told him we were resisting with love and music. I told him about the wall—the Stravinsky, the Brahms, the men on the other side. I told him about the promise I had made to myself and would never break: to build an opera house in Mosul, even if it cost me my life, and to invite the most famous musicians to play there. I told him I dreamed of the day he would play at that opera house—the house of music I promised to build myself. I told him that people would read, one day, that Mosul spoke to Itzhak Perlman, and that this great violinist helped this city triumph over terrorism and war, and was capable of spreading love and music to the world.

I signed the letter the only way I could. Not with my name—I was still anonymous, still the hidden man behind the account the world was reading. I signed it: *The Founder of Mosul Eye. Mosul, November 29th, 2016.*

The screen was still on when I finished. The battle had not paused for the letter. The sources had sent messages while I was writing. The map showed smoke over the eastern districts. I closed the letter, folded the pages, and turned back to the coordinates.

Five bridges connected the two halves of Mosul across the Tigris—the crossings that stitched the city into one place, the routes connecting markets to neighborhoods, the university to the residential districts, the modern eastern bank to the ancient western one. I had crossed those bridges hundreds of times. Alshuhada Bridge—the Martyrs' Bridge—where Adam and Samuel and Abraham and I had walked on late nights before the fall, when the river air was cool and the city was still a place where four friends could wander after midnight, talking about nothing that mattered, the water below catching light from the old city's lamps. The Fourth Bridge, which carried the commercial traffic between the business districts. The Old Bridge, the one the boat makers could see from the fish market, where the current ran strong and the smell of grilled *masgouf* drifted across the water on summer evenings.

The coalition struck four of the five bridges during the eastern campaign, targeting the spans to prevent ISIS from reinforcing the east with fighters from the western bank. Each strike disabled a crossing. Each strike also severed the city. Families on one bank who had relatives on the other could no longer reach them. A mother on the east side with a son on the west could not cross. A merchant whose shop was on one bank and whose home was on the other had no way between them. ISIS destroyed the fifth bridge themselves to prevent the military from using it as a crossing point. By late January, all five were gone. Mosul without its bridges was not one city but two halves separated by a river that had sustained it for thousands of years, and that now functioned as one.

And then the Shia militias completed the seal from the other side.

The Hashd al-Shaabi—tens of thousands of paramilitary fighters organized under an Iraqi government umbrella but answering to commanders in Tehran—had been advancing toward Tel Afar, a city sixty kilometers west of Mosul on the road to Syria. By late November, they had cut the highway. By late January, they had encircled the western approach entirely. Their stated mission was to prevent ISIS from fleeing westward toward Raqqa, the group's Syrian capital. In practice, their positioning closed the only corridor through which the enemy might have been permitted to withdraw—and through which civilians might have escaped.

The coalition had discussed opening that corridor. The logic was straightforward and, to anyone who understood what the western old city contained, overwhelming: If ISIS fighters could retreat, the battle for the west would be fought with fewer combatants among fewer civilians. Fewer fighters meant less house-to-house combat, fewer booby traps, fewer families caught in streets too narrow to escape. Let the enemy leave, and the city might survive its own retaking. I had argued for this through every channel I had access to—through the United States Central Command, through journalists, through anyone who would listen. The population was the city. The city could not be saved if its people were sealed inside it by an enemy intent on using them as shields.

The militias rejected that logic. Whether by strategic calculation, sectarian intent, Iranian direction, or the fury of a war in which the Shia paramilitaries had lost thousands of their own fighters to ISIS, the corridor was shut. ISIS could not leave. The civilians could not leave. The western half of Mosul—its hundreds of thousands of inhabitants, its old city, its mosques and minarets and shared-wall houses and the leaning minaret of al-Hadba'—was sealed from every direction. The river to the east, with every bridge destroyed. The military from the south and the north. The militias to the west. There was no way in and no way out.

I looked at the satellite imagery of the western bank and understood what that seal meant. I had documented the tunnels ISIS had built beneath the old city. I had tracked their headquarters in residential buildings. I knew the streets—their width, their turns, their dead ends, the places where a mortar round would bring down not only the building it struck but the buildings on either side, because the walls were shared and centuries of construction made the old city into a single interconnected fabric that could not be struck in one place without the damage spreading to every place around it.

The east had been a battle—brutal and costly, but recognizable as urban warfare with front lines and advances and retreats. The west would be something else. A siege within a city. A grinding destruction of a civilian population sealed between an army that could not stop, a regime that would not surrender, a river that could not be crossed, and a corridor that had been shut.

By late January, the eastern half was declared liberated. The last pockets of ISIS resistance were cleared from the remaining districts in a final push that took ten days of house-to-house fighting. The university campus was recaptured—the campus where I had defended my M.A. thesis, where

ISIS had turned the laboratories into weapons workshops and the grounds into training fields where cows grazed on what had been lawns. My family drove through the eastern districts in those first days after the declaration. The city looked dead. Quiet. Buildings with their facades blown off, their interiors exposed to the street like open wounds—a kitchen, a bedroom, a child's room with the wall missing, everything visible from the road. Cars burned on roadsides; their frames twisted into shapes that no longer resembled vehicles. The silence of a place that had been fought through and had not yet understood what it had become.

In the liberated eastern districts, a man named Musab Walid—working under the Mosul Eye name—began conducting relief campaigns, distributing food and water and basic supplies to families emerging from basements into neighborhoods they barely recognized. The documentation network I had built for intelligence was transforming into a network for aid. The transition was not planned. It was demanded by the reality walking out of those basements: Families needed food, water, blankets, and information about where to go, and the channels I had maintained for two years were the channels that could reach them fastest.

On March 7, I wrote on Twitter: It is 1,006 days since ISIS occupied my city. I had been counting since the first letters to the German orientalist, since the signature from Mosul the Captive. The east was free. The west was sealed. The counting did not stop.

In the weeks after the east was liberated, while the west Mosul offensive was closing around the old city, I did something I had promised myself I would do.

Mosul has always lived with a story about itself. The story of Jonah—the prophet who came to Nineveh calling on its people to accept his message, and who almost left before they answered. The people accepted, just in time, and the city was granted divine protection. That is the story parents told their children in every generation. That is the story grandparents pointed to when they passed the shrine on the hill. In times of war, in times of economic collapse, in times when the future of the city seemed impossible, the people of Mosul said the same thing: No need to worry, this is the city of Jonah; we will survive, and this shall pass too. The shrine of Prophet Younis—sacred to Muslims, Christians, and Jews alike, built on the hill above the ruins of the palace of Sennacherib, the Assyrian king—was the place where the story lived. It was the city's proof that the divine protection held.

When ISIS destroyed it in July 2014—dynamited the shrine, collapsed the structure, reduced the hill to rubble—they did not only destroy a building. They destroyed the anchor of the city's confidence. If they could destroy the divinely protected place, then nothing was beyond them. That is what the people understood the day the shrine fell. It was the moment Mosul knew that what had taken it was intent on uprooting everything—not only the present, but the story the city had been telling itself for centuries in order to endure.

What ISIS had not known, or had not cared about, was that beneath the shrine lay the palace of Sennacherib—an Assyrian king who built Nineveh twenty-seven centuries before the men who destroyed it arrived. Their excavation after the demolition uncovered the palace. The destruction revealed what it tried to erase.

I wanted music to play on those ruins. Not as performance. As restoration of the story, of the protection, of the principle that the city had survived everything before and would survive this. A musician from Mosul named Ameen Mokdad—a violinist who had kept composing in secret through the entire occupation, who lost his instruments when ISIS raided his home, who escaped to Baghdad carrying nothing but the music he had written in hiding—agreed to return. I arranged it from Paris. He played on the ruins of the shrine on April 19, 2017, while across the river the shelling of the western city continued. The sound of a violin rose from the place where the divine protection had been destroyed, above the stones of the Assyrian palace, and for the first time in nearly three years Mosul heard music in the open air.

About twenty people stood among the rubble and listened. It was not a large crowd. It did not need to be. What mattered was that the site was no longer silent—that the place where the city's oldest story had been anchored was carrying sound again. A woman who had been forced to abandon her studies said afterward: The performance was like a dream.

Ameen and I finally met in person nine years later, at the Owl Shop, my favorite bar in New Haven, Connecticut. The man who played the violin on the ruins and the man who put him there had never been in the same room until then.

Ahmad was in the north of Mosul's Old City. Western half. The neighborhood that sat directly on the line between ISIS positions and the approaching Iraqi forces—the neighborhood that military planners were already identifying as the center of the coming battle for the west. My brother, inside the seal, with his wife and their four children. The eldest was ten. The youngest was two. I had told him to leave. I told him what I could see, what the pattern of the operation meant, what was coming for his street. He did not listen. He said the house would hold.

The west Mosul offensive was set for February 19, 2017. What was coming would be unlike anything the city had endured in its thousands of years of continuous habitation. Not the Mongol sack of the thirteenth century. Not the Ottoman conquests. Not the British mandate. Not even the fall to ISIS. What was coming was the destruction of Mosul by the forces that had come to save it. The old city—the city of shared walls and narrow alleys and the leaning minaret and the churches beside the mosques and the shrines beside the markets—was about to be fed into the machinery of liberation, and the machinery did not distinguish between the enemy and the place the enemy had chosen to die inside.

The time had come to end ISIS. The price of ending it was Mosul.

THE BATTLE FOR THE SPIRIT OF MOSUL

For more than two weeks after my brother was killed, I did not say a word.

I had spent three years speaking—documenting, recording, publishing, sending coordinates, giving Mosul its voice when the city had been silenced. I had spoken through the occupation and the exile and the eastern campaign and the west Mosul offensive. I had spoken when speaking could have killed me and I had not stopped. After Ahmad died, the voice stopped. For more than two weeks I was as silent as Mosul had been before I began.

But before I can explain the silence, I must explain what was destroyed. Not only Ahmad. The city itself.

The western Mosul offensive began on February 19, 2017. The first satellite update after the advance started showed smoke over the southwestern neighborhoods—a different density of smoke from the eastern campaign, darker, wider, rising from positions deeper inside the residential fabric. By the second update the smoke had spread across the southern approaches. By the third, I could see it: the first blocks of the old city were beginning to change shape on the imagery. Rooftop lines I had been tracking for months—broken, collapsed, replaced by the gray uniformity of rubble. In the east the streets were wide enough for the military to function as a military. In the west the streets closed around the advancing forces the way a fist closes around something it intends to crush.

Iraqi counterterrorism forces and federal police advanced from the south and southwest, pushing through the outer western neighborhoods—the airport district first, then al-Mamoun, al-Tayaran, Wadi Hajr—before colliding with the ring of ISIS defenses around the old city. The Ninth Armored Division swung from the southeast. The advance was methodical and brutal: a block at a time, a building at a time, each block containing booby traps and each building potentially containing snipers and each advance requiring air strikes or artillery to dislodge an enemy that fired from one position and disappeared through tunnels to reappear behind the force that had just passed. The soldiers moved through streets where their armored vehicles could not fit, where they pressed against the walls on foot, exposed to fire from every direction in a three-dimensional environment that the defenders knew intimately, and the attackers were learning one fatal step at a time.

By late February, the forces had captured the airport and were pressing into the southwestern districts. By early March, they cut all roads into western Mosul, trapping the remaining ISIS fighters inside the old city and the neighborhoods immediately around it. By mid-March, the advance reached the government buildings—the provincial headquarters, the train station, the museum—landmarks that I had passed a thousand times in the years before the fall. But the advance into the old city itself, the historical core, the dense residential heart of west Mosul—that advance was something different. That advance was the one that would break the city.

I must explain what was being destroyed. Not the idea of a city. Not a name on a map. Not an abstraction called the old quarter. What was being destroyed was a place I had walked through so often that my feet knew the turns before my mind did, a place where the act of moving through space was also the act of moving through time, because every step took you past something that had been built by someone who had been dead for centuries and that was still in use by someone who was alive that morning.

Old Mosul sat on the western bank of the Tigris. Its neighborhoods had been built over centuries in a pattern that no planner had designed—families adding rooms to houses already connected to the houses beside them, houses growing upward and inward as new generations occupied the same footprint, the city accumulating density the way a language accumulates vocabulary, word by word, generation by generation, until the result was a fabric of construction so intimate that one building and the next shared not only a wall but a structural logic. You could enter through one family's door and walk through three connected houses before reaching the street again. The alleys turned and narrowed and turned again, passing beneath arched overhangs where upper floors bridged the gap between buildings on opposite sides, creating covered passages where the light came through in slants and the air carried the combined smells of the houses above—cooking, coffee, soap, the sweet tobacco of the water pipes that men smoked in the evening.

The souks—the covered markets—ran through the center of the old city like arteries. They were not shopping districts in the modern sense. They were civic organisms—corridors of commerce and conversation where the copper workers hammered their trays in one section, and the spice merchants weighed their saffron in the next, and the textile sellers displayed fabrics that had come through Mosul from as far as India and Iran, and the barbers cut hair and exchanged gossip, and the tea sellers poured from brass pots that had been used by their fathers and their fathers' fathers. The souks were not ancient in the way a museum is ancient. They were ancient in the way a living body is ancient—still functioning, still inhabited, still warm.

Around the souks clustered the *khans*—the old commercial courtyards where caravans had once rested and where traders still stored goods and conducted business in rooms built during the Ottoman period, the centuries when Mosul was a provincial capital of the empire that governed it from Istanbul. Sufi shrines occupied corners that had been sacred for generations, their small domed chambers holding the memory of saints whose names the neighborhood children knew the way they knew the names of their own grandparents. Churches shared walls with mosques—not as a political statement about coexistence but as a physical fact of proximity, the natural result of centuries of building in a space where everyone lived close, and the sound of the church bell and the call to prayer occupied the same air. The Shrine of Prophet Younis—the Prophet Jonah, sacred to Muslims, Christians, and Jews alike—had stood on its hill overlooking the city since antiquity, a place where, during Eid, the children played in the park outside while their families prayed inside. ISIS destroyed it in July 2014, one of their first acts of cultural obliteration. But the memory of it remained in the old city the way the memory of an amputated limb remains in the body—you could still feel it, even after it was gone.

The smell of cardamom from the coffeehouses mixed with the smell of baking bread from the houses above and the faint mineral dampness that rose from the stone walls in the early morning before the sun reached the narrowest alleys. Everything was closed. Everything touched. The old city had been built by people who lived in proximity as a condition of life—families layered over families, generations layered over generations, the city growing upward and inward because there was nowhere else to grow. It was not a planned city. It was not an efficient city. It was not a city that made sense on a grid or a satellite image. It was a city that made sense only if you walked through it, if you knew which alley led to which courtyard and which courtyard led to which street and which street brought you out next to the mosque where your grandfather had prayed and where the minaret of al-Hadba' leaned over the skyline the way it had leaned for eight hundred years.

This was not a city built for war. It was a city built for life—for the slow accumulation of memory, for the intimate adjacency of families who had known each other for generations, for the daily passage of human beings through spaces designed to be walked through at the speed of a person carrying bread home from the baker or a child running to school through an alley too narrow for anything but a child's body. A military force entering the old city was entering a space that would resist it not through fortification but through its own organic density, and the only way through that density was to destroy it.

The shared-wall construction that had made the old city intimate now made it catastrophic. A mortar round that struck one house brought down the house and the houses on both sides, because the walls between them were the same wall—one continuous structure supporting the weight of everything on either side. An air strike that targeted a building where ISIS had placed a sniper collapsed that building and the buildings adjacent, and the rubble buried whoever was inside all of them—fighters and families alike, indistinguishable under the stone. The precision that the coalition claimed was a physical impossibility in a quarter where the distance between one building and the next was the thickness of a shared wall. You could not strike one and spare the other. The architecture built for intimacy now guaranteed that violence traveled the same way warmth had traveled—through the walls, from house to house, family to family.

ISIS spent two years turning this architecture into a weapon. The tunnels I had reported on in April 2015, expanded into networks connecting entire neighborhoods—underground passages that allowed fighters to appear behind advancing troops, fire from one building, vanish into the earth, and reappear a hundred meters away in a position the attackers had already cleared. They mined doorways, stairwells, windows, entire buildings. They placed snipers on mosque minarets that the coalition would hesitate to strike because destroying a mosque produces images that serve the propaganda of the side being struck. They parked car bombs at intersections, wired motorcycles with explosives, positioned suicide bombers in civilian clothing at the points of maximum exposure. They moved headquarters into residential buildings, weapons into schools, command posts into hospitals. They told the civilian population that anyone who tried to flee would be shot—in the street, in the home, in front of the family. The civilians believed them. They had watched the executions for two years and they knew the men who gave the orders meant what they said.

The civilian population was sealed inside it. Hundreds of thousands of people trapped by the river on one side and the militia cordon on the other and the battle itself closing around them. Iranian-backed militias blocked the western borders of the city—the corridor that the coalition and the Iraqi security forces had planned to leave open so that ISIS fighters could flee rather than fight to the death among the population. The militias closed that corridor, and the consequence was that the battle could end only one way: in total destruction, with the population still inside. Some families tried to flee, and ISIS shot them at checkpoints inside the neighborhoods, in the streets, in the houses of those caught gathering supplies for the journey. Others ran toward the Iraqi lines and were caught in cross fire—running through streets where the forces on one side were advancing and the forces on the other were firing and the families in between had no cover and no direction that was safe. Others made it through to the displacement camps that by now held more than a million people from across Nineveh province. But many could not leave—the elderly who could not walk fast enough, the injured who could not walk at all, the families with infants who could not be silenced, the people who did not know which direction led to safety because the front line moved every day and the map of the city was being rewritten in real time by the pattern of destruction.

I tracked it on the satellite through March and April and May. Each update showed less of the city I had known. Streets I could identify in one image were featureless gray rubble in the next. Blocks that had contained dozens of houses became flat expanses of broken stone. Image by image, update by update, the old city was being subtracted from the map. I would open the application in the morning and look for a street I had walked and find that the street was no longer there—not damaged, not partially collapsed, but erased. The route from the university to the market. The alley where the barber had his shop. The corner where the tea seller kept his brass pot on a stand outside the door. Gone. Not as metaphor. As fact. The satellite confirmed it with the indifference of a machine that does not know what it is showing—that cannot distinguish between a house and the rubble that was once a house, that records the surface of the earth without understanding that what has changed between one image and the next is not only a rooftop but a family, a history, a claim on continuity that took centuries to build and seconds to destroy.

In April, the battle entered its attritional phase. Rain turned the rubble to mud. The advance measured progress in meters, not blocks. ISIS launched counterattacks nightly—suicide vehicles at dawn, tunnels opened behind cleared positions after dark, snipers who held buildings for days. The forces found themselves in a grinding stalemate in the neighborhoods surrounding the old city, unable to push through defenses ISIS had spent two years building. April was the month when the battle stopped looking like a battle and started looking like a demolition.

After the liberation, reading the final Mosul dispatches in *Al-Naba*—the weekly newspaper ISIS had published throughout the occupation—I encountered the battle described from the other side. Not as testimony deserving sympathy. As evidence.

They described the American B-52 craters that had turned entire streets of the Old City into impassable terrain. They described the coalition strategy of bombing approach routes to prevent suicide car bombs from reaching Iraqi positions—and they noted, with operational clarity, that the strategy destroyed the city faster than the forces could advance through it. They were not grieving the destruction. They were assessing it tactically. The city they had occupied for three years, whose heritage they had systematically erased, whose population they had terrorized and taxed and executed—that city's physical annihilation registered in their accounts only as terrain.

They wrote about their medical personnel—doctors who had served in the Diwan al-Siha, the health administration—abandoning their clinics in the final weeks to die as suicide attackers. The head of the health diwan killed himself in a solo assault against Iraqi forces in the Shifa neighborhood. His wife died the same day under mortar fire in the Old City. Three senior medical officials dead within two days, all by choice. *Al-Naba* reported this with pride. I read it as the final corruption of a profession—men trained to preserve life choosing to end it, and to end the lives of the soldiers who were coming to liberate the city these men had helped destroy.

An elderly fighter was quoted saying a single sentence: "Our religion deserves it."

No. Mosul deserved better than what they did to it. The religion they claimed does not belong to them. And the city they reduced to rubble while reciting scripture was not theirs to destroy. That old man died in the ruins of a civilization he had spent three years dismantling, and the newspaper that printed his words presented his death as martyrdom. It was not martyrdom. It was the last act of an occupation that had consumed everything it touched—the city, its people, its history, and finally its own fighters, who were sent to die in the wreckage they had created.

Their testimonies are useful to this book for one reason only: They confirm, from the enemy's own records, the scale of what was done to Mosul. They confirm the B-52 craters I tracked on the satellite. They confirm the tunnel networks I had reported. They confirm the weaponization of the medical infrastructure I had documented. They do not deserve to be read as the words of men who fought bravely for a cause. They deserve to be read as the final entries in the ledger of a criminal enterprise that destroyed one of the oldest cities in the world and called the destruction holy.

By May, the advance had slowed to a crawl. The streets were too narrow for vehicles. Soldiers moved on foot through rubble-choked alleys, clearing one building at a time. ISIS held less than five square kilometers. But those five square kilometers contained the densest, oldest, most historically layered part of Mosul, and tens of thousands of civilians were still inside them.

On June 18, the Iraqi forces launched the final assault to retake the old city. The United Nations estimated that more than a hundred thousand civilians remained trapped as human shields. The advance moved from block to block through streets that were no longer streets but corridors of rubble. The soldiers advanced through holes blasted in shared walls because the alleys were impassable—filled with debris, blocked by collapsed buildings, seeded with explosives. They moved from house to house, passing through living rooms and kitchens and bedrooms in houses no longer inhabited by families but by fighters or by the dead or by the dust of collapsed ceilings. The fighting in June and early July was the most intense of the entire nine-month campaign. The old city was being pounded into a consistency that the satellite could not distinguish from the rubble around it.

On March 17, in the neighborhood of Mosul Jadida—a modern residential district on the western side, its name meaning simply "New

Mosul"—a single American air strike struck a building where families had gathered for shelter. The building had been identified as an ISIS position. Two snipers were firing from its upper floor. A five-hundred-pound precision-guided bomb was dropped on the structure. The bomb detonated a cache of explosives that ISIS had placed inside the building, and the secondary explosion brought the entire structure down on the families sheltering on the lower floors.

More than a hundred people were confirmed dead by the Pentagon's own investigation. Local civil defense officials counted far more—some estimates reached two hundred, others higher. The Iraqi Civil Defense Department cited 531 bodies recovered from the broader al-Jadida neighborhood in the days following the strike and the fighting around it. The people inside the building had been invited there by a neighbor who told them it was safer than their homes. They crowded together the way people crowd together under bombardment—seeking proximity, seeking walls, seeking the illusion of collective safety that comes from being near other human beings in a situation where no safety exists. The families had not been identified by the coalition. The snipers had. The bomb was precise. The building collapsed on everyone inside, indiscriminately.

My two cousins were killed with their wives and children—seven people—in an air strike on their house. There is nobody left of them. All of them. Children, wives, the mother, my cousins. Our neighbor, whose house held five families—roughly thirty to thirty-five people—was struck. All of them died. I can name more. I can name more and more. The names are in the record. The coordinates are on the map. What the record cannot contain is what those coordinates meant when they were not coordinates but addresses—places where people answered when you knocked, where tea was offered before questions were asked, where the door was open because in old Mosul the door was almost always open. Now the coordinates mark rubble. The door is rubble. The people who opened it are beneath it.

The numbers kept changing—first dozen, then a hundred, then two hundred, then the Iraqi Civil Defense counted over five hundred bodies from the broader neighborhood. The Americans investigated and confirmed 105 dead from their strike alone. The bomb had been a single five-hundred-pound GPS-guided munition, aimed at two snipers. Two snipers. A hundred and five confirmed dead. And those were the confirmed. The bodies that were never pulled from the rubble were never counted. The families that disintegrated entirely—no survivor to report them missing, no name to add to the list because the people who knew their names were dead beneath the same concrete—those families became gaps in the record rather than entries in it. The precision of the bomb and the imprecision of the death. The two snipers eliminated and the families beneath them eliminated and the word precision used to describe the operation as though precision and 105 dead civilians could exist in the same sentence without one canceling the other.

After Mosul Jadida, I understood that the battle was not a battle in which civilians were unfortunately dying. The civilians were dying because the battle had been designed to accept their deaths. The accelerated pace of the air campaign, the hundreds of munitions unleashed over the closing weeks of March alone—these were not accidents. They were policy. The policy was annihilation, and the annihilation included the population that the battle was supposed to liberate. I had known this analytically. After Mosul Jadida I knew it in my body.

The morgue list I later obtained from the city itself recorded more than fifty thousand names.

Fifty thousand people killed in the battle for Mosul. Not ISIS fighters—those numbers are separate. Civilians. Counted not by an international organization estimating from a distance, not by a monitoring group extrapolating from samples, but by the hands that received the dead and wrote the names in the city's own registry. This figure must be understood for what it is: a document I obtained after the battle from Mosul's own records, compiled by the people who processed the dead. It is not a projection. It is a count. Each name was a person who was alive when the battle began and dead when it ended, and most of them died inside the buildings where they had been living, in the neighborhoods where they had been surviving, in the city they had not been able to leave because the bridges were destroyed and the militias had sealed the western corridor and the battle itself turned the city into a cage from which there was no exit that did not cross a front line.

The Iraqi security forces would later call it the cleanest battle they had ever conducted. The Americans would be proud of the precision of their targeting. The record I kept had a different number.

What happened to Mosul was a punishment. I say this not as rhetoric but as the considered judgment of a man who documented every phase of the occupation and every phase of the battle. It was a punishment the way Berlin was punished—the Nazi regime destroyed, yet the bombing did not stop, because the destruction of the city was not incidental to the victory. It was part of the victory. It was the message. A collective punishment. An example made of a city so that no other city in Iraq would allow itself to become the capital of such an organization. You want ISIS, this is what you get. This is the fate of any city that permits it. In the years afterward, whenever Iraqis in other cities protested for clean water or basic services—in Basra, where people asked for drinking water because the taps ran dry—the answer from the government and the media was the same: Keep your head down. Do you want your city to be like Mosul? They made us an example. They made the destruction of Mosul the argument against protest, against rights, against the expectation that a government should serve its people. The punishment did not end when the battle ended. It was designed to last.

The news came daily. Sources reported neighborhoods I had walked being fought through, buildings I had mapped being struck, streets I had documented becoming front lines. Each day the satellite showed more of the city gone, and I sat in the apartment in Paris and received it the way a body receives blows—one after another, each one landing on the same bruise.

But I was not only receiving. Through the CENTCOM channel—the direct line I had established with the United States Central Command, the military headquarters coordinating the coalition campaign—the intelligence I had been building for three years was being used in real time. Target assessments I had provided identified ISIS command positions. Coordinates I had transmitted from the source network helped locate facilities that the coalition's own collection systems had not been able to find from the air. The methods I had developed—the fusion of satellite imagery with ground-level source reporting, verified through the cross-referencing system I built inside Mosul and maintained through exile—were producing consequences I could see on the screen: a compound struck, a command post neutralized, a weapons depot destroyed. The scholar's work became the instrument of the city's liberation and its destruction simultaneously—the same coordinates that helped the coalition find ISIS also defined the geography of what would be hit, and what would be hit included the city I was trying to save.

I could not stop a mortar round. I could not stop an air strike. I could not reach through the screen and pull people out of the buildings that were about to collapse on top of them. But I could—and did—provide the information that helped the forces distinguish between the positions that needed to be struck and the buildings that held only families. That distinction was not always honored. The helplessness was not total. But it was becoming more total with each passing week, because now the city I had been trying to preserve was being erased faster than I could document its erasure, and the intelligence I provided could not prevent the collateral destruction that the battle's own logic demanded.

Ahmad was my eldest brother. He was also my friend. He was also, in the ways that mattered most, my father.

Our father was not always present, and Ahmad became the compass—the one who oriented the family, who made the decisions, who carried the weight that falls on the eldest when the father is absent. He taught me what I needed to know before I knew I needed to know it. He was not gentle about it. He was short-tempered. He could flare at small provocations—a misplaced word, a broken promise, a failure to show the respect he believed was owed to the order of things. He was proud. He was stubborn. He was the kind of man who, once he had decided something, would not be moved from it by argument or evidence or the desperate pleading of a younger brother calling from Paris to tell him he was going to die.

But he was also the one who presented me to his friends as the scholar and the historian. He said those words—the scholar and the historian—long before I had earned either title, before I had finished my doctoral thesis, before I had published anything that would justify the claim. He said it because he believed I would earn it, and his belief was the kind that makes the thing it believes in more likely to become true. He said it with pride. He said it the way a father says my son the doctor or my son the engineer—not as description but as declaration, as though by naming what I would become he was helping to create it. He was right. The title he gave me is the title I carry.

During the occupation I had begun attending a secret weekly meeting at the house of Junaid al-Fakhry, the archaeologist who had spent decades preserving Mosul's material past. Seven to twelve of us—artists, scholars, historians, archaeologists—gathered there to talk freely while one of ISIS's informants sat on the street corner outside the building, watching the entrance without knowing what was happening on the other side of the walls. We discussed everything. ISIS. Abraham. The origins of art. The nature of history and the fate of nations. The meaning of what was happening to us and to the city. Everything that the regime had forbidden us to think aloud, we thought aloud in that room, once a week, with the spy on the corner and the conversation behind the walls. It was one of the only spaces in Mosul where speech was still speech and not performance—where a man could say what he believed without first calculating whether the words would kill him.

I invited Ahmad to join me. He came. He came back the next week and the week after that and the week after that. He was not a scholar. He was not an artist. He was not an archaeologist. But he sat in that room and listened and talked and argued—about Abraham, about the origins of nations, about whether art had a purpose beyond beauty, about whether ISIS could be understood historically or only condemned morally—and he came alive in a way that the occupation had been slowly extinguishing in everyone. The meetings gave him something that the occupation had been taking from all of us—the knowledge that the mind had not been conquered, that the city's intellectual life had not been killed, that somewhere behind a door in Mosul people were still thinking freely while the regime controlled everything on the other side of that door.

I never smoked in front of Ahmad. It was a matter of respect—he was the eldest, and in our family the younger brother does not smoke in the presence of the elder. This was not a rule anyone had written down. It was understood. It was part of the order of things that Ahmad himself embodied. But during ISIS, when tobacco became scarce and the regime taxed or confiscated what little was available, I gave him from my supply. The younger brother supplying the elder brother with contraband cigarettes under a regime that punished smoking—this was what the occupation had done to the ordinary hierarchies of a family. It had reversed them without either of us acknowledging it. He took the cigarettes. I did not smoke in front of him. The form of respect was preserved even as the substance of the relationship shifted beneath it.

Ahmad suspected what I was doing. I am sure of this now, though we never discussed it directly. He never asked. He never said the words Mosul Eye. He never confronted me with what he must have understood from the pattern of my behavior—the absences, the secrecy, the devices, the way I moved through the city with a purpose I could not explain. He knew. I believe he knew from early on. And he chose not to ask—not because he did not care but because asking would have meant confirming, and confirming would have meant sharing the danger, and sharing the danger would have meant that I would carry not only the weight of the work but the weight of having placed my brother inside the knowledge of it. He protected me by choosing not to know. That was Ahmad. The brother who loved me enough not to make me tell him the truth.

By the end of the occupation, over the phone from Paris, Ahmad had become calmer. The two years under ISIS had changed him the way they had changed everyone who survived them—worn away the sharp edges, replaced the quickness of temper with something quieter, something that might have been patience or might have been exhaustion or might have been the particular stillness that comes over a man who has lived under a regime that kills people for small things and has learned that surviving means letting the small things go. He kept checking on me. He called to make sure I was eating, sleeping, working. He said he wanted to come to Paris—to see the city, to sit with me, to hear everything I had lived through on the other side of the screen. He wanted to come.

The phone calls from Paris to Mosul followed a pattern. I would call at hours when I thought the shelling would be less intense—early morning, sometimes late at night, the timing shaped by what the satellite and the ground reports told me about the rhythm of the fighting. Ahmad would answer and his voice would carry that new calm—the occupation calm, the calm of a man who has accepted that the world outside his door is no longer a world he controls. He would ask about my studies. He would ask if I was eating. He would tell me about the children—how the eldest was growing, how the youngest had started to walk, how the middle ones were managing in a city where school had been replaced by the sound of shelling. He never complained. He never said he was afraid. He spoke about the future as though there would be one—the trip to Paris, the things he would see, the conversations we would have in person. The future he described was the future of a man who believed he would survive, and I listened to him describe it while the satellite on my screen showed his neighborhood closing like a wound around the forces advancing toward it.

He did not come.

The neighborhood sits in western Mosul, and by spring 2017, it had become the precise center of the war zone—the front line where the Iraqi security forces and ISIS met in streets too narrow for retreat and the civilians between them had nowhere to go. The fighting in Zanjili was among the worst of the entire battle. At least sixty people waiting to flee—standing in the open, carrying their belongings, trying to reach the Iraqi lines—were killed there.

I contacted my mother. I told her: There will be mortar shelling in this neighborhood. Do not stay. She said: No, we are fine. I said: I have information. This part of the city will be attacked by the federal police. I was following everything. The pattern of the operation was logical—I could read it from the satellite imagery and the ground reports the way a historian reads a document, tracing the sequence, anticipating the next movement, understanding the logic of the advance before the advance itself confirmed it. I knew what was coming for Old Mosul. I had the information. I had the coordinates. I had the pattern. I had everything except the ability to make the people I loved act on what I knew.

I told Ahmad: You are going to die. Listen to me this time. Just move to another house. Do not stay.

They did not listen.

In May 2017, a mortar shell hit Ahmad's house in the north of Mosul's Old City. A small piece of shrapnel entered his chest and stopped in his heart. There was no blood. He was thirty-six years old. He left four children—the eldest was ten, the youngest was two. We still do not know who sent the shell. We do not know if it came from the Iraqi security forces or from ISIS. He was sitting in his house. He was not fighting. He was not running. He was not standing in the street trying to flee. He was sitting in his house because he had not listened to me and because he believed, the way our mother believed, that the house would hold, that the walls would protect him, that staying was safer than running. The walls did not protect him. A piece of metal smaller than a coin entered his chest and stopped his heart and he was dead at thirty-six in a house in a city that was being destroyed by the forces that had come to save it from the men who had occupied it for three years while I documented every day of the occupation from inside and then from exile and could not save my own brother from a mortar shell I had predicted was coming.

They buried him in the garden. The streets were too dangerous to carry a body to the cemetery—snipers, shelling, the front line that ran through the neighborhood like a wound that would not close. So they dug a grave in the garden of the house where he had been sitting when the shell came, and they put him in the ground outside the door, and the family went on living in the house with Ahmad buried beneath the earth they walked on every morning. The children played in the garden where their father was buried. The family cooked and slept and waited for rescue in a house whose garden had become a cemetery because the city could not even give its dead the dignity of being carried to the place where the dead are supposed to go.

I never wrote Ahmad's eulogy. I never stood at his grave and said the words that are supposed to be said when a brother dies. I have not been to the grave. I do not know what the ground looks like where they put him. This is his eulogy. I am writing it here because this book is the only place I have.

Ahmad, you were the first person to see what I might become. You called me the scholar and the historian when I was neither—when I was only your younger brother trying to understand the world you had already learned to navigate by the time I was old enough to watch you navigate it. You taught me what our father could not teach me because he was not there, and you did it without ever saying that is what you were doing, without ever naming yourself as the one who had stepped into the space our father left, because naming it would have been a kind of accusation and you were not the kind of man who accused. You simply did what needed to be done.

You were impatient and you were proud and you were stubborn and you did not listen to me when I told you that you were going to die, and I was right, and being right is the most worthless thing I have ever possessed.

I would give back the entire archive to have you alive in a house that held.

You sat in Junaid's house every week and argued about Abraham and the origins of art with scholars and archaeologists, and you belonged there—not because you had a degree but because the life of the mind was never something that required a degree, only the willingness to sit in a room and think freely, and you had that willingness, and you exercised it while an ISIS spy sat on the corner outside and the conversation carried on behind the walls as though the walls were stronger than the regime.

You knew what I was doing and you never asked.

You protected me by choosing not to know—the silence of not asking, the silence that says I trust you and I will not make it harder by making you explain.

And now you are dead at thirty-six with four children who will grow up without you the way I grew up without our father, except that you were better at being present, and your children lost more in you than I lost in him, because you were the one who stayed, you were the one who showed up, you were the one who filled the space that needed filling, and now that space is empty and your children will have to learn to navigate without the compass that I had and that they will not have.

Your youngest child will grow up without a single memory of your face.

I owe you this book. The title you gave me—the scholar and the historian—is the title I carry. I carry it into the rooms where I speak about Mosul and into the pages where I write about it. When I say it, I will be saying what you said first.

You named me before the world did.

The news reached me in Paris. I do not remember who called or what words were used. I do not remember the hour or the light in the room or what was on the screen when the phone rang. I do not remember whether I was sitting or standing, whether the satellite application was open, whether I had been tracking the advance into Zanjili at that moment or whether I had stepped away to do any of the ordinary things a person does between one catastrophe and the next in a life that has become a sequence of catastrophes separated by intervals of waiting. I do not remember the words that told me Ahmad was dead. I was standing in the courtyard of the École des Hautes Études en Sciences Sociales on the Boulevard Raspail. The building was constructed on the site of the Cherche-Midi prison, where the Nazis held members of the French Resistance before their executions. A section of the original prison wall is still visible from the courtyard—the stone face of it, the mortar lines, preserved inside a modern building the way a wound is preserved inside a body that has healed around it. I was standing in front of that wall when the call came. What I remember is what came after.

I stopped speaking. I have said this already—it is where this chapter began, because it is the truest thing I know about what the battle did to me. For more than two weeks I did not say a word. Not to anyone. Not on the phone. Not in the apartment. Not to the people at EHESS, the graduate school in Paris where I was pursuing my doctoral research on Mosul's chronicle tradition—who did not know what had happened and could not have understood if I had told them, because they did not know who I was. They did not know that the man sitting in the reading room, the doctoral student working on the history of Mosul, had a brother who had just been killed by a mortar shell in a city they knew only as a name in the news. They did not know that the same man had spent three years documenting that city from inside and from exile, that he had built an intelligence operation from a laptop, that he had warned his brother and his brother had not listened and now his brother was dead and the man in the reading room had stopped speaking because there was nothing left to say.

I have not cried for Ahmad. Not then. Not in the years since. The tears have not come because the conditions for them have not been met. I have not seen his grave. I do not know what the ground looks like where they buried him. I do not know who sent the shell. No one has been held accountable—not the commander who ordered the shelling, not the soldier or the fighter who fired the round, not the war that placed a mortar inside the range of a house where a man was sitting with his family because he believed the house would hold. No one has answered for Ahmad's death. No one has been made to say: We did this, and this is why, and this is what we owe the family of the man we killed. Until then, the tears remain where they are. I carry them the way I carry the archive—encrypted, stored, waiting for the conditions under which they can finally be opened.

There was not a day in my life in Mosul when I did not pass by al-Hadba'. If I had a memory of my first days as a child—my earliest days, the days before memory becomes reliable—I believe I would find al-Hadba' in it. The minaret was not something you went to see. It was always there, the way the sky was always there, the way the Tigris was always there. You did not notice it the way you notice a monument. You noticed it the way you notice the horizon—it was the background against which everything else was placed.

It leaned. That was what everyone knew about it first—the gentle tilt, the inclination that had given the city its name: Mosul al-Hadba', Mosul the Hunchback. It had been built in 1172 by Nur al-Din Zangi, a Zengid ruler who governed Mosul during the era of the Crusades and who commissioned the minaret as part of a religious complex that included the al-Nuri mosque. Forty-five meters tall, its cylindrical shaft decorated with ornamental brickwork in patterns that caught the light differently at different hours of the day. By the fourteenth century, when the great Moroccan traveler Ibn Battuta—who journeyed across the entire Islamic world documenting what he saw—visited the city, the lean was already pronounced and the nickname already established. Over the following centuries the lean increased. The minaret tilted nearly three meters off vertical by the time I was born. Engineers worried about it. UNESCO planned a conservation project. The project was announced just days before ISIS seized the city in June 2014, and the conservation never happened.

But for the people of Mosul, the lean was not a structural deficiency. It was identity. It was the thing that made al-Hadba' al-Hadba'. Children grew up seeing it from their rooftops and from the streets of the old city, where it rose above the low skyline as the one vertical that was not quite vertical, the one structure that could be seen from almost anywhere and that told you where in the city you were. It was the landmark you pointed toward when giving directions. The shape you looked for when you were coming home. It appeared on postcards, on official seals, on the ten-thousand-dinar banknote, in the drawings that schoolchildren made of their city when asked to draw what Mosul looked like. It had stood through the Mongols, through the Ottomans, through the British mandate, through Saddam, through the American occupation, through the insurgency, through everything Mosul had survived across eight hundred years. It was not a symbol of the city. Symbols can be replaced. Al-Hadba' was the city's physical continuity made visible—the proof that something had endured across eight centuries and that the city was therefore older and more durable than anything that happened to it. As long as al-Hadba' stood, Mosul could say: We are still here. We have survived before. We will survive again.

The al-Nuri mosque beside it was where Abu Bakr al-Baghdadi had declared the caliphate in July 2014—the building from which the catastrophe had been announced to the world, the place where a man in a black turban had stood at the pulpit and declared himself the leader of the faithful and the city his capital. Baghdadi had not chosen the mosque by accident. It was the mosque of Nur al-Din Zangi, the ruler who had fought the Crusaders, and by claiming that pulpit Baghdadi was claiming that history—wrapping his caliphate in the authority of an eight-hundred-year-old war against the West. For three years the mosque and the minaret stood under ISIS control. The regime reportedly rigged al-Hadba' with explosives in 2014, but the residents of the old city formed a human chain to prevent the detonation—a rare and brazen act of collective defiance in the caliphate's three-year rule. The minaret survived that attempt. It would not survive the second.

On the twenty-first of June 2017, as the Iraqi forces closed in on the last ISIS positions in the old city, the mosque and the minaret were destroyed. ISIS detonated explosives placed inside the structure. The Iraqi government said ISIS had blown them up rather than let them be recaptured. ISIS said an air strike had hit them. Eight centuries of standing ended in seconds. At approximately nine-thirty in the evening, the structure that had defined Mosul's skyline since the twelfth century was reduced to its square base and a pile of ornamental brick.

I was in Paris when the news came. I sat at the desk in the apartment where the light was always off and I looked at the screen and I understood that the question I had been asking on all those nights walking past Notre-Dame—two structures built in the same century, one in a city at peace, one in a city under siege, the question of what survives the catastrophe—had been answered. Al-Hadba' did not survive. The minaret I had passed every day of my life in Mosul, the shape I had looked for when coming home, the structure that had told me where I was in the city since before I could remember—it was gone. And the city it had anchored, the city whose continuity it had proved, was gone with it. Notre-Dame still stood by the Seine. Al-Hadba' was rubble in the old city of Mosul, and no one could rebuild the eight centuries it had carried.

Ahmad was dead. Al-Hadba' was rubble. The person who called me the scholar and the historian, and the building that had been the city's proof of its own continuity. Both destroyed in the same weeks of the same offensive in the same part of the city I had been watching from a screen in an apartment in Paris where the light was always off. The part of me that had believed—through the occupation, through the exile, through the battle—that the record could protect the thing it recorded, that the archive was a form of survival not only for the chronicler but for the city: That part died with Ahmad and with the minaret. The record survived. The city did not. The brother did not. The belief did not.

On July 10, 2017, the Iraqi government declared Mosul liberated. The word was used. It was correct in the military sense: The territory had been retaken, the regime expelled, the flags replaced. I do not know if I can call what happened a liberation. It was the end of a battle between the Iraqi security forces, the international coalition, and ISIS. It was completely different from a liberation. Because they left a destroyed city behind them.

Seventy-five percent of the city was destroyed. Two million people were internally displaced. More than five thousand buildings were damaged in the old city alone. The estimated cost of rebuilding ran to tens of billions of dollars. Hundreds of people sat in prison accused of ISIS membership with no trial. Camps held families—mainly women and children—accused of being ISIS families, punished for acts they had not committed. They did not even try to save the people. I say this not as rhetoric but as the assessment of a man who documented every phase of the occupation and every phase of the battle. What is left of the city can give the answer that they did not care. If anyone has a good reason to tell me this is a liberation, I would say it is a liberation. But it is not.

Years have passed since the government declared victory. I have followed the reconstruction the way I followed the destruction—through sources, through images, through the reports of people who are there while I am not.

UNESCO has led the rebuilding of the al-Nuri Mosque and the al-Hadba' minaret. The Church of the Immaculate—the church I entered secretly during the occupation to see what ISIS had done—has been restored. Some of the old city's streets have been cleared. Scaffolding rises where rubble lay. The souks have partially reopened—not the same souks, but stalls in the same spaces, selling goods to people who remember what was sold there before. These are real achievements, and the people and institutions responsible for them deserve the recognition that repair has always deserved in a world that pays more attention to what is destroyed than to what is rebuilt.

From Paris, I launched a campaign to resupply the destroyed Central Library of Mosul University—the same library where I had spent years among the archives, where ISIS had forced the faculty to rewrite the textbooks, where tens of thousands of books had been burned. I called it Let There Be a Book, Rising from the Ashes. For so long, I had been focusing on death and destruction. Now I would focus on this—to rebuild the library, and to reconnect Mosul to its neighbors and to the international community. Volunteers entered the rubble and found thousands of books still intact behind the ashes. Over forty days, they carried 32,000 books to safety, one by one, while the battle for the west still raged. Donations arrived from across the world—from universities, from publishing houses, from a French association in Marseille that pledged twenty tonnes, from Baghdad residents who bought books at street markets and sent them north. The books ISIS burned, the world sent back.

But reconstruction is not restoration. The buildings can be rebuilt. The population that made Mosul what it was—the specific arrangement of communities that had lived together for centuries—has not returned, and most of it will not. The majority of the Christians who were expelled have not come back. The Yazidis have not returned to their villages in large numbers. The Shabak communities remain displaced. The Jewish community was already gone, emptied decades earlier. The city being rebuilt is a city with new walls and old absences. The stones are being restored. The coexistence that gave those stones their meaning is not.

I sat in front of the screen and tried to find the streets I had walked. The alleys of the old city. The souks. The route I had taken every day past al-Hadba' without thinking, because al-Hadba' was always there and I had never had to think about it. The neighborhood where Ahmad had sat in his house. The corner where Junaid's house stood, where we had discussed Abraham and the origins of art while the spy sat on the corner outside. I could not find them. Not damaged. Not altered. Gone. The satellite showed rubble where buildings had been, craters where streets had been, absence where eight centuries of continuous life had been. I looked at it the way you look at the place where something was—not searching for it anymore but confirming, with the patience of a man who has learned to confirm the worst, that it is no longer there.

I zoomed in on the satellite image until the pixels blurred and then zoomed out and then in again, trying to find the outline of a building I recognized, the turn of an alley I had taken a thousand times, the courtyard of a khan where I had once sat and drank tea, the rooftop of a house where I had looked out over the city as a boy and seen al-Hadba' leaning against the sky. I could not find them. The resolution was high enough to show individual cars, individual craters, individual piles of rubble. But it was not high enough to show what those piles had been—the homes, the lives, the centuries of accumulation. The satellite showed the present. It could not show the past. And the past was all that was left of the city I had known, because the present was rubble, and rubble does not remember what it was before it fell.

People were reaching me through the same channels I had used for intelligence—families trapped in the rubble, people trying to find relatives, voices carrying not information but appeals. The work was changing. The documentation was becoming intervention. The moral burden was widening into something I had not anticipated, and it would expand in the weeks ahead into a different kind of effort—geolocating the trapped, coordinating with forces on the ground, attempting to save from a screen in Paris what could still be saved in a city where most of what I had tried to save was already gone. That work belongs to the next chapter, because it required a different kind of effort and a different reckoning with what had become possible and what had not.

The archive I had carried out of Mosul on a hard drive in a bag thrown up from a trench—the encrypted files, the satellite imagery, the source reports, the coordinates, the names, the dates, the verified incidents, the photographs of streets that no longer existed, the records of neighborhoods that were now rubble—was now the memory of a place that existed only in the memory and in the record. The city I had documented from inside for eighteen months and from exile for eighteen more had been destroyed twice: once by the occupation that erased its diversity, its freedom, its public life, and once by the forces that came to end the occupation and erased its physical body in the process.

I thought about what it means to carry a city in an archive after the city itself is gone. The chronicle tradition I had studied at EHESS—Behnam Badriyya's Tawarikh al-Mawsil, the nineteenth-century historical record of a city that had survived its own catastrophes and continued—those chronicles had been written in the confidence that the city would outlast the document. The chronicler recorded because the city would remain to be recorded. My archive was different. My archive had outlasted the city. The document had survived what the city had not. The encrypted files on the hard drive were now more durable than the streets they described, more permanent than the houses they mapped, more real—in the sense that they still existed—than the neighborhoods they had been created to preserve. The archive was supposed to be the shadow of the city. Now the city was the shadow of the archive.

Ahmad was dead and I had not cried. Al-Hadba' was rubble. The souks were rubble. The houses were rubble. The streets were gone. The alleys were gone. The smell of cardamom and bread was gone. The sound of the church bell and the call to prayer occupying the same air was gone. The barbershop was gone. The tea seller's brass pot was gone. The record I had kept was no longer the shadow of a living city. It was the only proof that the city had ever been what it was.

The archive survived. The city it described did not.

NOT BAD FOR A HISTORIAN

I could not save Ahmad. Ninety-two other families, I saved.

The first message came while I was still unable to speak. A man in New Zealand, using a fake name, wrote to Mosul Eye. His first words were: Is this conversation private?

I was at the desk in Paris. The apartment with the light always off, the satellite application open, the phone beside the screen. Ahmad had been dead for weeks. The two-week silence was over but the voice that came back was not the voice that had left. The old city—the dense Ottoman-era quarter on the western bank of the Tigris where my family had lived for generations, where the narrow streets folded into each other and the houses shared walls and the minarets marked the sky—was rubble. Al-Hadba', the leaning minaret of the Great Mosque of al-Nuri, where Abu Bakr al-Baghdadi had declared his caliphate in July 2014 and which had stood over Mosul for 840 years, was gone. And the messages were coming in—not intelligence reports anymore, not source updates about ISIS positions, but something else. Pleas. Fragments. Coordinates followed by names followed by the number of people in a house followed by the words please help us followed by silence when the connection dropped.

Only my body was in Paris. My nerves, my attention, my fear, my operational consciousness—everything that made me function—remained in Mosul. The machine inside me did not stop. I do not know what else to call it—the capacity that had been built over three years of clandestine documentation, the reflexive system of receiving information, testing it, and transmitting it. That system had been designed for intelligence. Now it began, without any conscious decision on my part, to try to prevent the deaths it had been recording.

I discovered during those months that grief and function could coexist in the same body. The grief did not lift—Ahmad's death, the minaret's destruction, the old city's erasure—heavy, constant, unresolved, stored in the body like a weight that shifted but never lightened. But the function continued around it the way blood circulates around a wound. The hands moved. The eyes tracked the screen. The mind assessed the coordinates. The voice answered the phone. The rescue work became the form grief took when it could not remain still—the conversion of mourning into action, the redirection of helplessness into method, the insistence that if the city could not be saved then the people inside it might be.

I asked the man from New Zealand: How can you prove you are not ISIS? Because I kept receiving messages from ISIS—probing messages, test messages, attempts to identify who was behind the account. A rescue request could be a trap. A family described as trapped could be a fiction designed to draw out a response that revealed a phone number, an IP address, a communication pattern. I could not afford to trust the panic in a message simply because it sounded desperate. Desperation could be performed.

He started the conversation. He said: You are my only hope. I have been trying to help my niece, who is trapped in her house in Mosul, but there was no way to do this. Then I saw the name Mosul Eye in the media and I came to you.

His niece was in west Mosul—the half of the city that still lay under ISIS control, where the battle of liberation had become the most intensive urban combat the world had seen since World War II. Trapped in her house. Her husband was dead. Her son was injured. Her daughter was crying. The house had been hit by an air strike—not destroyed entirely, but damaged, and the family was inside it with no way out, in a neighborhood where the battle was ongoing and the streets were impassable. He was asking me to rescue his niece with her children. I was in Paris. I was an anonymous account on the internet. I had no soldiers, no vehicles, no authority over any military force. What I had was the satellite, the phone, the encrypted channels, and a knowledge of the city that no one outside it possessed.

I asked for her phone number. He gave it. I called her on Skype—not from my own number, which I never used. I had subscribed to Skype specifically so my private number would not be exposed. I used temporary numbers for every new case. I used multiple communication applications and never relied on one channel for all exchanges. When a new case came in, I compartmentalized it—one channel for the family, a different channel for the military coordination, a third for the intermediary who had brought me the case. Every new contact was a potential exposure. Every phone number was a potential trace. ISIS still controlled parts of the city. Any communication that reached the wrong hands could lead not to rescue but to execution. The rescue work did not make me less clandestine. It made me more exacting. The tradecraft that had protected me under the occupation became the tradecraft that protected the people I was trying to save. The purpose had changed. The discipline had not.

I talked to her. I said: Can you geolocate your house? She said: I have no internet. I have no access to the internet. So I asked her to describe what was around her house—what she could see, what landmarks were nearby, what direction the shelling was coming from. She described it. I matched her description against the satellite imagery and against my memory of the city—the mental map I had built over a lifetime of walking through Mosul and two years of tracking it from above. I identified the house. I said: Is it this place? She said yes.

That was the geolocation method. Not GPS. Not a pin dropped on a phone. A woman in a damaged house in a war zone describing what she could see through a window, and a man in Paris matching her description against a satellite image and a memory of streets he had walked before they were destroyed. Sometimes the process took minutes—the person described a mosque, and I knew the mosque, and I could place the house within a block. Sometimes it took hours. The landmarks had been destroyed. The streets were rubble. The mosque was gone. In those cases, I worked from what remained: the direction of the river, the direction of the sun at a given hour, the number of turns from the front door to the basement. I reconstructed the location from fragments the way an archaeologist reconstructs a vessel from shards.

Now came the hardest part: How to rescue her? I went back to the man in New Zealand. I said: Can you give me more information—anything, documents, papers, something that can help. He said: What do you want? I did not know. I said: Just tell me something. He said: She was born in the United States.

That was all I needed. I contacted the coalition—the US-led military alliance supporting the Iraqi forces' assault on the city—through email and through their Twitter account. I told them: A US citizen is trapped in her house in west Mosul. ISIS might take her at any moment. I gave them the number of her birth certificate and her social security number so they could verify her citizenship. How I had built the channel to the coalition is a story I am not yet ready to tell in full. What matters here is that the channel existed, that it carried trust, and that when I transmitted verified coordinates of a trapped civilian, the information was acted on.

Those three hours were among the longest of my life. I had transmitted the information. The chain was in motion—the data moving from my screen to the coalition's operational channels to the units on the ground. But between the transmission and the confirmation there was nothing I could do except sit at the desk in the apartment with the light off and wait. I could not speed up the military. I could not open the door of her house from Paris. I could only check the satellite, which updated too slowly to show real-time movement, and refresh the channels for any message from the coalition confirming that the extraction had been attempted. The waiting was the price of distance—the tax the rescuer pays for not being in the city he is trying to save.

Within three hours she was rescued. Moved to a hospital. I contacted Médecins Sans Frontières—the international medical organization that was among the few operating near the front lines—so they could be aware of her situation. Her family came from Jordan and met her there. The next day I called to ask how she was doing. She did not believe I existed. She made a joke: Are you CIA? I said: No, I am Mosul Eye.

That was the first one. I kept a record of each case—the coordinates, the names, the outcome. Ninety-one more would follow.

After that first case I understood what was possible. The system I had built for intelligence—the layered communication, the geolocation from description, the satellite cross-referencing, the transmission to military channels—could be used not only to document death but to prevent it. The same methods that had allowed me to track ISIS from inside the city now allowed me to locate trapped civilians from exile. I began searching Iraqi social media the way I had once monitored ISIS propaganda—scanning for actionable specificity, filtering out duplication, testing credibility. Coordinates posted publicly, family names shared, appeals tagged to any account that might have influence. Some of the pleas were posted to Mosul Eye directly. Others I found by searching. The digital layer of the war was also the digital layer of rescue: the same platforms ISIS had used for propaganda were now carrying the coordinates of trapped families. Twitter, Facebook, WhatsApp—the channels carried both the war and the attempt to survive it, and I was reading both streams simultaneously, separating the noise from the signal, converting the signal into the operational format that the coalition could use.

The information came in fragments. A neighborhood name. A street. A description of the area around the house. The number of people. Whether there were children. Whether someone was injured. Whether the husband was dead. Whether they had water. Whether they believed anyone was coming. The fragments arrived at all hours—three in the morning, during the day when I was supposed to be at EHESS, In the middle of a bus ride across Paris my phone vibrated, and I stood in the aisle speaking quietly in Arabic, geolocating a house in al-Mashahda while the bus passed the Jardin du Luxembourg and the passengers around me read their books and lived in the city they were in.

I verified each case with the same discipline I had used for intelligence. Who sent the message, and through what channel. Whether the person was speaking freely or under coercion. Whether the description of the location matched what I knew of the city. Whether the coordinates were consistent with the front lines—was the house in a zone the military was about to enter, or had it already been passed. Was it about to be struck. I cross-referenced against the satellite, against the ground reports, against the known positions of the Iraqi forces and of ISIS. I tested for duplication—several relatives abroad sometimes contacted me about the same house, each using different names. I had to determine whether ten messages meant ten families or two.

The rescue requests formed a dense map of civilian entrapment across western Mosul. Cases in al-Mashahda came in clusters—three families in one block, four in the next, a mosque nearby where civilians had gathered for shelter. In Tawalib, near al-Faruq Street, the entrapments were dense—families in basements beneath partially collapsed houses, exit routes blocked by rubble. In the Shifaa neighborhood the reports were especially urgent—close to the front line, shelling continuous, secondary collapses days after the initial strikes. There were children in almost every case. The elderly in many. One man in a wheelchair who could not be moved through the rubble.

Each cluster required its own verification. The families in one block might confirm the presence of families in the adjacent block, and by combining fragments I could construct a rescue map for an entire section of a neighborhood—the number of civilians, their conditions, the obstacles, the routes still passable. I plotted the coordinates on the map I had been maintaining since 2014—the map that had tracked ISIS positions, checkpoint locations, execution sites, tunnel entrances. Now it carried a second layer: the locations of the living.

Eighteen people in a basement in al-Mashahda—the house bombed above them. Thirteen at the coordinates next door, including three children in critical condition. Fifty trapped under rubble in a third house in the same cluster. Seventy people in five families on al-Faruq Street in

Tawalib. Nineteen at another coordinate—the message said please, nineteen people will die. A man in a wheelchair among them, with a request not only for rescue but for deconfliction—avoid accidental targeting. More than ninety people under heavy bombardment at another location, with a note that they could not use their phone—the request was to stop the bombardment first, then evacuate. The numbers added up to hundreds of people across a few square kilometers of western Mosul, each entry a coordinate, each coordinate a cluster of lives.

One of the families I rescued was the family of Junaid al-Fakhry—the archaeologist in whose house Ahmad and I had gathered every week during the occupation. The house where seven to twelve of us had discussed Abraham and the origins of art while the ISIS spy sat on the corner outside. Junaid was one of the people who had sustained the city's interior life under the regime, one of the memory-bearers—a man who carried in his knowledge the archaeological and historical depth of a city that ISIS had been trying to erase.

If Junaid died in a basement in the old city, something more than a single life would be lost. The memory he carried—of the excavations, of the sites, of the historical layers beneath the streets that were now being destroyed above them—would die with him. The rescue work was usually about bodies. In Junaid's case it was also about memory.

Now his family was trapped. A sniper was positioned in a building nearby, preventing the Iraqi forces from entering the area. There was another route—a way to reach them that avoided the sniper's line of fire—but the forces on the ground did not know it existed until I told them. I knew the streets. I knew the turns. I knew the old city's architecture from the inside.

I was on the phone with Junaid's family. They were afraid. They were crying. They asked for water. I called the Ninth Division of the Iraqi Army and the Federal Police—the two forces operating in that sector—and told them: There are civilians at this location who need water. I was talking to all of them, the families and the security forces, without any of them knowing who was on the other end. They sent the water. When I called the family back, the voice said: Can you send some bread?

I cried. He was not asking to be rescued. He was asking to eat. The scale of the request against the scale of the catastrophe was more than I could hold. But I held it. I said: Can you wait? You will not just get bread. You will get your life. Can you hold it with me for a few minutes?

The coalition told me to tell the family to move away from the windows and to get ready. They also asked for the geolocation of the building in front of them—the building where the sniper was. I got the coordinates from the family. I sent them to the coalition. They struck the building. The family was rescued.

Junaid's family knew me. They knew Omar Mohammed. But they did not know they were talking to Omar Mohammed. They did not know that the anonymous voice on the Skype call—the voice that had told them to wait, that had coordinated the water and the bread and the strike on the sniper's building—was the same man who had sat in their house every week and argued about Abraham and the origins of art. I knew them. They did not know it was me. The clandestine identity that had protected me under ISIS was now protecting me while I rescued the people I loved.

Then a case came through that was different.

I cannot say how it was different. The information arrived in the same format—coordinates, a neighborhood, the number of people trapped, the condition of the house. The chain was the same: verification, geolocation, transmission to CENTCOM, confirmation that the information had been received and relayed to the forces on the ground. I had done this dozens of times by now. The procedure was established. The language was established. The distance between my desk in Paris and the basements in Mosul was the same distance it had always been—measured not in kilometers but in the gap between a voice on a phone and a body under rubble.

But something in this case sat differently inside my chest. I worked it the way I worked every case. I verified. I cross-referenced. I sent the coordinates to CENTCOM and waited. The waiting was always the worst part—the minutes between transmission and confirmation, when the information had left my hands and entered a chain I could not see or control, and the family was still in the basement and the only thing connecting them to survival was a sequence of numbers I had sent into a system that might or might not act in time.

CENTCOM confirmed the rescue. The forces had reached the location. The extraction was complete.

I felt something move through my body—not joy, something less nameable, something closer to the moment when a muscle that has been clenched for hours finally releases and the release itself is a kind of pain.

Then I learned they had gone to the wrong house.

In the geography of a destroyed neighborhood, where walls had collapsed into neighboring walls and rubble had made one address indistinguishable from the next, the forces had extracted a family from an adjacent house. The coordinates had pointed them to a location, and they had entered it, and the people inside were alive and grateful and rescued—but they were not the people I had been asked to save.

I contacted CENTCOM again. I said: This is not the right family. The one you have just rescued—they are another family. You have to go back. Not only the family I was coordinating for was still trapped—three neighboring families were also inside, in basements along the same row of houses, waiting.

Special forces went back in. The streets were impassable—snipers controlled the sightlines, and the rubble had sealed the normal approaches. So they went through the walls. They breached the interior walls between the houses, cutting through plaster and brick and concrete, moving from structure to structure without ever stepping into the open street. They tunneled through the row until they reached the house. They reached the family. They reached the neighbors.

Everyone came out alive.

I sat at my desk afterward for a long time. The screen was still open. The satellite image of the neighborhood was still visible—the gray and white and black of a place that had once been houses, that had once been a street a person could walk down, that was now a topography of collapse through which soldiers had burrowed like men moving through the interior of a wound.

The system had held. The chain had held. But for the minutes between the first confirmation and the discovery that the forces had entered the wrong house, I had understood something about the rescue work that I had not understood before. The verification, the geolocation, the transmission, the coordination—all of it could be perfect, and the outcome could still fail, because between the precision of a coordinate and the reality of a destroyed city there was a gap that no amount of care could fully close. A house that existed on the satellite was not always a house that existed on the ground. An address that was legible from six thousand kilometers away could be illegible to a soldier standing in the rubble of the street it had once been on.

I did not sleep that night. Not because the case had failed—it had not failed, the family was alive, the neighbors were alive, the soldiers had done what soldiers do when the first plan does not hold: They adapted, they went back, they cut through walls with their hands and their tools until they found the people they had been sent to find. I did not sleep because for those minutes I had felt something I had trained myself not to feel in the rescue work—something beyond operational concern, beyond the discipline of the chain, beyond the analyst's distance that allowed me to function.

I had felt it before in Mosul, in the years when the knowledge I carried could have killed me and the people closest to me did not know what I was doing. The feeling of being unable to protect what mattered most, while being the only one in a position to try.

I moved to the next case. There were always more cases.

The hardest part of the rescue work was not the verification or the geolocation. It was the talking.

Talking to people who were trapped in basements, who had been there for days, who had not eaten, who were injured, who had watched their neighbors die, who believed that no one was coming and that they would die in the rubble of houses they had lived in for decades. Talking to them and making them believe that someone was trying. Making them stay alive long enough to be reached.

I said the same things over and over, to family after family, in call after call. Wait. Do not give up. Someone is coming. Stay away from the windows. Stay in the basement. Do not go into the street. Do not try to run. Help is being coordinated. I am talking to the forces. I said these things from an apartment in Paris to people who were dying in Mosul, and the distance between my voice and their bodies was the distance between a man in front of a screen and a family in a basement with the ceiling cracking above them.

There were families I spoke to for hours. Not because the verification required it—the coordinates were transmitted, the chain in motion—but because the family could not be left alone. They needed a voice on the other end of the phone that had not hung up. Some were mentally collapsing—the sustained terror of days in a basement, the sound of shelling that never fully stopped. I gave them instructions. I told them where to position themselves in the house. I told them which walls were safest. I was giving tactical advice to civilians over the phone from six thousand kilometers away, and the advice was sound because I knew those houses, I knew those walls, I knew the old city's architecture from the inside.

I remember specific voices. A woman in al-Mashahda whose voice was so flat with exhaustion that at first I thought the call had connected to a recording. She had been in a basement for five days. She described a school to the east, the remains of a shop to the north, the sound of the river when the shelling paused—and I placed her within a block. A man near al-Faruq Street who called not for himself but for the family next door, whose shared wall had collapsed and who were trapped in a space between the rubble and the surviving structure. He could hear them. He could not reach them. An elderly couple near Shifaa, the husband unable to walk, the wife trying to describe their location while the phone cut out every few seconds. I reconstructed their position from fragments she gave me between explosions.

The ones who survived often called back afterward. They did not know who I was. They knew only that a voice had told them to wait and that they had waited and that they were alive. Some thanked me with a formality that was almost unbearable. Some wept. Some asked: Who are you? I said: Mosul Eye. They did not know that the anonymous voice that had guided them through the worst hours of their lives belonged to a man who had walked their streets and lost his brother in the same battle that had trapped them.

A house in the Mashahda district. Seven families inside. Among the people was Carter's pregnant wife. I verified the case. I geolocated the house. I transmitted the coordinates and the description to the coalition. The pregnancy compressed every element of the rescue into a narrower window—the shelling could not wait, the verification could not take hours, the coordination could not tolerate delay. Inside that building was a future—a life that had not yet begun and that would end before it started if the bombing continued.

The bombing of the area was stopped. A US Army officer, whom I had provided with the coordination and details of the location, on the ground made the decision to halt the strikes because civilians were confirmed present. The family survived. The pregnant woman survived. Then the officer was accused by the Iraqi forces of supporting ISIS, because he had stopped the bombing. The logic was: If you stop bombing, you are helping the enemy.

He asked me to write a letter explaining what had happened. That he had stopped the bombing because there were civilians inside. That I had provided the civilians' names. That the decision to stop had been a decision to save lives. I wrote the letter. I provided the names. I provided the geolocations. An anonymous person on the internet is writing an official letter to support a US Army officer accused of supporting ISIS because he chose not to kill a pregnant woman. That was the war. That was what the rescue system looked like from inside—a system where saving a life required locating and verifying and transmitting and then defending the person who did the saving from being punished for it.

One call I cannot set down.

A family near al-Mashahda. A woman's voice. Three children. The husband is already dead. The coordinates were verified. Transmitted. The chain was in motion. I told her to wait, to stay in the basement, to keep the children away from the walls. She said: They are not crying anymore. I said: That is good, keep them calm. She said: No. They are not crying because they have stopped.

The line went quiet. Not dead—quiet, the way a phone goes quiet when the person holding it has set it down or has stopped being able to hold it. I called back. No answer. I called again. No answer. I called the next day. No answer. The coordinates remained on my map. The entry was never updated. I do not know what happened to that family. I know only that the voice stopped and that I have not been able to forget the sentence.

They are not crying because they have stopped.

The information moved from me to the coalition to the operational units on the ground. The team I communicated with could read my messages in Arabic instantly—no translation delay, which in a rescue context means the difference between life and death. The units deconflicted the location—ensuring it was not about to be bombed, that the area could be safely approached. When the troops were close enough, they attempted extraction. The process was sequential and real: I received the plea. I verified. I transmitted. The coalition acknowledged. The coalition relayed to the relevant units. Units deconflicted. Units approached. Civilians extracted if possible. I received confirmation—or waited without confirmation, or called the family and discovered the phone no longer answered.

In one case the soldiers could not enter through the front, the roof, or the basement—every approach was rigged with explosives. So they dug through the shared wall of the adjacent house, broke through the old city's intimate architecture from one living room into the next, and reached the family through a hole in a neighbor's wall. I was on two phones for that one. On one, the special forces—reporting minute by minute as they broke through the wall, as they entered the room. On the other, the family inside—telling them to hold together, to stay calm, that help was coming through the wall. Two phones. Two voices. One in each ear. The soldiers telling me what they were doing. The family telling me they were still alive.

Whatever I did from Paris—the geolocation, the verification, the transmission—it was those soldiers who converted my coordinates into rescued lives. They carried children out of basements. They broke through walls. They walked into kill zones where a wrong step could detonate the floor beneath them. The bravery was theirs. The risk was theirs. They went in. I could only tell them where.

I was at the desk at two in the morning. Multiple screens open—the satellite on one, the messaging applications on another, the phone between them. A case in Shifaa. A case near the old bridge. A voice note from a family that had been in a basement for four days and whose youngest child had stopped crying, which the mother interpreted as a good sign and which I interpreted as dehydration. I was triangulating coordinates, checking them against frontline reports, preparing the information for transmission, and the apartment was dark and Paris was asleep, and I was the only person in this building—possibly on this street, possibly in this arrondissement—trying to keep a child alive in a basement six thousand kilometers away.

I was on a date. An evening that was supposed to be ordinary—dinner, conversation, the simulation of a life that existed in Paris rather than in Mosul. The phone rang. A rescue case. A family. Coordinates. I excused myself. I stood outside the restaurant and called the family on the Skype number and talked them through the protocol—describe the house, describe the landmarks, describe the direction of the shelling—and geolocated them and prepared the information and sent it to the military channel and went back inside and sat down and the person across the table asked if everything was all right and I said yes. I did not say that I had just been talking to a man in a basement in west Mosul whose wife was injured and whose children were under a table and who believed he was going to die and I had told him to wait and I did not know if he would.

There were nights when I would finish a rescue call at three in the morning and lie in the dark and listen to Paris outside the window—the distant sound of a car, the silence of a city asleep—and try to reconcile the two realities I occupied. My body took the Métro and bought groceries and sat in cafés. My body occupied space in a city at peace. But the rest of me—the part that could not stop, the part that had been built by three years of clandestine work and that could not be switched off because the city was still dying—that part was in Mosul. Always in Mosul.

The cases multiplied. Ten families. Twenty. Thirty. Forty. Each requiring the full cycle—verification, geolocation, transmission, coordination, follow-up. Some succeeded. The family reached. The civilians extracted. The voices on the phone changing from desperation to disbelief to gratitude. When I heard their voices afterward and compared them to the voices during the rescue calls, the difference was the difference between a person who believes they are going to die and a person who has been told they will live. That comparison became the meaning of why I was alive. From that point I understood the reason.

But the failures accumulated alongside the successes. There were calls that ended mid-sentence and never resumed. There were coordinates that led to rubble so total that no one could determine whether the people inside had been alive when the building fell. I carried those failures inside the method, inside the operational consciousness that could not afford to grieve because the next call was already coming in.

Ninety-two families. That was the final count. I kept a record of each case—the coordinates, the names, the outcome. The list runs to ninety-two families rescued through a system built from a desk in Paris with a satellite screen and a phone and a knowledge of the city that no briefing could replicate.

And there was the boy from the orphanage.

During the battle, a photograph reached me. I do not remember how—whether it came through social media, through one of the channels that had opened between the advancing forces and the civilians emerging from the ruins, or through someone who knew what I had been documenting and thought I should see it. What I remember is the face.

It was a child I had seen inside Dar al-Bara'im—the orphanage I had entered secretly in 2015, pretending to be staff, in a city that was still occupied, in a year when the battle had not yet begun. A Yazidi boy from Sinjar. ISIS had renamed him Abdullah. His family had believed he was dead.

I recognized him from the inventory I had made inside that building—the names, the ages, the origins I had recorded while the children looked at me without knowing why I was there or what I was writing down. I had preserved who he was before ISIS finished erasing it. I had noted the name they had given him and the place he had come from. The information had traveled from my notebook to the encrypted file to the hard drive I carried out of Mosul when I crossed into exile. It had survived the occupation, the escape, the battle. And now his face was in a photograph, and the boy I had catalogued as a line in a file was alive.

His family had believed he was dead. That is what happens when a child disappears into an occupied city that the world cannot reach—the family that survives, if any family survives, eventually stops waiting. The distance between Sinjar and Mosul under ISIS was not measured in kilometers. It was measured in silence. The boy had been taken, renamed, placed inside an institution that looked like a prison, and lost to everyone who had known him by his real name. His family had grieved him the way you grieve someone who is gone.

I made an announcement. I put his photograph out through the channels Mosul Eye had built over three years—the networks of followers, the contacts inside and outside the city, the infrastructure of attention that had begun as one man's blog and became something large enough to carry a boy's face from a war zone to the eyes of the people who were looking for him. The message was simple: This child is alive. He is from Sinjar. His family should come.

They came. His family came and took him.

I was not there for the meeting. I was in exile—in the apartment, at the desk, in the city that was not my city. But somewhere, in a place I have never seen, a family that had mourned a child was handed back the child they had mourned, and the name Abdullah fell away, and the name he had been born with was spoken again by the people who had given it to him.

That is what the inventory was for. Not for the daily reports, not for the blog, not for the encrypted file that would one day be evidence in a courtroom. It was for this: a name preserved against its erasure, carried through an occupation in a notebook, surviving the battle that destroyed half the city, surfacing in a photograph at the right moment, and returning a child to the people who had lost him.

I had entered the orphanage because the children were being taken and no one outside knew their names. The method—the historian's method, the archivist's method, the method that kept me recording the dead when the recording itself was a death sentence—had, in this single instance, worked in reverse. It had not preserved a death. It preserved a life.

And then there were the animals.

The Montazah al-Morour zoo sat in the eastern part of Mosul—a small public park on the road between the city center and the university that before the war had held roughly forty animals: lions, bears, monkeys, tropical birds, rabbits. When ISIS seized the city in June 2014, they used the grounds as a staging area and, according to sources I trusted, as a site of detention. The animals were abandoned. No one fed them. No one cleaned the cages. Over two and a half years, the animals died one by one—some from shelling that tore open enclosures, some from starvation, some eaten by predators that had escaped damaged cages. Simba's mother—a lioness—starved to death. The locals buried her in a shallow grave beside her son's cage. He could see the mound of earth from inside the bars.

By the time the eastern side was recaptured in January 2017, only two animals remained alive: Simba, a young male lion, and Lula, a female bear. They were in their cages, covered in their own feces and the debris from shelling. Simba had a joint condition. Lula had pneumonia. Both had rotting teeth and severe diarrhea from malnutrition. Neighbors had tried to feed them—throwing scraps over the fence—but when the fighting became too intense the neighbors could not leave their houses and the animals went without food for days. They were alive. Barely.

I learned about them through the same channels that brought the civilian rescue cases. And I understood—without deliberation—that I could not ignore them. After so much death, after Ahmad, after al-Hadba', after the fifty thousand names in the morgue, the instinct to rescue expanded beyond ordinary categories. These animals had been kept in captivity because of us. They did not have the luxury to escape. They could not run through the streets or cross the front lines or find their way to a displacement camp. They were locked in cages in a destroyed zoo in a destroyed city, and if no one acted they would die the way their cage-mates had died—slowly, in filth, surrounded by the carcasses of the animals that had not survived.

The coordination required for the animals was different from the civilian rescues but no less exhausting. The animals could not walk out. They required sedation, crates, vehicles, veterinary support, permits, checkpoints, and a destination. What I could do was what I had always done: work the channels, make the calls, apply pressure through persistence, keep the case alive in the operational chain until it moved from intention to action.

The key military coordination was with Abdul-Wahab al-Saadi—a senior Iraqi counterterrorism commander whose forces had been central to the liberation campaign. I contacted him through the channels I had built. The conversations were among the most surreal of the entire rescue period. I was calling a military commander in the middle of the deadliest urban combat since World War II and asking him to help save a lion and a bear from a zoo. The requests were specific: access to the zoo site, security for the veterinary team, coordination with checkpoints, clearance for the animals to be moved out. Each request required follow-up. Each follow-up required another call—at the same hours I was coordinating civilian rescues, talking families in basements out of giving up, geolocating houses from the satellite screen.

Abdul-Wahab al-Saadi engaged with the effort. He did not dismiss it. At one point, after days of calls about security and access and transport, he asked me—with the dry humor of a man who has seen too much to be surprised by anything—do you also want us to bathe them?

I laughed. It was one of the only times I laughed during those months. The absurdity of a general in the middle of the deadliest battle in modern Iraqi history being asked whether the lion and the bear could also be washed—the kind of absurdity only war produces, funny because the alternative to laughing is the recognition that the world has become so broken that bathing a lion is a genuine operational question.

The international animal welfare organization Four Paws carried out the physical rescue. Their veterinarian, Amir Khalil, entered the zoo in February 2017 and found the conditions I had been told about—the filth, the debris, the carcasses. He sedated Simba and Lula, treated them, began arranging transport to a sanctuary in Jordan. The first attempt failed—the convoy was stopped at a checkpoint two hundred meters from safety and the animals were sent back. It took a second attempt, nine days stuck at the border, and finally clearance to cross before Simba and Lula reached the Al Ma'wa sanctuary in Amman in April 2017. Lula took a bath when she arrived. Simba stepped out of his crate, looked at the grass, and retreated to his shelter. He had never walked on grass.

Ninety-two families. And a lion and a bear. Not bad for a historian.

The coalition's final message about the rescue work, months later, carried a line I have not forgotten. They said they were happy that many families had been rescued by the Iraqi forces. By then I had revealed my identity. By then they knew who they had been talking to. But during the rescue itself, they did not. They were communicating with an anonymous account that sent them verified coordinates of trapped civilians, and they acted on the information because the information was good—because the method was the method of an intelligence professional even though the person behind it was a historian with a satellite application and a phone.

The rescue work did not heal the grief. Ahmad was still dead. Al-Hadba' was still rubble. The old city was still gone. The tears had not come—not fully, not in the way grief is supposed to arrive and be carried and eventually transform. The rescue became the thing I did instead of crying, the place where the energy went, the form the mourning took when the body would not let it sit still. Ninety-two families was what grief did when it had coordinates and a phone.

But the rescue work widened my footprint. Under ISIS my survival had depended on invisibility—the anonymous account, the hidden identity, the discipline of leaving no trace. In exile the anonymity had persisted. But the rescue operations expanded the number of people who interacted with Mosul Eye. The families I rescued knew my voice. The coalition knew my method. The journalists who covered the battle knew my reliability. The circle was growing, and with it the pressure of a hidden identity that was becoming harder to sustain because the work it protected was becoming impossible to do in shadow.

I had been anonymous for more than three years. Even my family had not known I was the person behind Mosul Eye until the battle forced the secret open. The families I had rescued—the woman who asked if I was CIA, Junaid's family who knew me personally without knowing it was me on the phone—none of them knew. The world had been following an anonymous account that had become one of the most cited sources on the battle for Mosul, and behind it was a doctoral student in Paris who had not cried for his dead brother and who carried the locations of ninety-two rescued families on a map he had been building since 2014.

The battle ended on July 10, 2017. The Iraqi prime minister declared victory from the ruins of the Great Mosque of al-Nuri—the same mosque where Baghdadi had declared the caliphate three years earlier, now destroyed. ISIS was defeated. The city was in ruins. And the anonymity was fraying. The world was beginning to ask who was behind the account. The question had been asked before—journalists had probed, intelligence services had wondered, readers had speculated. Now it was becoming unavoidable. The decision I had known was coming since the fall—the decision I had deferred through the occupation and the exile and the battle and the rescue—was approaching: to reveal my face, to say my name, to step out of the shadow and into the exposure that would make me permanently visible.

The hidden chronicler had become a rescue node. The rescue node was becoming a public figure. And the public figure would have to decide whether to remain a mechanism or become a man again.

THE IMMORTAL RIVER

The Tigris remembers everything.

It is older than the name Mosul. Older than the Arabic word *al-Mawsil*, the place of connection, which the city has carried since the seventh century. Older than the Assyrian settlement on its eastern bank, which the Greeks called Nineveh and which had already been a ruin for six hundred years when Islam arrived. The river was flowing through this valley before anyone built anything on its banks, and it will be flowing long after the last wall standing today has returned to the earth it was cut from. It carries all of it—every city that was ever built on its banks, every city that fell, every name the land has worn and shed and worn again.

I say this not as poetry. I say it as a historian, because it is the truest thing I know. The river is the only truthful witness of the whole history of Mosul. It has seen everything that happened in this city since the beginning. We call it the immortal river. That is why I went to it when I had nothing left. That is why I dedicate this book to it now.

It was there when Sennacherib built the walls of Nineveh and diverted the water to irrigate his gardens. It was there when the city fell to the Medes and Babylonians in 612 BC and the Assyrian empire ended in a single season. It was there when the Arab armies arrived and built mosques alongside churches that were already five centuries old. It was there for Badr al-Din Lu'lu', who raised the Qara Serai—the Black Castle—on its shore in the thirteenth century, and it was there when Hulagu Khan's armies burned the castle so completely that the white stone turned black and the name changed with it, and the castle carried the mark of its burning for eight hundred years afterward. It was there for the Ottomans. For the British. For the wars, one after another, that I was born into and that I have never lived without.

And it was there in June 2014, when everything this book has described began. The river did not stop flowing. It does not stop for anything. That is what makes it immortal—it records nothing, judges nothing, and cannot be silenced, because silence is not a condition that applies to moving water.

I am not the river. I record. I judge. And I can be silenced—was nearly silenced, more than once. But I learned something from it that has shaped every page of this book: The record does not stop. Not because the person keeping it is brave, but because stopping is a form of death that the living cannot afford.

The old city of Mosul sits on the western bank, facing Nineveh across the water. On the river shore you would find the Qara Serai, and very old houses built of Mosul marble—a pale stone, cream-colored, cut from quarries north of the city—and a mosque next to a church next to a shrine, the architecture of coexistence built into the physical structure of the streets. The sound of church bells and the call to prayer occupied the same acoustic space every morning and had done so for longer than most nations have existed. When the early sunlight came, it struck the old stone and the river at the same angle, and the colors of history and water and inhabited time mixed into something that was beyond explanation because it was very old and you could only feel it.

That is where I belong. Not to a coordinate on a map. To that specific convergence—the river, the ancient city, the sunlight on stone—which existed as a single experience and which I have carried in my body since before I knew what history was.

When someone says the word *Mosul*, my mind goes only there. To the oldest part. To the river shore. To the place where the identity lives.

What was lost is not the buildings. What was lost is the souls. The particular arrangement of lives that created a place where a church rings its bells and one minute later you hear the call to prayer from the mosque next door, and the people in the street hear both and think nothing of it because it has always been so, because coexistence was not a policy in Mosul but a fact of architecture.

And here is what terrorism does that no bomb, no army, no invasion has ever done: It takes the architecture apart from the inside. It does not only destroy the building. It destroys the principle that allowed the building to stand beside the other building. It does not only kill the person. It kills the relationship between people that made the city a city and not merely a collection of structures on a plain. When ISIS expelled the Christians, they did not only empty neighborhoods. They severed a coexistence that was older than Islam itself in this city. They cut a thread that had been woven into the fabric of Mosul for seventeen centuries. And the cut cannot be repaired by rebuilding the houses, because the houses were not the thread. The people were.

I do not know if it is possible to understand this without having lived inside it—without having walked through the emptied Christian quarter and seen the crosses spray-painted with the Arabic letter *nūn*, for Nazarene, marking each home the way a disease marks the body it intends to consume. Without having known the families who lived in those houses. Without having eaten at their tables, argued in their shops, grown up hearing their church bells as part of the sound of your own mornings.

Terrorism does not only kill the people it kills. It kills the world that existed between people. And when that world is gone, it does not come back, because it was not built by anyone in particular. It grew. The way a language grows, the way a neighborhood grows, the way a child's understanding of home grows—without a blueprint, without a plan, by the accumulated weight of ordinary life lived over centuries. You cannot rebuild it. You can only remember that it existed, and that someone destroyed it, and that the destruction was deliberate.

What does it do to the person who documents it?

I will tell you as a historian, because the historian's discipline is the only tool I have left that I trust. The feelings are unreliable. The method is not.

It restructured me.

Not damaged—that word is too simple, too clinical. What happened was not damage. It was architecture. The occupation built something inside me—a second structure, a parallel self, designed for survival—and that structure did not dissolve when the conditions that built it ended. It is still here. I live inside it the way I once lived inside the occupied city—adapting to its rules, navigating its checkpoints, performing for its surveillance, even though the surveillance is now only my own.

I do not always know which of my feelings are real. After years of manufacturing the exact expression each situation required—calm at checkpoints, interest in conversations designed to extract intelligence, piety in mosques where the words being spoken were being used to justify the murder of my neighbors—the mechanism became so deeply installed that it no longer requires my permission to operate. It runs now the way breathing runs. I do not decide to perform. The performance decides for me.

That is what living underground does. It does not only hide you from others. It hides you from yourself. The mask becomes the face. The cover story becomes the story. And the man who was there before the cover was built—the man who put a rose in a vase every morning, who listened to Perlman with his eyes closed, who sat with friends and meant every word without first checking the words for what they might reveal—that man is somewhere inside the structure, but I cannot always reach him. When I do, I cannot always tell whether it is him or the mechanism producing a convincing simulation of him.

The river does not have this problem. The river does not perform. It flows, and the flowing is identical to what it is. I envy the river this. I have not been identical to what I am since June 2014.

And faith. I must speak about it, because what terrorism does to faith is the deepest wound of all, and the wound no one asks about.

I am a Muslim. I was raised in the sound of the call to prayer the way I was raised in the sound of the river—it was the atmosphere of my life, not a doctrine I adopted but a world I inhabited. Prayer was not performance. It was breath. The mosque was not ideology. It was the place where my grandfather's voice was, and his father's before him, and the rhythm of prostration and rising was the rhythm of a city that had been praying in this way for fourteen centuries.

And then men came who used that rhythm to kill.

They did not invent a new religion. That is what no one outside Mosul understands, and what everyone inside it understood immediately. They used the existing one. They used the words. They used the prayers. They used the gestures. They used the architecture—the same mosques, the same minarets, the same call that had been part of my mornings since birth. They filled the familiar forms with new content, the way you might fill a familiar cup with poison, and the poison worked not despite the familiarity of the cup but because of it. People drank because the cup was the cup they had always drunk from.

What does that do to a man's faith? Not to his beliefs—beliefs can be defended, argued, revised. To his faith. The thing underneath the beliefs, the thing that is not intellectual but physical, the feeling of being at home inside a tradition that is older than your ability to question it.

It made prayer into performance. It made the mosque into a surveillance site. It made every gesture of devotion into a potential signal—too much piety and you were performing for them; too little and you were suspect. The occupation colonized the space between a man and his God and filled it with calculation. And the calculation did not leave when the occupation ended. I carry it still. When I pray now—if I pray—I cannot always tell whether I am speaking to God or whether the mechanism is producing the appropriate gestures because the situation requires them. The occupation did not take my faith. It did something worse. It made my faith indistinguishable from the performance of faith. And the difference between the two is the difference between being alive and being a very convincing copy of alive.

I do not say this to indict Islam. I say it to indict what was done to Islam in my city, and to every person who carried it as something precious and watched it be wielded as a weapon against the people it was meant to shelter. That is the crime that has no court. The crime of taking a thing that belongs to the interior of a human being—the most private, most sacred, most vulnerable thing—and turning it into an instrument of power. Every religion has been used this way. But I am speaking of mine, because it is mine, and because the damage was done to me, and because the historian's duty is to speak from the evidence he carries in his own body when no other archive survives.

I went to the river once to die. I have told that story in this book and I will not tell it again here. What I have not said is why I chose the river.

It was not sentimentality. It was precision.

The river had Nineveh on one bank and the old city on the other. The immortal elements of Mosul—the things that were older than any occupation, older than any flag, older than the idea that this land could be owned by the men who had seized it. If I was going to leave, I wanted to leave in the company of the only things in this city that could not be conquered. The river knew what the occupation did not: that conquerors are temporary. That the water outlasts the men who try to own its banks.

I did not die that afternoon. And what I understood, sitting on the bank with the taste of forbidden tea and the warmth of forbidden sunlight, was not a decision to live but something closer to a recognition—that I did not have to die to join the continuity of Nineveh. That continuity was not reserved for the dead. It was available to the living, if they were willing to carry it.

I have been carrying it since.

A close friend of mine—one of those people who has known me long enough to understand both my seriousness and my absurdity—saw the book cover. She noticed it carried a foreword by Pope Francis and an introduction by General David Petraeus, and then, with the timing of someone who has been sharpening her wit for years, she said:

Only you could put the Pope and the CIA on the same page.

Pun intended.

I laughed out loud, the kind of laugh that catches you off guard and fills the room even when you are alone in it. She had sent the message the night before, late, probably smiling to herself as she typed it, and I had only just woken to find it waiting. I called her. We spoke on the phone, still laughing, the way old friends do, where the laughter carries more meaning than the words between it.

The laughter surprised me. Not the joke—the joke was excellent. The surprise was the laughter itself: spontaneous, unmanufactured, arriving before the mechanism could intercept it. For a few seconds I was simply a man laughing at something a friend had said. The ordinary human act of being amused—it felt like finding a room in my own house that I had forgotten existed.

The river carries everything. It carries the bodies thrown into it during the occupation, and it carries the reflections of children swimming on summer afternoons. It carries both without preference. Perhaps that is the lesson I am slowest to learn—that the man who documented atrocity and the man who laughs at a friend's joke about the Pope and the CIA are the same man, carried by the same current, and neither one cancels the other out.

People call what I did heroic. The image they create of heroes is itself a kind of violence. The image says: This person did not feel what you feel. This person was stronger than ordinary life. This person operated above the human. And the image erases the person inside the hero the way the word *refugee* erases the person inside the asylum papers. Both are cages. One is made of pity. The other is made of admiration. Neither one has room for the man who laughs at a joke, or the man who cannot tell which of his feelings are real, or the man who loves a woman who went to fight her own war. The hero is supposed to be complete. The man is not. The man is standing inside an incomplete life, carrying what he can, and the distance between what the image requires and what the man contains is a distance he crosses every day, because the expression gives nothing.

From the outside it looked like courage. From the inside it felt like the progressive disappearance of everything that once made me a person. The feelings go. The dreams go. The capacity to sit with a friend and be fully present goes. These things are replaced by competence, by method, by the discipline that keeps you alive and useful. The system works. But the person who operates the system is no longer the person who started it.

To save what you love, you must become unrecognizable to it. That is the law, and no one who has obeyed it has returned whole.

No one asks about that person, because the hero is more useful than the man, and the story is more portable than the truth.

I would do all of it again. I would do it because it was necessary and because I was the one who could do it and because the alternative was to let the city be silenced and the dead be unnamed. But I will not pretend it did not cost me. And I would ask the reader—you, holding this book, wherever you are—to consider what you hold. You hold the record. You also hold the man who made it, and the man is not the record. The record is clean. The man is not.

The historian in me knows that Mosul has been here before. Not the specific events—the events are always specific, always someone's individual suffering, someone's name—but the pattern. The city besieged, the city occupied, the city burned, the city rebuilt. The Mosul historian Yasin al-'Umari, writing in the eighteenth century, recorded that when Hulagu Khan's armies took Mosul, they massacred the inhabitants and plundered for nine days and razed the town to the ground, and the survivors fled. That was the thirteenth century. The city came back. Not the same city—never the same—but a city on the same river, carrying in its rebuilt streets the memory of what had stood there before.

This is not consolation. A historian who uses deep time to diminish present suffering has failed at both history and compassion. But the river's indifference to the suffering on its banks is itself a kind of testimony. It says: I have carried all of it—the bodies and the prayers and the reflections of burning buildings and the silence of emptied neighborhoods—and I am still here, and I am still flowing south toward Basra and the Gulf, and there is no force on earth that can make me stop.

The record is like that. It does not stop. It does not comfort. It does not avenge. It only continues, carrying what was given to it, delivering it downstream to whoever is waiting to receive it. That is what I have done. Not heroism. Hydrology.

I sit now in a city that is not Mosul. *Refugee*—that is the word that follows me. The word I hate most. Not because it is inaccurate but because it erases everything else I am. I am a historian. I am a scholar. I am a man who documented the occupation of his city and preserved its memory and carried an archive out of a war zone. But the word does what ISIS could not do. It reduces me to a single category.

I have a hard drive. I have notebooks and encrypted files and names and dates and charges and prices and the record of everything I could carry out of a city that was being forced to forget itself. The hard drive is small enough to hold in one hand. It contains the memory of a city of two million people across three years of occupation. A small, scratched rectangle of metal and plastic, and inside it the proof that Mosul existed as itself and not as what its conquerors said it was.

The archive will outlast me. That was always the point. Not that I survived—though I did, and I am grateful in ways I cannot always feel—but that the record survived. The evidence that when the conquerors tried to rewrite the city, someone was in the room taking notes. Someone refused to let the only record be the one written by the men with guns.

But here is the question I want to leave with the reader, and it is not comfortable. What did you do with the record while it was being made? I wrote the dispatches at two in the morning. You read them over coffee. I documented the executions. You shared the posts and moved on to the next thing in your feed. I do not say this with bitterness—I wrote for you, I needed you, the work had no meaning without the world receiving it. But I want you to sit, for a moment, with the distance between the writing and the reading. A man was producing these words from inside an occupied city where the production of them was a death sentence, and the words traveled through a screen and landed on a desk in a country where the electricity never goes out, and the person reading them was free to close the screen and walk away. I could not walk away. I was still there.

That distance is not your fault. It is the condition of the world. But the condition of the world is part of the record too. I do not ask you to feel guilty. I ask you to feel the weight of the distance, and to carry it for a moment the way I carried the hard drive—not because carrying it changes anything, but because the carrying is the proof that you have understood what you are holding.

I do not know when I will go back to Mosul.

The death threats have not expired. The city I would return to is not the city I left. But the river is there. It is there this morning, as I write this, flowing past the ruins of the Qara Serai, past the place where the al-Nuri Mosque stood before it was blown up in retreat, past the rubble and the scaffolding and the children growing up on its banks who will carry their own version of Mosul forward into a future I cannot see.

I think about those children. They will not remember the occupation the way I remember it, because they were too young or not yet born. They will know it the way I knew the Iran-Iraq war—as a weight carried by the generation before them. They will walk along the river, and they will not know that a man once sat on its bank in a red sweater, drinking tea he was not permitted to drink, waiting for a death that did not come. They will not need to know. The river will be enough.

But I want something for those children that I did not have. I want them to pray—if they pray—without the calculation. I want them to sit with a friend without assessing the friend for intelligence value. I want them to love someone without the mechanism intercepting the love and converting it into the appropriate response. I want them to walk through a city where a mosque stands next to a church stands next to a shrine and think nothing of it, the way I once thought nothing of it, before the thinking became the last thing left.

I want for them the ordinary life. The life that is not heroic, not documented, not carried on a hard drive. The life that does not require a man to become two men in order to survive. The life where the expression gives everything, because there is nothing that needs to be concealed.

I do not know whether that life is possible in Mosul again. The historian in me says: It has been possible before, it was destroyed before, it came back before. The man in me says: I cannot feel whether it will come back, because the part of me that would feel it was the part I traded away. But the river does not trade anything. The river carries everything and loses nothing and keeps flowing regardless.

I dedicated this book to the river.

I did that before I wrote the first word, because I knew that whatever I managed to put on the page, the book would be incomplete. Every book about a living city is incomplete, because the city continues after the last page. The river was the only dedication that could hold that incompleteness without pretending to resolve it.

For the river.

Meaning: for the witness that cannot be silenced. For the continuity that no occupation can break because it is not human and therefore cannot be threatened or deceived or forced to walk in the shadow of anyone's wall. For the immortal thing that I sat beside on the worst afternoon of my life and that taught me, without language, without argument, without comfort, that the record does not stop.

I am still writing the record. I am writing it now, in my own name, which is both a freedom and a strange exposure. The record is not finished because I am not finished and Mosul is not finished and the river is not finished. None of us are finished. That is not a promise. It is a fact, stated by a historian, in the only language a historian trusts—the language of what can be verified.

The river is still there.

I am still here.

The record continues.

STATEMENT OF ENDORSEMENT

GENERAL ABDUL-WAHAB AL-SAADI HEAD OF THE COUNTER-TERRORISM SERVICE, IRAQI SPECIAL OPERATIONS FORCES (CTS-ISOF)

I fought to liberate Mosul. Omar Mohammed fought to keep it from being erased. We were on the same line.

The liberation of Mosul is among the defining events of modern Iraqi history. It was not only a military operation. It was a test of what a state owes its people when it fights to recover them. Many commanders took part in that battle. I was one of them, and I know what it cost.

In 2014, Daesh seized Mosul, Iraq's second city, after the sudden collapse of our security forces. For more than two years, the people of Mosul endured what no population should endure: repression, forced conscription, the destruction of their infrastructure, and an extremist rule that reached into every corner of their daily lives. In October 2016, we began the operation to retake the city. The Counter-Terrorism Service, the Iraqi Army, the Federal Police, and our partners in the international coalition fought side by side. It was one of the most complex urban battles of this century. Daesh had turned a city of millions into a fortress, and its civilians into human shields.

We planned the operation to win. We also planned it to protect. That is not a contradiction. In dense urban terrain, with a civilian population trapped among the enemy, the two had to be held together at every moment, or both would have been lost. We observed international humanitarian law not as a formality but as a discipline. We opened safe corridors. We delivered food, water, medicine, and emergency care neighborhood by neighborhood, in coordination with the United Nations and the Red Crescent. We treated detainees as human beings, not as trophies. The pressures were immense—human shields, mass displacement, the devastation inflicted on the Old City—but the standard did not shift. Even the welfare of animals was taken into account.

We fought house by house. The hardest decision we faced, day after day, was the line between combatant and civilian. There were advances we delayed for hours to ensure that families had made it out. There were losses we accepted among our own forces rather than place civilians in harm's way. That was not sentiment. It was doctrine. Our mission was not only to defeat the enemy. It was to return the city to its people.

When we entered the neighborhoods, the people were afraid. What surprised them was how we treated them. For the first time in years, they understood that someone was there for them—for their lives, for their homes, for what remained of what they owned—in the darkest circumstances they had known.

I owe Mosul a personal debt. I studied at the university. I lived among its people. I know its neighborhoods, its social fabric, the depth of its history. The Moslawis are a people of rare awareness and principled conviction, and they hold to the law and to the order of their city as few others do.

During the battle, I received calls from a voice I did not know—a voice reaching me from outside the city, anonymous at the time, carrying information from inside. That information was accurate. It was timely. It saved lives, and I acted on it. Some of those calls concerned civilians trapped in basements beyond the reach of our corridors. Others concerned matters no one would have expected to reach a commander in that battle—including, at one point, the animals left behind in the ruins of the city's zoo. In the deadliest urban battle of this century, one of the calls I answered was from a historian asking me to save a lion. I took it seriously, and I still do.

A war of that scale tests what a commander is willing to protect, and the answer cannot be selective.

It was not a voice from afar. It was the voice of Mosul itself, reaching me from the heart of the city when its streets had been silenced. Only later did I learn whose voice it was. It was Omar Mohammed—the man the world knows as Mosul Eye.

For this reason, I believe this book matters, and I stand behind it. The account of what befell Mosul in those years must be written by one of its own—by a man who was there, who saw, who recorded, who bore the cost of bearing witness. Omar Mohammed is that witness. This is the record Mosul deserves, and I am proud to add my name to it.

INDEX

C

N

Y

Z